Nicaragua's Mosquito Shore

Nicaragua's Mosquito Shore

The Years of British and American Presence

Craig L. Dozier

The University of Alabama Press

Passages from the Daniel Cleveland diary are quoted
by permission of The Bancroft Library

Library of Congress Cataloging in Publication Data
Dozier, Craig L. (Craig Lanier), 1920–
Nicaragua's Mosquito shore.

Bibliography: p.
Includes index.
1. Mosquitia (Nicaragua and
Honduras)—History.
I. Title.

F1529.M9D68   1985   972.85′3   84-237
ISBN 0-8173-0226-3

To my wife, Virginia,
and to my friend, Dr. Franklin D. Parker

Contents

Illustrations

Preface

I first visited eastern Nicaragua in 1957, after a lengthy trip down the San Juan River in a motorized flatboat, pulling barges loaded with empty coconut-oil drums. With that visit began a lasting interest in this unique part of Latin America, for I have always been fascinated by obscure corners of the world which were not once so—with places that have a history, if they seem to have no present. The result, many years later, is this book, which is intended to be a narrative of the years of foreign presence in this once-important region: the stimuli, and economic and political relationships, the international rivalry, the problems, the ways of life, the events, the people and their perceptions.

My objective throughout has been to emphasize the internal history of the region (a rather neglected segment) through extensive use of British and American archival sources and other firsthand accounts, while placing this history within the framework of the better-known external political and economic relations. In the concluding chapter, the narrative is brought up to the present and the region depicted as foreign influence faded.

When the manuscript was begun, there seemed little likelihood that the region would gain prominence in modern-day affairs. The foreign interlude had ended and the Nicaraguan revolution had not yet come. However, with the coming of the Sandinista regime to power, the east has new relevance. Of all regions of the country, its inhabitants have proved most resistant to the new revolutionary government and its policies. Despite top-priority efforts by the government, they have remained unassimilated, and constitute a major element of the opposition. Consequently, despite its small population and undeveloped economy, the region has commanded an uncommon amount of attention from the Sandinistas, and the reasons are not difficult to find. The government has become painfully aware that this is a "soft spot" in its aim to unite the country behind its socialist objectives.

There was recognition of a number of disturbing facts: most east coast inhabitants were never strong opponents of the previous dictatorship, and had almost no role in its overthrow; the Protestant-Moravian missionaries, who have significant influence over the inhabitants, are strongly anti-Communist; the old American ties still prevail among the people; and their strong sense of ethnic identity and separatism poses obstacles to the achievement of government objectives. The remote and lightly populated frontier, with its nonsupportive inhabitants, is, in brief, perceived as a troublesome region by the regime. There is the ultimate threat that it might become a haven and base for counterrevolutionary forces.

In this uncertain period in Nicaragua's internal affairs and international relations, therefore, the isolated east is once again significant. For that new role this book provides a background.

I am indebted to the entire staff of the Reference Department of Jackson Library at the University of North Carolina at Greensboro for its assistance in the acquisition of materials through interlibrary loan and to readers of the manuscript for their invaluable recommendations. The sources of loaned materials are too numerous to mention, but I should like especially to thank the National Archives in Washington, the Bancroft Library of the University of California at Berkeley, the Wilson Library of the University of North Carolina at Chapel Hill, and the Perkins Library at Duke University.

I am grateful to John Thomas Minor, Assistant Director of the Jackson Library and formerly Reference Librarian, not only for his assistance but also for his continuing interest in the project. Mr. Minor knows eastern Nicaragua well, since he has been involved in mission work for the Moravian Church and the region is his wife's native land.

Cartographic work on the maps, in their finished form, was done by my faculty colleague, Dr. Jeffrey Patton, and by Lorna Lilly. I thank them both for their services. Finally, I wish to express my appreciation to Mrs. Shirley Brown, Secretary of the Department of Geography at the University, for typing several drafts of the manuscript and for various other tasks which she cheerfully performed in its preparation for publication.

Nicaragua's Mosquito Shore

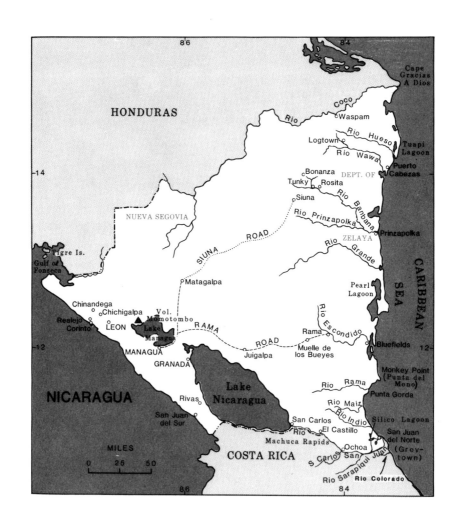

HONDURAS

—14

Cape
Gracias
A Dios

Rio   Coco
          oWaspam
      Rio Hueso
Logtown o   Tuapi
     Rio Wawa   Lagoon
       Bonanza   DEPT. OF   oPuerto
  Tunky oRosita   Cabezas
      oSiuna   Rio Banbana
NUEVA SEGOVIA   Rio Prinzapolka
                        ZELAYA   oPrinzapolka
              Rio Grande

Tigre Is.
Gulf of
Fonseca   SIUNA   ROAD
                                    Pearl
         oMatagalpa   Lagoon

Chinandega
  oChichigalpa   Vol.
Realejo   oMomotombo   RAMA
Corinto oLEON Lake   Rama o Rio Escondido
—12   Managua   ROAD   Bluefields 12—
       MANAGUA   Muelle de
       GRANADA   Juigalpa   los Bueyes
                                    Monkey Point
NICARAGUA   Lake   (Punta del
            oRivas   Nicaragua   Rio Rama   Mono)
      San Juan   Punta Gorda
      del Sur   Rio Maiz
              San Carlos Rio Indio Silico Lagoon
MILES   El Castillo   San Juan
0   25   50   Machuca Rapids   del Norte
                            Ochoa San   (Grey-
       COSTA RICA   S. Carlos   town)
              Rio Sarapiqui Juan Rio Colorado

86   84

CARIBBEAN
SEA

Introduction

Across the mountains, eastward from Nicaragua's well-settled Pacific plain, is a much larger plain of sparse population and persistent isolation, yet one not overlooked in history (as have been so many similar tropical frontier zones). This remote stretch of Caribbean coastal plain, in latter years forgotten and bypassed, has not only an eventful history but is unique in all of Spanish America in the dominant role formerly played by British and North Americans—not only on the scene as inhabitants and transients but also at high levels of international politics. Geographically, it was unlikely to attract foreigners: a wide, low-lying tropical plain of extreme flatness, broken only occasionally by low spurs of a central mountain range, with temperatures averaging 75° to 80° year-around; one of the wettest regions of Latin America and the world, where some parts received over 200 inches of annual rainfall; a dense tropical rainforest in the south and up the flanks of the wet eastern mountain slopes, grading into pine-forested savannas in the northeast; leached, sandy, or gravelly soils (except in the river valleys and well-drained sites around lagoons); shallow, reef-strewn coastal waters; a lagoon-studded shoreline with poor harbors, obstructed by bars and silting up, surrounded by swamps, marshes, and mangroves. Because of its latitude, orientation, and configuration, however, it was fully exposed to the onshore easterly trade winds, and this offered some compensation: as in the West Indies, it made the heat and humidity more tolerable.

Except for one lowland break, provided by the San Juan River (connecting with Lake Nicaragua), this most extensive plain of the isthmian countries was separated from the rest of Nicaragua by a rugged backbone of mountains. Down from the mountains and across the plain flowed Nicaragua's longest rivers, broken by numerous rapids. The region has never experienced significant Hispanic settlement or influence, under Spain or independent Nicaragua. For various economic and strategic reasons, the area's defense and control were recognized as vital, but its lands and climate never appealed to settlers from the west. They were driven away by the difficulty of access and the hostility of the natives, and there appeared to be no significant wealth in precious metals (some were discovered later, but not until the nineteenth century by foreign prospectors).

On the other hand, the productive potential of the Pacific plain, with its volcanic soils and dry season, became a magnet for Hispanic settlement and assured that area's economic preeminence. All tropical lowland plantation crops that were in demand—sugar cane, cacao, indigo—could be grown there, amid the best cattle-raising lands. Meanwhile, accessibility to the Caribbean coast by non-Hispanic foreign elements was easier by sea, and for different reasons they began to come in the late sixteenth century and did not stop until the twentieth.

Thus was the enclave nature of eastern Nicaragua reinforced and a cultural dichotomy established which has prevailed until today. Spain and, later, Nicaragua never relinquished their territorial claims, but the region remained non-Hispanic. Through the decades of Spanish colonial rule in Central America, the struggles for independence, and the turmoils of internal Nicaraguan politics, it was, with its special external relationships, always a region apart. Its story became, in large degree, one of British and North American involvement—their objectives, perceptions, experiences, and conflicts—superimposed on a receptive native culture.

The natives of eastern Nicaragua during the British and American presence were members of the same groups who live there today. Originally, there were the Miskito Indians. (Although the correct anthropological term for this dominant and indigenous Indian group is "Miskito," the term invariably used by foreigners—British and Americans—for the people and the area they inhabit was "Mosquito," and this is the designation that this study will use. Nevertheless, it is a corrupt form, not acceptable to present-day Miskito people and considered degrading.) Later, a sizable Creole population developed. ("Creole" came to be applied to people of dominant African ancestry, both mixed bloods—products of interbreeding of early slaves with Indians and whites—and the more recent black immigrants, mainly from Jamaica, who began to immigrate as wage laborers in the last century.) The Mosquitos were descendants of tribes thought to have migrated from South America, up the Caribbean coast, prior to European contact. They usually acquired some admixture of African and white blood over the generations. By long presence among them, foreigners have left a decided cultural imprint upon these people, which has passed down to the present-day descendants. This is manifested in their general use of the English language (Mosquitos use their native language in addition), the adherence of the majority to the Protestant religion (introduced by Moravian missionaries in the last century), and their enduring Anglophilia and Americanism. In a way that Spanish-speaking Nicaraguans from the west have never been, the British and Americans, though foreigners, were welcomed and accepted. After their departure, nostalgic affinity for these former employers lingered among the natives. Indeed, for the Mosquitos and Creoles of the east the true foreigners and outsiders have been not from overseas but from the other side of the mountains.

Although these opposing relationships with the native people constitute only part of the story of the British and North American presence, they were vital.

1

Early British Entry
and Spanish Resistance,
1633–1800

"Thanks to God" was the name the seamen of Christopher Columbus' fourth and last voyage gave the cape they rounded along the Caribbean coast of Central America in September of 1502. Turning from an easterly course to one almost due southward, they were now in a smooth stretch of sea with favorable winds, having suffered severe gales for many days. They were sailing along a wide, low-lying tropical shoreland from which, unlike the shore farther north, the mountains retreated in the distance. This was the eastern part of the territory which would later be known as Nicaragua.

In late September the ships anchored near the mouth of a river where Columbus and his men rested several days in what they considered a veritable garden. They were received hospitably by Indians in their villages, and attempted to gain information about the country. On this voyage, Columbus was seeking a strait through the landmass he had encountered, which, he hoped would lead to the "coreland" of India. The river off which his ships were anchored was the closest approximation to the long-sought strait ever to be discovered, for its source lay close to the Pacific in a large freshwater sea (it was the river later called the San Juan). But Columbus remained unaware of the river's uniqueness, apparently receiving no information from the natives to encourage investigation beyond a short excursion to the interior. In early October the expedition again sailed southeastward, still seeking a strait into the vast ocean rumored to be across the mountains. It would be another quarter century, after Vasco Nuñez de Balboa's discovery of the Pacific and the settlement of Panama, before the Spaniards rediscovered the San Juan (from the other side of the isthmus) and recognized its significance.

In 1519 Gil González Dávila, of the colonial government in Santo Domingo, was given authority by the Spanish court to explore the areas bordering the South Sea (Pacific) north of Panama. After many delays, partly occasioned by lack of cooperation by the governor of Panama, the expedition departed from Panama City in January 1522. An arduous journey, part by sea and part overland, brought González, several weeks later, to a rich, volcano-studded plain surrounding a freshwater sea (Lake Nicaragua), the homeland of one of Central America's largest and most culturally advanced Indian groups. Unlike other groups of South American origin that inhabited the lands east of the Pacific plain, these Indians had moved south, from Guatemala and Mexico. Their culture included weaving and pottery making and they were skilled in fashioning ornaments made of gold, of which they seemed to have an abundance. Their economy was agriculturally based, and although they practiced a slash-and-burn, shifting cultivation, it was productive in the rich volcanic soils.

Meeting Nicarao, one of the Indian chiefs, the Spaniards were initially received with friendliness and presented with gifts of gold. They were fascinated with the freshwater, inland sea, and González was the first Spanish explorer to hear reports that this body of water was connected by a river to the "North Sea" (the Caribbean). He commented that "if so it is a great discovery," for it meant that the land distance between one sea and the other was only "two or three leagues of very level road."[1]

Relations with the Indians ultimately deteriorated and, as animosities developed, the expedition returned to Panama, carrying much gold. Almost immediately, bitter rivalry developed between González and Pedrarias Dávila, then in control of Panama, over the newly discovered Nicaraguan plain. Governor Pedrarias, renowned for his cruelties, had previously shown his jealousy of González when he refused to assist in the original expedition, so that González had been forced to set out in unseaworthy vessels, which had to be abandoned before he reached Nicaragua, and complete the journey overland. It was evident from the Indian ornaments brought back to Panama that Nicaragua had gold, and this incited Pedrarias to challenge González' claim. He dispatched a large army to Nicaragua, commanded by Francisco Hernández de Córdoba, and in 1524 Hernández founded Granada and León, two of Central America's first permanent Spanish settlements.

González, who fled to Hispaniola with some of the riches he acquired in Nicaragua, later attempted to regain control there by marching overland from Honduras, but was unsuccessful. Meanwhile, Hernández turned against Pedrarias, wishing to secure exclusive control of Nicaragua for himself, but Pedrarias marched northward from Panama and defeated the rebel in 1526. Hernández was executed for his treason, and Pedrarias set himself up in León as governor of Nicaragua. His rule was harsh. Not only were the Indians of the plain enslaved, but slave-hunting expeditions were sent into the mountains to the east to round up scores of natives. León and Granada were regularly filled with captives, slave markets abounded, and shiploads of natives were sent to Panama. Gladiatorlike games were staged for Pedrarias' amusement in León, where Indians and their chiefs were forced to fight packs of wild dogs.

During the next five years, until his death in 1531, Pedrarias consolidated his hold on the Nicaraguan plain and extended his control into parts of Honduras, while his authority was challenged from the north by Hernán Cortés and Pedro de Alvarado. In the early years after its discovery, Nicaragua was caught up in a scramble for control of various parts of the isthmus by the *conquistadores*, and their jealousies and geographic barriers conspired to prevent administrative unification for many years. Along with Guatemala, Honduras, Chiapas, and Panama, Nicaragua functioned as a separate administrative entity. After the strong-handed rule of Pedrarias, poor government and disorder prevailed. A schism soon developed between León, the provincial capital, and Granada, which became the principal commercial and agricultural center. It was unfortunate for Nicaragua's political future that two cities, instead of one, constituted its Spanish-settlement core.

Pedrarias was particularly interested in the reports that Lake Nicaragua had an outlet to the Caribbean. By this time, the Panama crossing to Peru was well established, but it was always his hope that an alternative route through Nicaragua could be developed, thus improving the economic prospects of his province. At the time, there was also revived interest on the part of the Spanish crown, since the Panama route was so difficult. Pedrarias' predecessor, Hernández de Córdoba, had made a reconnaissance of the lakeshore in 1524, in reassembled brigantines he had brought piece by piece from the Pacific, and had discovered that a river indeed flowed, in an easterly direction, out of the south end of the lake. The river was first given the name Desaguadero, or "drain," and the area was traversed by a number of expeditions in the years to follow. (A famous explorer, Hernán de Soto, who had accompanied Hernández de Córdoba to Nicaragua, led one of these expeditions downstream.) All had been greatly handicapped in the type of vessels they employed, by the rapids, frequently having to abort their journeys.

The most successful expedition was in 1539, long after Pedrarias' death, led by two lesser-known explorers, Alonso Calero and Diego Machuca, who volunteered to make the journey for the governor of Nicaragua, Rodrigo de Contreras, at their own expense. Careful preparation appears to have been a major factor in the success of this expedition. Appropriate vessels were constructed near Granada, consisting of a large, decked bark and two lateen-rigged lighters, supplemented by four large canoes. Carpenters, blacksmiths, and caulkers were obtained for the journey and ample supplies of food, stores, arms, and medicines were loaded.[2] Setting out from the lake in April of 1539, the expedition passed the rapids and finally reached the Caribbean, which was first thought to be another large lake. Later both explorers, in separate journeys, ascended the river. They had proved that it could be navigated in both directions in small vessels, though with difficulty. They learned—as did their predecessors and all who used the river subsequently—the problems of the rapids (one of which was named for Machuca) and the bar at the river's mouth.

After its conquests in Latin America, Spain for a while was untroubled by foreign competition as she pursued her monopolistic control of trade with the colonies. The northern European powers–Britain, France, and the Netherlands—also interested in finding a sea route to India, confined their search to the upper latitudes while they explored North America. But Spain's freedom from intervention in its southern domain did not continue long. Europe's growing demand during the sixteenth century for the goods which Spain's large overseas empire in the Americas could provide complemented the Spanish colonies' demand for goods which could be obtained only from the northern European countries. Spain's weakly commercialized economy could neither meet the needs of its colonists nor totally absorb colonial products, and it was ineffective in marketing them elsewhere in Europe. As the century advanced, first the French, then the British and Dutch, resorted to contraband trade with the Spanish colonies, then to raiding Spanish ships and attacking weakly defended parts of Spanish America, ushering in the age of buccaneering. Monarchs did little to discourage such activities, for Catholic Spain was hated and buccaneers were valuable allies in times of war. During the sixteenth century, Spain was engaged on the Continent in almost continuous warfare with the northern European Protestant countries. These wars were costly and a severe drain on Spain's resources, many of which were derived from her American empire.

The British attempt to disrupt the monopolies of Spain and Portugal had begun during the reign of Queen Elizabeth, and Sir Francis Drake was one of the first of a long line of Englishmen to descend in piratical raids on Spanish-American ports. In the early 1570s he led an expedition to New Granada and preyed upon Spanish treasure shipments from Cartagena and the Panama isthmus. During his voyage around the world (1577–1580) in the service of his queen, he attacked and looted at various points along the Pacific .coast, including Realejo in Nicaragua. Such actions persuaded Philip II that he had to defeat England or yield control of the sea. However, the large Armada he launched against his enemy a few years later met with disaster, and this momentous British victory (1588) opened the way to a further, more effective challenge to Spain's commercial supremacy in Latin America. The Caribbean became the major arena as buccaneering depredations continued for more than a century (except for a brief period in the early seventeenth century, coinciding with European peace settlements prior to the outbreak of the Thirty Years' War). The British, with the French and Dutch, gained control of small islands and occupied marginal areas of the mainland of Central America from which to launch their plundering expeditions.

By the end of the sixteenth century the San Juan River (as the Desaguadero was subsequently named) was frequently used as a Spanish trade route between Nombre de Dios, Panama, and the Nicaraguan lake plain. The latter, with its productive soils and Indian population, was a source of food and slaves, some of which were sent to Peru. Granada, with its lakeshore location, was a principal beneficiary of this trade, and during the first half of the seventeenth century additional impetus developed for the city's commercial growth. It was to profit from the insecurity of seaports more accessible to pirate raids, and trade was diverted from all parts of Central America for shipment down the San Juan. Although the San Juan, and especially its lower course, continued to be threatened, the lake district and Granada were protected by their inland location and distance from the sea. The Granada–Cartagena link with Spanish ships proved to be the safest and most reliable route, and the lake port became the regional entrepôt, particularly for the Guatemalan trade. Precious metals, major plantation products, and food staples were transported with regularity by mule train along rough roads and trails from Costa Rica, Honduras, El Salvador, and other parts of Nicaragua to Granada's warehouses.

Navigating the San Juan was not easy during this busy period. There were problems even for large, specially constructed flat-bottom vessels; and canoes (which carried only a third as much cargo as the *bongo* of the nineteenth century) handled much of the commerce. Because of the rapids, it sometimes took two months to travel the full length of the river; and Indians, mules, and warehouses were necessary where goods had to be portaged. The rapids later known as Castillo, because of an unusually large drop of the riverbed over a short distance, could be passed only by "tracking" from the shore with hawser and towrope. The difficulties were noted in letters to the Spanish government. Juan López de Velasco had written in 1574: ". . . the navigation from Granada to the Mar del Norte is not very secure,"[3] and Diego de Mercado wrote in 1620: ". . . these ships ascend and descend the river with great effort and difficulty."[4]

Despite the difficulties, Granada's trade flourished into the mid-seventeenth century. Thomas Gage, writing his classic account of a decade of travels in Central America, had this to say about his sojourn in Granada:

> The houses are fairer than those of Leon, and the town of more inhabitants, among whom there are some few merchants of great wealth . . . who trade with Cartagena, Guatemala, San Salvador, and Comayagua, and some by the South Sea to Peru and Panama. At the time of the sending away the frigates that town is one of the wealthiest in all the north tract of America. . . . That year that I was there, before I betook myself to an Indian town, there entered in one day six *recuas* (at least three hundred mules) from San Salvador and Comayagua only, laden with nothing else but indigo, cochineal, and hides, and two days after from Guatemala three more came in. One was laden with silver, which was the King's tribute from that country; the other with sugar; the third with indigo.[5]

Gage hoped to gain passage on one of the frigates, despite the inconveniences of possibly a two-month journey, with numerous physical handicaps and loadings and unloadings en route. However, the report of pirates lurking at the mouth of the Desaguadero caused cancellation of the scheduled sailing from Granada, and he proceeded to the Caribbean via Costa Rica and Panama.

One of the first British intrusions on the Central American mainland occurred when traders from Providence Island contacted the Indians at Cape Gracias a Dios in 1633 and laid the groundwork for a lengthy and useful liaison. In the years immediately following, small numbers of Englishmen settled at the cape and at the mouth of the Escondido River farther south, where a Dutch pirate, Abraham Blauvelt, had established a buccaneer haven. (Later, the settlement became known by the English as Bluefields.) They cut mahogany and dyewood and grew sugar cane on scattered plantations, using imported blacks for both operations. Thus began a mixing of African and Indian races (Sumus in this region, ethnically related to the Mosquitos farther south) which continued for decades, the African component becoming more pronounced. An early derivation of significance occurred when a Portuguese ship, loaded with African slaves, was wrecked in 1641 on the offshore keys. The slaves had revolted, taken over the vessel and, without knowledge of navigation allowed themselves to drift with the trade winds until wrecked. Then, reaching the mainland, they were made slaves by the Indians; but through intermarriage their descendants became free members of the tribes. Members of the mixed race came to be called Sambos, while the Mosquito Indians south of the cape remained of purer blood. There is no doubt that the Sambo mixture contained white blood as well, since these initial English settlements (and many of those to follow) contained few white women.

The colonists established good relations with the Indians. Trade eventually turned from trinkets and beads to firearms, and the British acquired faithful allies against the Spaniards. Spanish hating and with a craving for the things, especially guns and rum, furnished by the British, the Indians assisted by furnishing dugouts, guiding buccaneers along the easiest routes to the interior, and fighting alongside them. In fact, the first threat to western Nicaragua came in 1645, when a band of British and Indian raiders ascended the Rio Escondido and pushed overland to attack Matagalpa. This was the unofficial beginning of a relationship, later made official and lasting over two and a half centuries, of the British with the natives of this area. They called it the Mosquito Shore and its native inhabitants, both Sambos and Miskitos, Mosquitos.

Once the large island of Jamaica was won during Oliver Cromwell's trade war with Spain in 1655, it became the nucleus of British empire in the West Indies, and thenceforward Britain posed the greatest danger to Spain. During this latter, intense phase of sea warfare, most attacks were accomplished by freebooters—and if they were not officially sanctioned, they were tacitly approved by their governments. Many of the buccaneers had bases in Port Royal, Jamaica, but others set out from smaller Caribbean islands (Roatan, close by the Honduran coast, had been taken by the British in 1642) or from Belize, which, like the Mosquito Shore, was being settled by English logcutters. The Spaniards constructed forts in coastal sites along the Caribbean and rivers of penetration, but initially they were ineffective in repelling the often devastating raids. At times, British and French buccaneers mounted daring joint attacks on the interior mainland, such as the ascent of the Rio Coco and the plundering of Nicaragua's Nueva Segovia in 1654.

Granada's inland position did not protect it from pirates indefinitely. Because of distance and river rapids, it was not an easy target, but the lake port, after all, was accessible by a water route, and the insecure and rapidly deteriorating fortifications along the river offered minimal defense. Moreover, there were no populous areas between Granada and the sea. Pirates first reached and attacked the city in 1665, causing widespread destruction. The sackings, highly profitable to the buccaneers, continued until the completion of Fort Inmaculada Concepción a few years later, on an elevated site overlooking one of the San Juan rapids, which was thereafter called Castillo. There were weaknesses even after that: the climate of the isolated fort, in the middle of the rainforest, made disease rampant and equipment and materials subject to rapid deterioration. Moreover, garrisons depended upon the river for water, and access to it could be cut off by enemy forces. Nevertheless, with increased manmade obstructions in the river, the fort proved to be a deterrent for the next 100 years.

The sacking of 1665 was effective in ending Granada's most active and prosperous period. Even though the city's appeals to the Spanish crown for protection had resulted in a fort that was capable of resisting upriver pirate incursions, ships entering and leaving the river's mouth were still preyed upon and fear of attack was never completely removed from the minds of Granada's inhabitants, many of whom abandoned the city. By the end of the seventeenth century the lake-river waterway was hardly used, despite the new and elaborate fortifications at Fort Inmaculada Concepción. Meanwhile, piracy was in its twilight. It was too disruptive for all of the countries involved (freebooters attacked ships of any nation), and Britain and France finally joined with Spain to terminate the lawless practice.

The last efforts of the buccaneers came from the Pacific side, and Granada was again vulnerable. A joint British-French band attacked and occupied it. The French prayed in the cathedral, then feverishly pursued their plunder and terrorizing of the population. Before they left, they burned the cathedral and principal buildings. For all of this, little booty was obtained since Granada was by that time no longer a thriving trading city.

However, the British retained their hold on the Mosquito Shore and continued to incite Mosquito raids upon Spanish settlements. In 1720 the British governor of Jamaica negotiated a treaty with the Mosquito Indians by which the natives received arms for the avowed purpose of assisting in the capture of fugitive Jamaican slaves who had recently come to work on Shore plantations. However, there is little doubt that the arms were intended for broader, offensive purposes. Attracted by an abundance of free land for sugar plantations, as compared with Jamaica, Englishmen began to settle along the Shore in ever-increasing numbers, swelling the colonies at the cape and Bluefields and creating new ones at other points. Some of these settlers were former buccaneers, who knew the Shore and its isolated coves very well and were acquainted with the natives. These men particularly were unable to fit into the system of large sugar plantations that was being established in the West Indian islands. Logwood, for the dyes in demand by British textile mills, was exceptionally profitable; so most settlers engaged in its cutting. Not overlooked was the pine forest, whose logs were in demand for ship outfitting (keels, sterns, sternposts, deck planks, masts) and as a source of naval stores. Additional income came from trade in tortoise shell, sarsaparilla, sugar, and rum. Besides the products of forest and soil in their areas, a major source of income for the British settler was smuggling. Contacts were established with the interior Spanish frontier at many points, and there was a steady flow of contraband back and forth. Few settlers were not directly or indirectly involved in this illicit activity, along with their local pursuits, and it became a way of life: a sort of substitute for the plundering of buccaneer days.

Most settlements were small and crude and the settlers generally of modest means, employing only a few poor whites or Indians as labor. However, along with expanding Bluefields, the Black River settlement was an exception. This settlement was about 15 miles up the river of the same name, between Trujillo and Cape Gracias a Dios in the Honduran portion of the Mosquito Shore. It was founded by William Pitt, a young immigrant of means (with an illustrious name, but no kinship with the great English statesmen to follow). Arriving from Bermuda in 1699, he and others established sugar plantations up and down the river valley for miles, engaged in logwood and pine cutting, raised herds of cattle, and carried on general trading. The upriver site selection was fortunate for the Mosquito Shore; the valley was by all accounts uncommonly productive. Scores of African slaves provided most of the labor. With Pitt's impressive manor house and extensive holdings as centerpiece and with him as leader, the settlement grew rapidly in size and influence. For a number of decades, it presented the appearance of stolid, relatively prosperous stability. (By 1750 the population of this and adjacent settlements was estimated to approach 3,000.)[6] With its neat, substantial, white-washed houses of wood or wood and plaster, some shingled and often with two stories, it had an air of permanence that set it apart from other settlements. For all this, it became in Spanish eyes the most visible sign of more than passing British encroachment on the Shore. (It is no wonder, then, that it became the object of major assault almost a century later.) Through most of the eighteenth century, Black River quietly thrived and Pitt advanced to old age.

During the first 100 years, until almost the middle of the eighteenth century, the British settlement on the mainland of Central America had no official link with either London or Jamaica. It was during this period, however, that the British settlers manipulated the natives in the interests of British occupants and their lucrative trade, which was highly dependent upon the good will and assistance of the Indians. The system of control began by "crowning" a Mosquito native "king." This was first done when Jeremy, the Sambo chief, was taken from Cape Gracias a Dios to Jamaica in 1687, a "cocked hat" was placed on his head, and he was presented with a certificate. Thenceforward, the native "kings" were chosen by the governor of Jamaica and dressed up with silk hat, red coat, shirt, and broadsword by a British clique of advisers. Control was administered by "governors," "generals" and "admirals," and "dukes" in various subregions. The system quickly evolved into a hierarchy, with all the appurtenances of high office. The king and his staff, flattered by their counterfeit titles and subject to intense rivalry among themselves, were puppets of the British. However, they were highly influential, commanding scores of natives whose assistance was essential in economic activities and military operations.

This system continued almost without break after the protectorate was made official (several decades later) and into the nineteenth century. The way was prepared for the later claim by Britain that the Shore was a separate, sovereign part of Central America to which Spain and Nicaragua had no claim. As for the privileged position of the British, it became firmly established with the first Mosquito kingdom and was still intact over a century later, as this commentary reveals:

> During the lifetime of the late king, George Frederick, any Englishman could traverse from one end of the country to the other, without the expense of a yard of cloth, for the king's orders were to feed and lodge them, and provide them with horses when they wanted.[7]

The natives, growing significantly in number and establishing numerous towns of their own near the British settlements, especially Black River, Cape Gracias a Dios, and Bluefields, turned increasingly to predatory incursions into Spanish Nicaragua for their livelihood. With their newly acquired tastes for things which only the British could provide—clothes, firearms, and drink—but not inclined to become agricultural laborers, such plundering was "essential." Moreover, they had become accustomed to this while the buccaneers held sway, and they were not inclined to more peaceable pursuits. The British, interested in the contraband trade across the frontier and not wishing to see it endangered, now found it difficult to control the Mosquitos.

In the early eighteenth century there were repeated Sambo-Mosquito raids on isolated villages of the Spanish frontier in the interior. The purpose was not only booty but also Indian slaves, profitable human items for trade. In this frontier zone were weaker tribes of Indians who had been pushed into the interior wilderness by the coastal Sambo-Mosquitos. The Spanish were attempting to pacify them, convert them, and win their allegiance against outside, opposing forces. In this, they employed the mission system, as in other thinly populated frontier zones of Latin America. However, it was not successful. Not only were many of these Indians carried off in raids, but others scattered in fear of attack, died from epidemics, or remained hostile to missionary efforts. Some even joined the Sambo-Mosquito enemy.

The Spanish military were not able to protect the frontier from raids, which at times went well beyond the frontier, even to the shores of Lake Nicaragua. Having started the Indians on this course by encouraging the raids, the British later were able to interest their allies more in participating in contraband activities than in sheer destructive plunder. Even then, though diminishing, the raids did not cease. The Spanish became convinced that they must go on the offensive if they expected to prevent attacks upon their frontier and to control the rampant smuggling. This meant a return to the coast, to the source of the trouble, and dislodging the enemy there, where he had become entrenched over the previous century.

It was 100 years after the first British settlers came to the Mosquito Shore and the formation of their alliance with the Sambo-Mosquitos that plans for Spain's coastal offensive got under way in 1733. But it was another 50 years before it could be executed. Three general wars with Britain intervened, and the Spanish were repeatedly forced into defensive positions. An essential part of the plan for the Mosquito Shore was always construction of a large fort on the Caribbean, which could be used both to launch an assault on Black River, the key point of British encroachment, and to control the contraband traffic. A proper site was finally selected at Omoa Bay, near the mouth of the Ulua River in Honduras, but during the War of Jenkins' Ear, beginning in 1739, Spain's attention was diverted to other parts of the Caribbean (Panama, Costa Rica, Belize) and the world.

With *de facto* control of the Shore well established when the war broke out, Governor Edward Trelawney of Jamaica decided the time was ripe for formalization of the protectorate. He sent one of his subordinates, British Infantry Captain Robert Hodgson, to Black River in 1739 as the Mosquito Shore's first superintendent. Hodgson's instructions were to cement the relationship with the Sambo-Mosquitos, to use them in repelling Spanish advances toward the Caribbean, and to stimulate more British trade in the region. During the War of Jenkins' Ear he was the British counterpart of Spain's Luis Diez Navarro, an engineer who had been dispatched to reconnoiter the Mosquito Shore with the objective of improving Spanish defenses. Defense of the thriving upriver settlement of Black River was on Hodgson's mind also: a priority after his arrival was construction of two fortresses, one at the mouth of the river and another on a nearby lagoon. While Hodgson directed numerous Sambo-Mosquito raids in the interior, Diez Navarro sent his reports on British activity along the Shore and recommendations for meeting the threat.

Meanwhile, the new superintendent diligently promoted British interests in other ways, as well. He cultivated Spanish merchants at the other end of the contraband trade and occasional Spanish officials who were willing, for favors and bribes, to render aid. He also attempted to ensure that Britain would be the beneficiary of most of this trade and that little was diverted to competing foreign nations. He was initially successful in improving the British liaison with the Sambo-Mosquitos, upon whom he exerted impressive control. The fact that he was married to Isabel Pitt, daughter of the esteemed William and his Spanish wife, was an advantage.[8] Upon Pitt's death, however, the unreliable natives rebelled against the governorship of the son-in-law, and the family was forced to withdraw from the Shore temporarily. After its return, one of Hodgson's four sons (also named Robert) succeeded to the superintendency but was unable to reestablish his father's firm hold on the Indians.

In spite of official links with the home country, some British settlers seemed to wish for a less tenuous connection which might encourage greater colonization and give more hope to settlers already there. There was a feeling of isolation and much uncertainty as to the region's future political status and development. Writing in 1766, one member of the Hodgson family, whose report was unearthed by proponents of renewed British colonization in the next century, called it a "shadow of a colony," the great potential of which was not realized for want of encouragement from London.[9]

A conciliatory period between Spain and Britain followed the War of Jenkins' Ear. The Spanish crown had authorized the construction of Fort Omoa, recommended by Diez Navarro in 1743; he directed the work (begun in 1756) and remained until the fort was completed, twenty years later. However, the Spanish government did not now see the fort's immediate purpose in terms of an attack upon the British; rather, it was to serve as a base for customs and controlling contraband. Fort Omoa was begun in the same year the Seven Years' War broke out between Britain and France in North America, and toward the end of that war, with the accession of a new king in Spain, a new anti-British policy prevailed. Spain entered the war in 1761, unprepared for the British strength that would be manifested during the next two years in the Caribbean. Spain had hoped to attack Belize and Black River, but the attacks never materialized. The British seized the initiative on several fronts in the Caribbean and elsewhere in the Spanish empire.

For a decade after this war, the Spanish attempted to win over the interior Indian tribes and the Mosquitos, not by missionary endeavors but by adopting the methods that had been used successfully by the British. Rivalry between the Mosquito and Sambo hierarchies and uncertainty as to continued British control had seemed to make them susceptible to defection. Therefore the Spanish began making overtures, making it clear that they could supply the Indians with rum, cloth, firearms, and other things the British had provided, in return for their friendship. Then in 1776 the Sambo king was captured and detained by the Spaniards. Since he had grievances against the British superintendent of the Shore, the younger Hodgson, the Spanish considered the king a possible convert—something much desired, since winning over the Sambos would be the greatest prize of all. But their entreaties, though at first encouraging, proved unsuccessful. Once more, war between Britain and Spain was threatening, and the Indians did not desert their old ally.

Unhappy with the results of the Seven Years' War, which had not ejected the British from the Central American mainland, King Charles III of Spain felt that the preoccupation of Britain with the American Revolution could be the long-awaited opportunity. As the British weakened in North America, the Spanish declared war in 1779. They had completed their construction of Fort Omoa, amassed a large Central American army, and seemed well prepared to reclaim the Mosquito Shore.

But again the British seized the offensive. Their prime objective, directed from Jamaica by the governor, was to capture Fort Inmaculada Concepción, thereby gaining control of the San Juan–Lake Nicaragua waterway, as well as a canal site, and severing Spanish Central America—a dream of British leaders that went far beyond Mosquito Shore colonization. This was a far grander goal—a decisive blow at Spain's hegemony in Central America, and not only along the Caribbean coast but across to the Pacific as well. An attempt had been made in 1762, during the Seven Years' War, but the aborted mission and failure to capture the fort had apparently not convinced everyone that it was invulnerable. Rather, the contrary.

Before this offensive was mounted, however, attention was directed northward, where the British believed Belize was in danger. The first action along the coast was consequently an assault upon the supposedly impregnable Fort Omoa, which faced its first test. With troops brought from Jamaica, supplemented by troops from Black River (including Sambo-Mosquitos) and the Bay Islands, British forces overcame the undermanned fort and forced its surrender within forty-eight hours, before reinforcements could arrive from Guatemala. When the Spanish troops arrived—who had been intended for the great Spanish offensive, "so often planned . . . and so poorly executed or postponed," as one historian puts it[10]—they faced the necessity of recapturing the fort. After a month of preparations and gathering additional troops, the Spanish forces, now greatly superior in number to the British defenders, were able to do so, but the British escaped by sea before the abandoned fort was reoccupied.

The British now turned to their ultimate goal and what was probably their most dramatic action in more than two centuries of Mosquito Shore occupancy: control of the San Juan–Lake Nicaragua waterway. Its control was of international significance, for had the British expansionist plan succeeded, Central America's history might have taken quite a different course and resulted in a much different political picture from the one we know. The expedition, directed by Governor John Dalling of Jamaica and commanded by Captain John Polson, arrived at the mouth of the San Juan in March of 1780. Horatio Nelson, then a captain, was in command of supporting naval forces aboard the *Hinchinbrook*. After several days of establishing a supply and reinforcement base at the mouth of the river and securing it against Spanish assistance that might be sent upriver from the Caribbean, the expedition departed for Fort Inmaculada. As planned, a large contingent of colonists and Sambo-Mosquitos (including King George) from Black River and other points along the Shore joined the force. Nelson, whose duties were to carry part of the troops and to convoy the ships to the coast, volunteered to go upriver with his sailors.

Two weeks later, the siege of the fort began. It lasted seventeen days and was very difficult, with both sides running low on ammunition and provisions. No help for the Spanish defenders could get through from Granada, but notice of the attack on Fort Inmaculada had been received and hurried preparations were made to prevent the British from going beyond, to the lake. In case the fort should fall, the Spaniards immediately began to construct another strong stockade at San Carlos. When their water supplies, obtainable only from the river, were cut off by the British, the Spanish forces at Fort Inmaculada were doomed, and they surrendered on April 29. Nelson did not see the capture, although he distinguished himself in this campaign as he was to do later as admiral of the British fleet. His advice and exploits in the early stages were extremely useful to Polson, who later commended him highly and gave him much credit for the victory. However, Nelson was stricken with dysentery and had to be sent downriver after the siege began. In a very weak condition he arrived in Jamaica, almost dead. Too debilitated to take up his new command, Nelson had to return to England on leave, and it was a year before he fully recovered. He was only the first of many on this expedition, however, to suffer the effects of dysentery and fever, and before it was all over there would be few survivors.

The expedition coincided with the rainiest period of the year in an area which normally receives over 200 inches annually—a profound mistake in timing. Rain and disease were valuable allies of the Spaniards, who were holding at San Carlos even though Fort Inmaculada had fallen. In mid-May, Polson wrote to General Kemble, who was on his way to the fort to take command: "It is not in my power to send you Returns, every one being Sick, some Companies have not a non-Commissioned Officer that can come to a Parade."[11] Casualties on both sides had been few, but many Spanish defenders of the fort, sent as prisoners to Cuba, died at sea in a lengthy, circuitous voyage beset by delays and mishaps.

It is not primarily the taking of the fort, though it had been heroic, for which the 1780 San Juan campaign is remembered in British history. Indeed, there was little occasion for jubilation when, in a steady downpour, General Stephen Kemble arrived at the fort. Born in America of a British loyalist family, Kemble was commanding officer of the same regiment on duty in Jamaica that was sent on the San Juan expedition, but he had been serving as a deputy adjutant general of the British army in the American Revolution until the previous October. When, afterwards, he returned to Jamaica, it had already been planned that Polson would command the expedition, and Kemble graciously declined to take over. But after the expedition was under way, Governor Dalling sent Kemble—as brigadier general—to take command, carrying with him reinforcements. He was to be responsible for the next phase of the campaign, to be directed at the lake and the Pacific plain of Nicaragua. A realist with much military experience, he recognized the difficult odds and reported them regularly to Governor Dalling.

Kemble faced a dilemma from the moment he arrived. Under Polson's command, the Indians had begun to desert in large numbers and little assistance could be expected from them. "They received your presents, gave you fair words in the day, and deserted at night," reported Kemble.[12] Usually more reliable, the Indians were unaccustomed to this kind of operation and had not worked well with the cautious Polson, under whom they felt overly restrained. Many decades later, after Orlando Roberts, a trader and writer, encountered some Indians who had been on the expedition, Roberts wrote:

> They uniformly agreed that the expedition had been undertaken at an im-
> proper season of the year; that they had been restricted in their mode of acting,
> and obliged to conform to habits, discipline, and diet, which dispirited
> them.[13]

Reinforcements and provisions did not arrive from the coast. On the few occasions that river craft were able to get through to the fort, after many difficulties and long delays en route (some were thirty days on the river), provisions were damaged and spoiled, and troop replacements too sick to be of use. All the while, illness and death mounted daily in the fort. On June 9 Kemble wrote in his journal:

> . . . The Officers have been, to a man, almost all sick. The Men's Tents so bad
> that they keep out no water. My intention to build Huts, but have not Men to
> do it, and Provisions very scarce, So much so as to Alarm me. Relapses almost
> certain the moment a Soldier does any duty. The Troops so sickly that some
> Corps have not a Man fit for duty, and the few Guards we have obliged to
> remain from two to six days on duty.[14]

Even the task of burying the dead became too great for the few remaining men who were not ill, and corpses were thrown into the river or allowed to be devoured by vultures. Rations were steadily reduced, so that malnutrition made it difficult for those who were not ill to perform their duties. At times the troops had only weevil-filled "Indian corn" to eat, which the Spaniards had left at the fort.

It required almost three weeks to get the long-awaited *Germain*, a flat-bottom, armed vessel, which would be needed in the upriver and lake assault, over the rapids. Then it was damaged, and repairs by the few carpenters in the fort who were able to work consumed another two weeks. Finally, in early July, with the late arrival of reinforcements and provisions from the coast, Kemble apparently felt ready to proceed upriver to the lake with 250 men, "one hundred of them useless, being Convalescents in a weakly state."[15] (Meanwhile, scouts had been sent ahead to observe the Spanish installations.) It was an arduous journey. The rains were almost constant and the river was swollen, making navigation difficult against a strong current. Many Indians had deserted, so that boatmen were in short supply, and the substitution of British sailors proved unsatisfactory throughout. As Kemble observed later, "Whites receive no addition of Constitution from being called Batteaux Men, etc. and fall sick as fast as other, from whence disappointments daily happen, and Craft two-thirds up the River are sometimes obliged to return, which would not be the case were they manned by Blacks or People of Colour, who by Constitution are better able to bear the Climate."[16] Provisions arrived infrequently and in insufficient quantities from the fort, which had not received additional shipments from the coast. The men regularly went into the forest to kill game and collect plantains. In the almost incessant downpour, they were "scarcely able to crawl for want of Shoes and Stockings."[17] Each day, more and more sick had to be sent back downriver. Not surprisingly, there were morale problems. Often, it was difficult to get officers to obey orders and to perform their duties, and commanding officers were frequently in conflict with one another.

By July 24 the force, with only 80 men fit for duty, was within 8 miles of the Spanish fortifications, to which a reconnoitering party had been sent the previous day to obtain information on the best plan for attack. Its report was very discouraging: the redoubt, now completed, was strong, capable of holding up to 300 men, and well defended by armed vessels. Attack from the river would be very disadvantageous.[18] Moreover, the Spaniards had discovered the scouting party and given an alarm, so that a surprise attack was no longer possible. The condition of his troops, the weather, provisions, and the necessity of preserving enough food at the fort to maintain its garrison caused Kemble to abandon his plans for an immediate advance toward the lake. He and his weakened force returned to Fort Inmaculada the next day, and on July 31 he left the fort for the coast, with boatloads of sick men. A garrison of 150 of the least ill was left behind to maintain the fort.

This proved to be the end of the San Juan River–Lake Nicaragua offensive for the British. Although Kemble might have wished to send reinforcements and provisions from San Juan harbor to support further action up-river, he was not able to do so. Upon his arrival at the mouth of the river, he found everything in extreme disarray, and hardly one healthy soldier in the fortified base. He found

> the Sick in a Miserable, shocking condition, without any one to attend them, or even to bury the Dead who lay on the beach shocking to behold; the same mortality raging among the poor Soldiers on board ship, where Accumulated filth had made all air Putrid; officers dying daily, and so wore down with disorders, lassitude, etc. that they are even as filthy and regardless where they lay as the Soldiers, never stirring from their Beds for days, though they might walk.[19]

Meanwhile, in Jamaica, Governor Dalling was reluctant to see the grand plan unfulfilled. He had remained optimistic, and his every letter to Kemble urged him on, assuring him of reinforcements and supplies, including medicines. Even as late as July 28, after Kemble's abandonment of the lake offensive and his preparations to depart from the fort, Dalling, not knowing of these events, wrote and expressed concern for the sick troops. He hoped that the healthy ones might push on to the lake, where the climate was more favorable, and offered the encouragement of a convoy, expected any hour (in Jamaica) from England, loaded with provisions of all kinds for transshipment to the San Juan. That convoy, upon which so much had depended for the success of the plan, arrived on August 9, but it was much too late. Perhaps its earlier arrival would have been of little avail, in view of the fact that the season of excessive rainfall had started almost as the expedition got under way, and this was a major factor in its failure.

The day after the arrival of the convoy in Jamaica, Governor Dalling wrote to Kemble that he had received reports of an impending invasion of his island by the combined forces of France and Spain. Defense of the eastern Caribbean now became the vital matter at hand—there might be another use for the recently arrived troops and supplies. Now reconciled to temporary abandonment of the Nicaragua operation, he ordered Kemble to proceed with most of his remaining troops to Bluefields, the new British base, and stay there until such time that another strike across the isthmus could be mounted, via the San Juan or another route. Even now, the governor was not willing to forsake the plan altogether.

From October 1780 through January 1781, Kemble remained in Bluefields, in a sort of holding operation, uncertain as to what his course of action would be. While there, he attempted to regain support of the Indians, including those who had deserted the San Juan expedition. The British expected that they would be needed later. Although Kemble evidently thought little of the Indians as allies, and considered them to be too pampered, he adhered to policy. Also, there was the continuing task of seeing that the garrison at Fort Inmaculada was supported, at least minimally. Resources were limited; even conditions at Bluefields were marginal for the troops, many of whom were still sick. Without vastly more support for the fort, Kemble felt it should be abandoned, but knowing how important the San Juan–Lake Nicaragua objective was for his government, he was reluctant to come out strongly in opposition to further efforts. He nevertheless made clear to the governor his grave reservations and emphasized the extreme difficulties in either a return up the San Juan or a new expedition up the Bluefields (Escondido) River. Writing more candidly to the fort's commander, he confessed that he dreaded the undertaking, should it come to pass.[20]

By early November, however, Governor Dalling, evidently convinced of the futility of holding the fort any longer, made the decision that it be destroyed and evacuated. He wanted all retrievable supplies and equipment of the San Juan operation, as well as the evacuated troops, to be brought to Bluefields and then be sent to Black River to defend against an expected Spanish assault there. It was three weeks before Kemble received Dalling's order, and mid-December before the order was received at Fort Inmaculada. By this time, conditions at the fort were so deplorable that Kemble wondered if the garrison, so short of provisions, might not abandon the fort before it received the order to do so.

The remainder of his time in Bluefields was spent mainly in directing and expediting the evacuation. Continually concerned that the Spaniards might attack before his troops got out, he knew that, with the coming drier weather, this possibility became ever greater. It was early January 1781 before the last British forces left the fort, and, true to Kemble's expectations, the Spanish had set out from the lake four days previously with the objective of recapturing it. Although it had taken two weeks to place the charges for destroying the fort, this was insufficient time to prepare for blowing up such a massive structure. (It had been estimated that the job would require several weeks.) Only a small part of the fort had been demolished when the Spanish forces appeared on January 3, and under pressure of time, more charges were placed as the garrison prepared to withdraw that night. After the troops embarked, the fuses were lit, but the results could not be known. Later reconnaissance disclosed extensive damage to the tower and ramparts, and a huge accumulation of debris, but destruction had been only partial. The fort was not in ruins; it had been triumphantly reoccupied by the Spaniards.

When evacuation was completed, Kemble's successor at Bluefields was instructed to deploy the forces to Black River, and General Kemble returned to Jamaica—without regrets, we assume, for he recognized a lost cause when he saw one. "Never was there so complete a ruin," he wrote of the episode.[21] The fiasco was the last of Britain's attempts to accomplish her ends in Central America by armed invasion of the Spanish interior. Incidentally, it marked the end of the significance of the San Juan route until the mid-nineteenth century.

The consuming goal of the Spanish had been the regaining of Trujillo and expulsion of the British and their Indian cohorts from Black River, the capital of their unofficial colony. This was considered the key to establishing Spanish control over the entire Mosquito Coast. They had held up their larger offensive because of the attack on Fort Inmaculada Concepción, but nevertheless, early in 1780, as the British were preparing for the San Juan expedition, they had reoccupied Trujillo. This old port, important to the Spanish in early colonial days, had been repeatedly attacked and pillaged by buccaneers. In 1643 it had been abandoned, and most of the town destroyed, but some of its fortifications were still intact. Since that time, it and the Bay Islands had been controlled by the British. The recapture of this base put the Spaniards in a good position for an assault on nearby Black River, and a destructive raid in April 1780, doubtless to test its defenses, drove out its inhabitants. This was only temporary, but for many months the settlement was weakly defended while the British forces, some from Black River, were engaged on the San Juan.

The main offensive did not come until March of 1782. By this time the British had withdrawn from Fort Inmaculada, and expecting that Black River would be attacked, attempted to support it from their base at Blue-

fields. During the fifteen months between the reoccupation at Fort Inmaculada and the full-scale land and sea assault on Black River, the
Spaniards made elaborate preparations. They amassed troops by the thousands from all over Central America, sent arms and supplies to Trujillo, and
dispatched a large fleet of ships from various parts of the Spanish Main.
Finally, the force was ready. The American Revolutionary War had ended,
and further delay meant additional British forces would be available for
Caribbean duty.

After an easy capture of the Bay Islands, the expedition set out from
Trujillo on March 30. The vastly superior numbers of Spaniards overwhelmed the two British forts defending Black River, one at the mouth of
the river and the other a short distance to the south, on Brewer's Lagoon. A
large Spanish force, proceeding overland from interior Honduras to rendezvous with the sea force, met adverse weather and had to withdraw; but it
made no difference. The Spanish captured Black River in early April and
occupied its forts. Although most of the British defenders and inhabitants,
including the British superintendent and the Sambo-Mosquitos, escaped to
Cape Gracias a Dios, it was a great satisfaction to the Spanish to have
expelled them and to be in control of their major stronghold.

But the Spaniards were not to get farther down the coast than Black
River, and even it was not to be retained. Because of British victories in the
eastern Caribbean, Spanish forces and ships had to be diverted there, and
by the following August the British had so strengthened their position that
men and supplies could be spared to aid the beleaguered Mosquito Shore
protectorate. For more then four months of occupation at Black River, the
Spaniards were harassed by the Sambo-Mosquitos, and when the Indians
joined a new British expeditionary force, sent out from Jamaica, the first
engagement at Fort Dalling (on Brewer's Lagoon) was bloody. In a surprise
attack, the revenge-seeking Sambos, difficult to restrain, went on a rampage
and massacred almost all of the small Spanish force. The main fort at the
mouth of Black River, the next objective, was greatly undermanned and
short of supplies, and the British had cut its lifeline to Trujillo. Meanwhile,
news had come of the horror at Fort Dalling. When the fleet of British ships
arrived offshore on August 28, filled with additional troops and Sambo-
Mosquitos (still "uncontrollable," the Spanish commander was informed)[22]
acquired at Cape Gracias a Dios, defeat seemed certain; so the Spanish
surrendered. The English were back at Black River.

The Mosquito Coast dominion controversy was still not settled, but both
countries, weary of war, were ready for a negotiated settlement. The British

government was no longer certain that the area's economic value warranted continued struggle. The compromise in the treaty that ended the war in 1783 was that logwood-cutting rights for British colonists would be retained (within certain limits) in Belize, while Spain would have undisputed sovereignty over that area long occupied by English woodcutters. For the Mosquito Shore colonists, the agreement stipulated that they would be evacuated and resettled in Belize. (The agreement was liberalized in favor of British colonists by another pact, signed in 1786, that expanded cutting privileges in Belize, added mahogany as a wood that could be extracted, and assured that the Sambo-Mosquitos would not be mistreated after British departure from the Mosquito Shore.) Still, many settlers felt that they had been dealt a severe blow by their government: the Shore was home to them and they were reluctant to leave it. Young writes of this:

> All was going on prosperously; sugar works commenced; when the people were astounded to hear they were to leave their homes, and wander forth to distant countries; the British Government having agreed with Old Spain, that they should be removed. Since my residence on the coast, and during my various peregrinations, I have conversed with several who were born at Black River, and who remember with what sorrow and regret their parents were obliged to leave their houses and plantations.[23]

Moreover, what vexed many was the thought that the British government had been persuaded to abandon them in this manner because of pressure by West Indian plantation interests, fearful of competition from the Shore. They were alleged to have propagated false and malicious reports about its adverse climate, unhealthy conditions, and unproductive soils in an attempt to turn the British government and public opinion against further support of settlement on the Mosquito Shore. Nevertheless, most of the colonists, from Black River to Bluefields, numbering about 3,000, evacuated during the year 1786/87. For the majority, the destination was Belize, but a few went to Jamaica and other British Caribbean islands. A very small number, including Robert Hodgson the younger, who had been superintendent at Black River from 1768 to 1776, was allowed to remain if they swore loyalty to Spain.

During the next four years the Spanish attempted to colonize the vacated Mosquito Coast and to eliminate the hostility of the Sambo-Mosquitos. However—unfortunately for Spain and for the independent Nicaragua to follow—neither method secured control of the area.

It was easier to get colonists from Spain and the Canary Islands—as was accomplished by the early part of 1788—than to assure them security in their new homes. The plan was to distribute the colonists, numbering over 1,000, mainly in Bluefields, Cape Gracias a Dios, and Black River.[24] As it turned out, very few were attracted to those places, because of Indian hostility, and the few who settled at the cape and Black River, close to the garrisons for safety, were soon driven out along with the soldiers. They could produce little food on the sandy soils along the coast, to which they were confined, and had to be supported by food shipped in at government expense. Even so, they fell prey to disease. Most of the colonists who came to the coast and stayed there remained in Trujillo, contrary to the plan. But the town had attractions: a less oppressive climate, better soil, an active port, and the security that was deficient elsewhere. Doubtless the new settlers were an impetus for the port's resurgence during this period, the single contribution of the venture. From Black River to the San Juan, the coast was still devoid of the Spanish imprint.

In their campaign to win the friendship of the Sambo-Mosquitos, the Spanish tried to use the influence of Robert Hodgson the younger, who had defected to the Spanish during the war and been allowed to remain at Bluefields as a prosperous planter and trader. They appointed him governor of the Nicaraguan Mosquito Shore in 1787 and gave him wide control, since the Spanish had been unable to establish a military presence in that area. Hodgson claimed to have much influence with the Mosquito Indians, but it soon appeared that he did not. Thereupon, the Spanish dealt directly with the Sambo king, based near the cape, and the leading Mosquito chief (called governor), based farther south at Tuapi Lagoon.

These two men, King George and Governor Breton, had long been rivals for power. Breton had proved responsive to Spanish overtures before, but during the war had remained loyal to the British. At any rate, both chiefs were invited to Cartagena to receive many honors and gifts amid great festivity. King George, though accepting the gifts, again refused to give his allegiance to the Spaniards, for whom he could not relinquish an underlying hatred. Although the British were gone, he was still pro-British. Governor Breton, however, was pliable. His infatuation with a young Spanish girl, captured in a raid on the frontier, was used by the Spanish to win him over and, through his influence, possibly the rest of the Sambo-Mosquitos and interior tribes. He first took the girl as his concubine, but after his conversion to her Catholic faith promised to marry her. The Spanish had always believed that if the Indians could be converted to Catholicism, their hostility would cease; and the marriage of a converted Mosquito chief to a

Spanish Catholic seemed sure to accomplish this. But it was not to be.

Chief Breton, baptized and renamed Don Carlos in Cartagena, married the Spanish girl in a ceremony performed by the bishop of Nicaragua in León cathedral in January of 1789. Now firmly in the Spanish camp, he returned to the Mosquito Coast shortly afterward, accompanied by his new wife and missionaries. The Spanish hoped this would be the beginning of Indian pacification in that troublesome region; however, it soon became apparent that Don Carlos, like Hodgson, did not exert the powerful influence that was expected of him. The reaction on the coast was exceedingly negative. The chief found that King George's Sambos treated him as an emissary of the Spaniards and were, accordingly, unresponsive or belligerent. Returning to his home at Tuapi, he met rebellion among his subordinate Mosquito chiefs. Finally, with no following among his people, and the missionaries and his bride departed, he was murdered.[25] This, once again, was the Sambo-Mosquitos' answer to the Spanish. Soon afterward, Robert Hodgson was forced to flee from Bluefields.

As the eighteenth century ended there were no further efforts by the Spanish to control the Mosquito Coast. In fact, their defenses at the cape and at Black River were deteriorating, as were those elsewhere in Central America. The colonies reflected Spain's weakness at home, its administrative ineptitude, its involvement in Continental wars. In any case, it would not be long before the colonies would be aflame with revolution and Spain would be confronted with the more critical problems of a crumbling empire.

By 1800, the small garrison and the few colonists at the cape had been withdrawn, victims of Sambo hostility, and Black River had been invaded by Sambos and retaken. During Spanish occupation, the once-thriving English settlement of neat buildings had begun to fall into ruin, and now it became a Sambo village, like many another on the Shore, waiting for the British to return.

The Revival of British Influence, 1800–1844

From the onset of the French Revolution in 1789 through the Napoleonic Wars, Britain and Spain were embroiled in Europe for a quarter century. Twice Spain was bound to France against Britain, twice she was allied with Britain in a coalition of European powers against France. Throughout much of this period she was unable to maintain contact with her colonies in Latin America and thus was forced to tolerate their freer trade relations. Her monopolistic trade arrangements were suspended for long periods, and establishment of commercial representation, in the form of nonofficial "consuls" by neutral powers, was permitted. In this, the United States was a beneficiary. Its trade with Latin America, very minor before 1796, increased notably in the following decade, during most of which Spain was at war with Britain. Much of this was in the form of reexports on neutral U.S. ships. The British, meanwhile, established free ports in its Caribbean colonies, which permitted trade with the enemy. Also, between 1796 and 1808, Britain and France at different times, depending upon their alliances, instigated and supported early revolutionary activity in Latin America against Spain. Their contacts with such early revolutionary leaders as Francisco de Miranda and the influences that followed helped lay the groundwork for the ensuing wars of independence.

The catalyst for rebellion in the Latin American colonies was events in Spain after 1808: Napoleon's invasion, the forced abdication and exile of Ferdinand VII, the placement of Napoleon's brother, Joseph Bonaparte, on the throne, the outbreak of the Peninsula War (of resistance against the French), and the domestic and colonial discord created by the interim provisional Spanish governments. While the colonies were at one with the Spanish people in their rebellion against Bonapartist rule, many used the occasion of turmoil and political fluctuations in the mother country to launch revolutionary movements to achieve their own independence. As the provisional governments of Cádiz—first the central junta, then the regency, and finally the parliamentary Cortes itself, with its famed 1812 constitution—were weakened by persistent conservative opposition within Spain, they eventually lost support in the colonies also, despite liberal tendencies. With loyalty to a Spanish government of any sort faltering among Latin Americans, whatever encouragement had been offered by the 1812 Cádiz constitution disappeared upon Ferdinand's return in 1814, and the revolutionary movement intensified.

Throughout the Peninsula War, however, Latin American revolutionaries from Mexico to the Rio de la Plata could look to Britain for support no longer. Britain was now an ally of Spain's provisional government in the third coalition of European powers against Napoleon, and their armies were fighting the invaders together on Spanish soil. Britain's position was nevertheless ambivalent. She needed Latin America's trade, and was fearful of the United States' gaining advantages in this rivalry, but at the same time could not give official support to the independence movements (although many British citizens fought with the revolutionaries) while she was allied with Spain. Besides her opposition to the formation of democratic republics in the New World—Britain was long to hope that monarchies would evolve, even after it became apparent that the revolutions would succeed—there was the practical matter of needing Latin America's resources and bullion in the joint Anglo-Spanish action against Napoleon's armies. Also, there was no wish for Spain's resources to be diverted from that struggle. Opposed, however, to the rigid commercial restrictions of the Spanish colonial system, Britain pressed the Cádiz government for liberalization of these policies while insisting upon her right to trade freely with the rebellious colonies.

In the United States, there was no such lack of government support for the revolutionary movements. Expectations were that they would facilitate acquisition of adjacent Spanish territories in dispute after the Louisiana Purchase, curtail European influence in the Western Hemisphere, and bring about even more profitable trade relationships for the young republic. Moreover, the recent experience of their own revolution made Americans sympathetic to the overthrow of monarchical and colonial institutions and the formation of independent states to the south. However, as was the case with Britain, no material aid was forthcoming as a result of the entreaties of Latin American agents in Washington.

The War of 1812 temporarily diverted the United States from the matter of the revolting Latin American colonies while, at the same time, causing losses in trade with the region because of the British navy. When the war ended and Napoleon was overthrown (soon thereafter), both Britain and the United States continued a policy of neutrality (however violated) with respect to the wars of independence in Latin America and Spain's attempts to recover her empire. Both insisted upon free-trade access to the Spanish colonies, and committed themselves to thwarting any European assistance to Spain in the reconquest, but each continued to be apprehensive of the designs of the other with regard to political influence, territorial gains, and commercial advantage.

Mediation attempts by Britain began early, and intensified after Napoleon's defeat in 1815. However, Ferdinand VII, who returned to Madrid after the war and reclaimed his throne, was not interested in compromise on the colonial problem. He was determined on a course of reconquest in the colonies and reinstitution of autocracy and repression at home. The gains of liberalism during the Cádiz years were wiped out. The single instance of successful mediation by Britain was in the matter of East Florida, which Spain finally relinquished to the United States after she had grown fearful of the latter's threats to her elsewhere, possibly in Mexico and Cuba.

Meanwhile, the captaincy-general of Central America had been caught up in the independence movements after 1808. There, as elsewhere in Latin America, rights of American-born Spaniards against Iberian-born administrators became an issue as the former group pressed for greater power in its local government and affairs. When Central America's delegates to the Cortes at Cádiz were elected from the six provinces, they were of liberal bent and encouraged by the provisions of the 1812 constitution, which they signed. However, the new captain general of Guatemala, José de Bustamante, who arrived in 1811, had different ideas. He represented the old regime and resolved to preserve the authoritarian Iberian hierarchy and to prevent reforms, political or economic, in the colony. At first conciliatory, as time went on he not only resisted the liberal colonial measures of the Cortes government in Cádiz but suppressed a number of insurrections— which increased as repression increased—against his authority. He constrained Central America's independence movements until 1814, but subsequently, with the restoration of Ferdinand VII and revocation of the constitution of 1812, he felt safe to pursue with even greater vigor his vindictive defense of authoritarian Spanish rule. Finally, however, Bustamante incurred the disfavor of the crown because of his excesses. He had alienated not only the merchant class of the colony, with which the royal government wished to maintain good relations, but some of his more progressive fellow Spaniards in the *audiencia* of Guatemala, because of his policies. By royal order, he was removed from office in 1817.

Despite the "reign of terror," Bustamante had kept Central America— unlike other parts of the Spanish domain—relatively stable for Spain, not allowing insurrections to grow into bloody conflicts. It was after the Bustamante regime, with a liberal-dominated colonial government installed in Guatemala City, that the independence movement gained headway, and the transition was peaceful. A great impetus was the establishment of free trade with Britain, long a goal of liberal Central American merchants, which stimulated the economy.

While these events transpired, British influence on the Mosquito Shore quietly persisted. Although evacuation of British colonists was almost complete, the British were still in Belize and Jamaica, and when it became apparent, by 1800, that the entire Shore beyond Trujillo to Bluefields and the San Juan River was not effectively controlled by the Spaniards and not successfully settled by them, a slow regress began. As the British renewed their links with the Sambo-Mosquitos and again profited from contraband activities, a gradual influx of colonists occurred, who this time settled mostly in the Bluefields–San Juan area.

Optimism over opportunities afforded by the disintegrating Spanish hold on Central America soon led the British to reestablish the Mosquito "monarchy." The old "king," George, had died at the time of the bloody Sambo recapture of Black River in 1800, and his son, George Frederick, was taken to Belize to be "crowned" by his British friends in 1816. (This was the first step toward proclamation of a new, official protectorate, to come later.) Apparently, the proceedings were not lacking in pomp and ceremony, and probably more than Belize had known before. However, the city had reached unprecedented levels in trading, population, and general prosperity. After the restoration of Ferdinand VII, the rights of British settlers, within circumscribed limits (which had been granted in previous treaties), were confirmed along this stretch of coast. Belize thrived as the center of contraband, serving the restive colonists of Spanish Guatemala who were eager to engage in illicit trade. Thus established as Britain's remaining enclave of influence on the Central American mainland, the port became the base for regaining control farther south.

This account was given of the events in Belize on "coronation day" (though not by a firsthand witness). After cards of invitation were sent to the merchants, inviting them to the coronation of the new king of Mosquitia, the dignitaries and townspeople gathered for a parade on the appointed morning, then set out for the church. George Frederick, in the uniform of a British major, rode horseback between two attendant British officers and his chiefs followed in double file, dressed in sailors' trousers. At the church, the coronation service was read by the chaplain of the Belize colony in the name of the archbishop of Canterbury, amid the roar of cannon salutes by vessels in the harbor. The regalia were a silver-gilt crown, a sword, and a scepter of small value. The chiefs were not allowed to swear their allegiance to the new king until they were baptized (during the same ceremony). After retiring to a schoolroom for the coronation dinner, the new king and his subjects became intoxicated (King George Frederick II became a notorious drunkard and an ineffectual promoter of British interests during the eight years of his reign), then fell asleep on the floor. After this revelry was over, the British authorities put the king and his retinue aboard a British vessel, that took them back to Cape Gracias a Dios.[1]

In 1820 Ferdinand VII, under pressure of revolution at home, restored the liberal provisions of the 1812 constitution in Spain's Latin American colonies, but these conciliatory moves were too late. The effect in Central America, as elsewhere, was to encourage sentiment for independence through the open political discussions and free press that were now permitted. More encouragement came from Mexico, which, after a decade of struggle to free itself from Spanish rule, was successful under Augustín de Iturbide, a defecting royalist general. Mexico's independence (1821) was followed the next year by the crowning of Iturbide as emperor, but meanwhile, on September 15, 1821, delegates from the provinces of the captaincy-general of Guatemala met in Guatemala City and declared independence for Central America. Unlike the response toward Mexico, a rich and important colony, this did not provoke armed resistance by Spain. For a few months after independence, there was interprovincial strife, and none was greater than that of Nicaragua's León, a provincial capital in outright revolt against the central authorities in Guatemala. Finally, despairing of maintaining order and doubtful of Central America's ability to preserve itself as an independent republic, its authorities sought annexation to Iturbide's Mexico. This incorporation—welcomed by Mexico but with far from unanimous support in Central America's provinces—was proclaimed in January of 1822.

For fifteen months Central America was part of Mexico, but throughout this period interprovincial strife and antagonism toward Guatemala's hegemony (much of it economically based) continued. Few benefits were derived from the union, and Mexico's military control and taxes were causes for discord. However, events in Mexico soon forced another change. Political rivals overthrew Iturbide's empire in March of 1823 and his representative in Central America concluded that, under the circumstances, these provinces need not adhere to the annexation agreement with the former government. A constituent assembly of all the provinces, after meeting for several months, declared Central America's absolute independence the following July. The new republic was a federation of five states, including Nicaragua, and was called the United Provinces of Central America, with its capital in Guatemala City.

Meanwhile, the Mosquito Shore had remained free of control, except that of King George Frederick and his chiefs. British traders cultivated their contacts and encouraged cooperation in contraband traffic. Orlando W. Roberts, a scrupulous trader, who traveled widely on the Shore in the early 1820s and later wrote a book about his experiences, found that the young king's good resolutions "constantly vanished when they were put in competition with the pleasures of the bottle."[2] His subjects and opportunistic foreign traders applauded his lavish bestowal of favors during his frequent sprees.

Spring of 1823, on the eve of Central America's independence, saw the first attempt to replant British colonists on the Mosquito Shore in significant numbers. The recolonization scheme was one of a number of escapades devised by a wide-ranging Scottish adventurer, Gregor MacGregor, who had been involved in the attempt to wrest East Florida from Spain and more lately, in the independence movements of Venezuela and New Granada. In 1819 British merchants, with the promise of reaping rich commercial advantages in that area, once independence came, had financed a force of mercenaries to aid in the struggle. The recruits of this British "foreign legion" were a mixed lot, with varying motives. Many were motivated only by self-interest, particularly the pay (which was not forthcoming, once they were in the field, and thus did not reinforce loyalty), and had no scruples. MacGregor was one of these; and his record as commander of a mercenary regiment in the Panama campaign was not distinguished. Soon after its capture of Portobello, the Spanish stronghold that guarded the Panama isthmus, the Spaniards counterattacked and MacGregor had thereupon deserted the fort, leaving his men to carry on the battle while he sent directions for them not to surrender—from an offshore vessel. Receiving no aid, the British were powerless to hold out. The fort fell, its defenders became prisoners of the Spaniards, and the vessel, with MacGregor, put out to sea. In 1820 he had landed at Cape Gracias a Dios, where he stayed for a time with King George Frederick. While there, in return for rum and the items cherished by the Mosquitos, he obtained from the king a grant to a huge tract of land in the area of Black River, which included a tributary region called the Poyais, the homeland of a tribe of Indians called Poyers. Without funds but with the grant in his pocket, MacGregor set out for England, where he interested a group of merchants in forming a colonization company. Although a settlement of colonists was one objective, the directors of the company admitted that their main purpose was "the supplying of British dry goods to the revolted provinces."[3] Again, the commercial motive.

Based on the "information" supplied by MacGregor, the propaganda for recruiting colonists was ridiculous and fraudulent, but it aimed at exploiting the hopes of unaware Englishmen and Irish. Calling himself "His Serene Highness Gregor, Prince of Poyais, Cazique of the Poyer Nation, Defender of the Indians," MacGregor extolled the healthy climate, the rich soil, the abundant crops, woods, horses and cattle, the many gold mines, the variety of marine resources, the harbors unrivaled for shipping, and the Indians, who he said were affectionately attached to Britain, advanced in civilization, and more than willing to contribute their labor.[4] All of this sounded very attractive, and more than a few were willing to make down payments on land unseen and to migrate to this New World paradise.

The expectations of the more than 200 colonists who arrived during the late winter and spring of 1823 were cruelly dashed from the beginning. At the mouth of the Black River, where the first contingent of colonists landed (they never ventured beyond the coast, although the lands in the Poyais grant extended far to the interior), there were no houses or church, as they had been promised awaited them—only unbroken forest to the water's edge. A site was selected for settlement about two miles away, on Brewer's Lagoon, which by coincidence was the site of the last Spanish settlement and, probably, the destroyed Fort Dalling. The land had to be cleared immediately to make a place to pitch tents, or, as it turned out, makeshift wigwams of sheets and blankets or leaves of trees. Thus began many weeks of misery. Disappointment was so intense that the colonists did little to make life as bearable as it might have been, even in the tropics. The ill-fated nature of the undertaking was foreshadowed very early by the flight, without notice, of the ship that had brought them, which sailed away with a large part of their dry and unspoiled provisions—arms, spirits, merchandise, and medicines. The captain sent word that, fearing another norther like the one that assailed them upon arrival, he would stay no longer and would land the goods at Cape Gracias a Dios. The deserted colonists never saw most of their provisions again.

In the absence of adequate housing and sanitation, subject to fierce northers that blew their tents away, and without proper food and water, disease took its toll. In addition, the colonists were victimized by the Indians who demanded payment for the land they thought they had purchased from MacGregor; to the natives, his grant was invalid. The Poyais currency was bogus and not acceptable, and there was no money to meet these payments nor to buy food from the Indians. As illness set in almost immediately, no great amount of farming ever took place, nor hunting, fishing, or gathering of forest products. For a while, to augment their food supply, they traded rum, powder, and shot with the Indians, who included helpful Africanized Caribs who had been banished by the British to the Bay Islands from St. Vincent. But this supply was insecure, as the Indians sometimes disappeared for long intervals. The rum and other articles of trade undoubtedly had been a factor in the Indians' presence, but these did not last indefinitely.

There was no replenishment of supplies for the first contingent of colonists. When another group of settlers arrived, their ship brought no new provisions; only the surplus stores laid up for the passengers en route were obtained, and these did not last long. In all the annals of ill-fated tropical colonization schemes, it is difficult to match the horrors in the diary entries (April 25 through May 6, 1823) of the colony's surgeon:

> 25th.—Of 200 individuals all were sick, with the exception of nine. One family of seven persons—father, mother, and five sons—were all ill: they lay on the ground on cane leaves.
> 26th.—To-day, three of the men, while crossing the lagoon in front of my house, in a pitpan, upset. One of the party, a good swimmer, struck out for the shore: he had only proceeded a few yards when he shrieked out and suddenly sank. He had evidently been seized by one of the alligators, which were numerous in the lagoons. Alligator was shot the next day.
> 27th.—To-day, a highly respectable and very worthy man committed suicide. He had been ill, but was recovering, though still unable to rise. He insisted that he was going to die, and wished me to take charge of his little property, and of a letter to his wife. Last evening, I had given him a little wine; this morning, when on my way to visit him, I heard a shot fired, and on entering his hut, found that he had loaded a horse-pistol to the muzzle, and

had literally blown himself to pieces. Not being able to get anyone to dig a
grave, I collected some brushwood, which I piled in his hut, and set fire to it.
To-day, five men and a woman took a large dory, got safely through the surf,
and off to the northward.

28th.—The two young men who had been upset with me in the surf, and
another, left the settlement with some Indians who were going to Belize.

May 1st.—Another man died. To-day, Col. Hall returned, bringing some
of the medical and other stores with him. He had found the Honduras Packet
at the Cape, but could not induce the master to return to the settlement. He
announced an intended visit of the King.

6th.—Every one is sick and helpless, excepting Colonel Hall, myself, and a
rascal named McGregor. Colonel Hall and myself took some of the sick into
our houses, and attended them as well as were able.[5]

Once, toward the end of their ordeal, King George Frederick came to
visit and was of temporary assistance to the suffering colonists, as he made
his people do some hunting and fishing for them. With great enjoyment, he
described to the colonists the destruction of the Spanish settlement in the
raid on this site two decades previously, while the inhabitants were asleep.
In his words, no one escaped massacre and no buildings survived the fires.
He showed the colonists the few remains, almost completely overgrown by
vegetation. This convinced them that a good-size settlement had indeed
existed here, as depicted by Thomas Strangeways in his *Sketch of the Mosquito Shore* (Edinburgh, 1822)—one of the sources of company propaganda
and very effective. But it did not alter the fact that they had come to a place
now completely desolate. After a week, the king departed suddenly, taking
all the Indians with him. He was angry because these colonists would not
swear allegiance to him, as perhaps he had become accustomed to in other
dealings with the British.

With the Indians gone, the colonists' abandonment was final. For the
colonization company, it was a clear case of desertion, of leaving the colonists to their fate, with none of the promises fulfilled and no succor from
England. Fortunately for the colonists, notice of their plight had reached
Belize and, soon after George Frederick's departure, ships came to pick
them up. Even so, for many it was too late, and they were buried among the
earlier and successful settlers who had lived out their lives in the previous
century. For the survivors, it was evacuation to Belize, where they settled
under more favorable conditions. Still, they were not content, and did not
succeed in farming, and finally they dispersed, some to Belize City and
others back to Britain.

It is interesting to contrast this experience with the two generations of

British settlers who had made Black River their home in the eighteenth century and made it productive and self-supporting in terms of agriculture. However, that colony had settled in healthier country, many miles upriver, where the soils were good. Being forced by circumstances to remain at the coastal lagoon was unfortunate for the MacGregor colonists, for, as the Spanish colonists had discovered before them, this site was disease ridden and unproductive. But initial responsibility for the wretched project was Gregor MacGregor's. Much of the time, while the colonists were suffering, he remained in England, living well off the proceeds of the invalid land sales, distributing "titles of nobility" in his "Poyais Kingdom," and printing propaganda tracts.

The financial backers of the colonization company, however, probably acted in good faith—at least this was the opinion of the colony's surgeon who wrote of the experience many decades later.[6] Like the colonists, the backers appear to have been unsuspecting dupes. MacGregor served prison terms for his fraud, but news of the project's failure and the many attendant deaths dampened efforts in England to "push" Mosquito Shore colonization for many years to come, besides encouraging prejudice against the area by West Indies partisans in the government.

Britain's foreign policy, as reflected particularly in Lord Castlereigh's tenure as foreign secretary after 1815, affected relationships with other European powers, and especially Spain, with regard to Latin American affairs. Britain was less inclined to autocratic crushing of liberal movements than the other European powers. It was particularly in her interest to have peace, in order to promote her prosperity as an industrial and trading nation. A corollary was the free access to sources and markets that she assiduously pursued. She believed that peace could best be achieved by maintaining a balance of power, so that no one state became a threat to the rest. France, due to her record of belligerency, culminating in the Napoleonic Wars, was still the principal menace for Britain in Europe and overseas. Thus containment of French ambitions was ever paramount.

The other members of the Grand Alliance (Russia, Prussia, and Austria), which had, with Britain, defeated Napoleon, were autocratic and dedicated to the restoration of "legitimate" regimes, abhorring any forms of liberalism or nationalism. British policy was opposed to this, and the alliance began to crumble. The British were apprehensive that Spain would turn to the other Continental powers for aid in regaining the Latin American colonies. Meanwhile, the United States had recognized the first Latin American republics in 1822, and the British realized that this would adversely affect their commercial interests. The final shove in Britain's drift from the alliance and toward reorientation of her policy regarding Latin America occurred when France invaded Spain in 1823 to suppress a liberal uprising (one of several in Europe at the time). This appeared to have implications in the long-feared European intervention (in this case, possibly French) to force Spain's colonies back into their former allegiance.

George Canning, Castlereigh's successor as British foreign secretary, turned to the United States and proposed a joint Anglo-American declaration against intervention in Latin America by any European power. Suspicious of Britain's intentions in the area and jealously guarding its own prerogatives, the U.S. government rejected the proposal. Instead, the unilateral Monroe Doctrine was proclaimed in December of 1823. Although the perceived French danger might have seemed to make the U.S. declaration urgent, there was no proof that France (and certainly not the other Continental powers) ever seriously considered interfering with the independence of Latin America, particularly in view of British supremacy on the seas. Even while his joint declaration was being considered in Washington, Canning approached the French government directly, clearly voicing Britain's intentions to oppose any intervention in Latin America, and was sufficiently reassured that he abandoned his original proposal.

Nevertheless, the United States went on record in the Monroe Doctrine, stating that the American continents would not henceforth be considered subject to future colonization by *any* European power, that any attempt to extend Europe's political systems to the Western Hemisphere would be viewed as dangerous to the peace and safety of the United States, and that any interference by a European power to suppress the independence obtained by the emerging Latin American states, or to control them, would be seen by the U.S. government as unfriendly acts. For the next two decades, though the doctrine may have discouraged European incursions into Latin America, it did not prevent them. Britain and France violated it, and there were no protests from the United States. During those years the country had little inclination or the necessary power to enter conflicts not related to its own territorial ambitions, which now had shifted westward to the Spanish borderlands and the Pacific.

By 1824 the constitution of the Central American Federation was completed, with a strong liberal cast, having been modeled upon both the U.S. Constitution and the Spanish (Cádiz) constitution of 1812. There was a congress, with representation by states proportional to their populations; a senate, with two members from each state elected by the people; and a supreme court, also chosen by popular vote. Special rights of nobility and clergy were eliminated, slavery was abolished, freedom of trade and several types of civil rights were guaranteed. On paper, it appeared to offer a firm basis for union.

However, almost from the outset there were problems in the operation of the Federation. Some were economic, as the treasury became exhausted, revenues dwindled, and debts for the new government mounted. Some were political; and their seeds had long been germinating in regional and provincial antagonisms. Besides the interregional jealousy toward Guatemala and Guatemala City (always controversial as the choice of the capital), there was strife between opposing ideologies, which largely prevented the provisions of the constitution (reflecting mainly liberal philosophy) from being carried out. Conservatives, composed of landowners, churchmen, and merchants (particularly of Guatemala), had not wanted a constitution modeled along U.S. lines, giving much autonomy to the states. They had desired, rather, a unitary, highly centralized government. Liberals represented more the provinces and naturally adhered to the home-rule concept, while harboring deep suspicions toward Guatemala. Some of the conservative elements had gained privileges, wealth, and power under the traditional pre-independence Spanish system, and these were now threatened. Free trade, for example, was not of benefit to all. Some of the merchant-entrepreneurs were inevitably hurt as their "closed" systems of providing domestic markets disappeared with the rapid introduction of British goods.

The period between 1826 and 1838 was one of almost constant friction between Liberals and Conservatives for control of the Federation government, and much of it was consumed in outright civil war and chaos. The Liberals were initially in control, with a constitution largely of their making. Then, after three years of Conservative rule, from 1826 to 1829, Francisco Morazán led the Liberals in a return to power, which brought sweeping reforms, along with harsh treatment for leaders of the opposition. There was hope for greater harmony and for preservation of the union when the more moderate Liberal, José del Valle, was elected president in 1834; but he died before assuming office, and Morazán was reelected.

Although the Federation capital had been moved to San Salvador because of its more receptive political sentiments, Guatemala became an arena of violent opposition to Liberal policies as its governor attempted radical reforms of the economy, society, and culture. Anticlericalism, greater foreign influences, burdensome head taxes, forced labor, land-tenure problems, secularization of education and marriage, and revision of the judicial system were hallmarks of the alleged reforms. Besides the alienation of certain conservative middle- and upper-class groups, widespread dissatisfaction developed among the peasants, whose traditional, Church-oriented, and paternalistic pre-independence way of life was being overturned. They found a leader in Rafael Carrera, of peasant stock himself, who rallied them in guerrilla warfare against the government for several years in the late 1830s. In this struggle, the Church proved a powerful ally, and the insurrection in Guatemala sparked similar uprisings against Liberal reforms all over Central America.

The Guatemala government was increasingly harassed by Carrera's growing forces and, increasingly, repression was employed to force compliance with the reform measures, thus intensifying the discontent. By 1838, when President Morazán led a Salvadoran army in an unsuccessful campaign to crush the rebellion, the Federation was falling apart, and Nicaragua was the first state to secede. With its strong, uncompromising Conservative (Granada) and Liberal (León) antagonisms, it had never been committed to the Federation idea, and Carrera's revolt and the Federation's ineffectiveness encouraged the break. By 1840, all states except El Salvador had seceded, and Morazán was decisively defeated by Carrera, who then became *caudillo* of independent Guatemala—in the vanguard of separate Conservative governments throughout Central America. The Federation was never again to rise successfully.

Self-interest (meaning trade) had certainly been involved in Britain's desire to see the Spanish colonies become independent and to keep the other European powers from interfering in the process. Her trade with the colonies had not only prevailed but multiplied after 1808, especially after Napoleon's defeat at Waterloo. All through these years, British manufacturers became ever more interested in Latin America, as the Napoleonic Wars disrupted their European markets and then both Europe and the United States turned toward protectionism. The significance of the commercial factor had been manifested in Canning's decision finally to give formal recognition to the major Latin American republics in 1824. Prior American recognition and fear of resulting lost trade had made him realize that Britain could no longer delay recognition while entertaining hopes for monarchies to emerge. After 1824 it became Britain's objective to capitalize upon the beckoning commercial opportunities in a number of new countries that now were able to make their own trade policies.

In the years following Latin American independence there was considerable rivalry between Britain and the United States in some of the new republics that seemed to offer the greatest trade advantages. One of these was Mexico, where British agents attempted to capitalize on that country's suspicions of U.S. intentions regarding Texas. Here and elsewhere in Latin America, Britain was able to gain the upper hand in trade. She was, after all, advanced in her industrial revolution and the foremost world producer of manufactured products; and because of this, she offered the greatest market for Latin American raw materials. The United States, at the time, was no match.

During the 1830s, Britain expanded her commercial influence in Central America significantly. Free trade was one of the important reforms instituted by her government during that decade; so the British market for raw material imports, not only from her colonies but from other parts of the world, was steadily growing. As Britain was the world's leading maritime power with established international contacts, foreign countries were encouraged to use the kingdom as an intermediary in trade relations with each other. A rapidly industrializing Britain now perceived a system of non-protectionist trade as essential in a bid for worldwide markets for her manufactured products, and Central America was but one of many areas to which she directed her policy of expanding trade. At first there was little competition. Britain was the natural heir to the vacuum of dependency left by Spain, and she had control of Belize, well situated on the Caribbean to serve Central American trade with Britain and Europe. Because it had been the principal contraband port, its facilities were already established and it was familiar with isthmian trade interests, particularly those of Guatemala and El Salvador. Since controversy continued over British territorial rights in Belize, it is ironic that the Central Americans found little alternative but to channel their trade (mainly exports of cochineal and indigo for British textile factories) through this port and to rely upon a virtual monopoly of British mercantile houses there for import-export services. However, they were unable to develop any other arrangement as convenient, and during the 1830s Belize became the outstanding entrepôt. (Although the British attempted to form a slave-based agricultural colony there as well, these efforts were largely unsuccessful.)

Aside from Belize, resident British commercial interests operated within the Central American states. These merchants were particularly active in Guatemala City, but also in other areas where most of the people, markets, and plantations were and where political power and administrative functions resided, as in and around the lake plains of Nicaragua and in El

Salvador. Although encouraged by the British government, these private interests initially operated without its direct assistance. In fact, their government informed them that, in these times of extreme political unrest and civil war, they could expect no protection from London. Nevertheless, the eagerness of Central Americans to establish trade contacts apparently was considered worth the risk.

British influence through capital investment in Central America during the 1830s was not so auspicious, but nevertheless present. Despite default on a sizable loan of a British bank immediately after independence, which discouraged many potential investors, Britain was still the source of most foreign capital. The need was great, and the bond of indebtedness mounted.

The commercial significance of Central America in British eyes had become so great by 1834 that a very active and controversial consul, Frederick Chatfield, was dispatched to negotiate a commercial treaty with the Federation. Before his long tenure was over (1852), he proved that his intentions went well beyond a trade agreement and that he was singularly effective in promoting British interests generally, whatever they might be and whatever the political situation.

Throughout this postindependence period of British commercial ascendancy in Central America, attention was diverted from the Mosquito Shore. Not surprisingly, the handful of British residents who had established themselves on the Shore during the first three decades of the century wished for a revival of the old British influence. This began to manifest itself significantly by the late 1830s, when descendants of the Hodgson family (and others) started a campaign to attract more immigrants. The time was appropriate, for during this decade there was a notable movement in Britain to promote emigration to the colonies, with the double objective of lessening population pressure in the burgeoning cities at home and stimulating colonial development. This fell in line with the enlightened imperial policies of the government that were being formulated at the time, and also awakened considerable public interest. Agricultural colonization projects had involved Britishers and other Europeans in Central America earlier in the 1830s and been encouraged by the Federation government (though not without opposition). Such projects as that around Lake Izabal in eastern Guatemala had attracted very few, it is true, and had not proved promising, but they were evidence of official interest in emigration-immigration.

Effective settlement was seen as necessary to reinforce what had lately become a very marginal British presence on the Mosquito Shore. Propo-

nents of revived colonization resorted to all kinds of exaggerated propaganda, praising the "enormous possibilities" of this tropical cornucopia, as
in the following.

> No serious doubt, then, can be entertained of the intention of the British
> Government to open in the Mosquito Territory a new field for the emigration
> of our countrymen. Numerous and valuable as are the Colonies which are
> owned by England, it may be confidently asserted, that not one of them can
> compete with this territory in the fertility of its soil; the abundance and
> variety of its productions (for which every town in the eastern and western
> hemispheres offers lucrative markets); the salubrity of its climate; the extent of
> its water-communication; and its proximity to England. The Australasian
> Colonies supply us with their wools; Canada, with its timber; the West India
> Islands with sugar, rum, and coffee; and India exports its indigo, sugar,
> spices, and specie; but the land embraced by the Mosquito Shore can, with
> the solitary exception of wool, pour the whole of these articles, with many
> other peculiar to itself, into the lap of England.[7]

Despite this and many other encouraging reports concerning the Shore's
physical environment throughout the period of contact by foreigners, the
fact is that its excessively wet tropical conditions and poor soils (sand close
to the sea and highly leached clays in the interior) were seriously limiting.
There were all the problems of cultivation common to such climatic conditions, plus a profusion of crop-damaging insects and quick-growing weeds
and shrubs. The usual response of the natives, over time, was the same as in
similar climatic environments with fragile soils: extensive shifting cultivation of the slash-and-burn type. The food-crop staples were usually the
same: cassava (manioc), unirrigated rice, yams, bananas, and plantains.
With much higher rainfall than most other parts of the tropics, almost
incessant rain (for weeks on end), and the almost complete absence of a dry
season, many food crops grown elsewhere in the wet tropics did not do well
here. The Mosquitos grew very little maize or beans, for example, and
apparently for good reasons. The limitations of the environment on varied
food production induced the Mosquito natives to use the seas as a source of
much of their sustenance. (The green turtle was paramount.) Despite these
clues presented by the native inhabitants, outsiders who came to this Shore
were usually slow in perceiving the environmental limitation on food production and, instead, simply blamed the natives for their laziness.

The above account goes on to say that abundant labor could always be
relied upon because of the Mosquito Indians and other groups of natives
who would flock to the area from all over Central America, once assured of

British protection and employment. In actuality, obtaining adequate labor became a very serious problem in later years.

Such propaganda was apparently effective, but many of the colonists it attracted were not able to make a successful adjustment on the Shore. Such was the case with another problem-plagued, though in this case well-intentioned, colonization venture in the Black River area. The colonists sailed from England to Cape Gracias a Dios in 1839, then established a settlement, which they named Fort Wellington, on the Black River. Difficulties, stemming mainly from mismanagement and inexperience, beset the colony from the beginning. Much of the cargo brought from England turned out to be ill adapted to the uncultivated country and needs of the settlers. There were delays, lasting months, in the arrival of new supplies, while the colony depended upon provisions from the surrounding countryside, for which it had to pay with some of its nonedible goods. Of course, the colony attempted to cultivate as much land as possible, concentrating upon cassava as the staple food, but when the crop came in, it turned out to be the bitter variety and thus was not usable (without techniques with which they were unfamiliar). Finally, when the natives found the colonists without further goods to exchange for their labor, they quit work altogether. The superintendent of the colony was incompetent and neglected to order supplies from Trujillo and Belize, where they might have been obtained. According to one of the discontented colonists, "instead of Fort Wellington being a settlement, and a hostelry for new comers, it was completely disorganized, and with barely the necessaries of life."[8]

When the returning ship finally arrived from England, in early 1841, it brought foodstuffs and livestock in abundance, but it also brought disease. It was so overcrowded with livestock and additional passengers, taken on in the Canary Islands, that the brig arrived in a very bad sanitary condition, and the stench could be detected by the welcoming colonists from a great distance. Disease (typhus included) had broken out among the passengers, and was soon to overcome others. The new superintendent, who arrived on the ship, was an early victim, and several other deaths followed. Having brought both its life-sustaining and death-dealing cargo, the ship, before it could be unloaded, was pounded by a severe storm, beached, and broken up. The loss of supplies was not total, but the colony did not revive.

Thomas Young, an official of the colonization company and himself a colonist, made these comments about the recently arrived passengers:

Most of them were poor, not having the means of subsistence even for a short period, unused to the labour required in such climates, without goods where-

with to hire the natives to labour for them, and perfectly unacquainted with all
they should know.

. . . Many of those who came by the Rose, ought not to have left their
homes, being perfectly unfitted for a foreign shore, and expecting they were
to enjoy the necessaries of life without exertion on their parts.[9]

A record of the failure, and its causes, may be the most effectual warning to
others; and it may especially serve to shew that it is useless for persons,
without discrimination, judgment, perseverance, and sufficient means, to
leave their homes for this country.[10]

This was the last attempt to colonize the Black River region, which, aside
from San Juan del Norte (Greytown), probably has the most extensive
history of nonenduring settlement on the Shore. Reminders of earlier use
were noted by the ill-fated colonists of Fort Wellington, who visited the site
of Pitt's old settlement (which was taken over by the Spaniards):

Since then the bush has again overgrown the bank, and as we slowly cleared
away the ground, we discovered many relicts of the dead, and times gone by;
ruins of an old Spanish church, with huge roots of trees growing through the
brickwork, and numerous traces of houses, pits, ec.[11]

Despite this additional failure of systematic colonization (if it can be
called that), the Mosquito Shore again played a prominent role in British–
Central American relations during the entire decade of the 1840s, and
British occupancy became more pronounced than it had been since the
evacuation of 1787. The initial impetus for resumed official interest came
from Belize in 1837. The aggressive new superintendent at Belize, Alexander MacDonald, wished to expand mahogany cutting to the Honduran
portion of the Mosquito Shore, despite Central America's claim to the
territory as inherited from Spain. Much to the concern of the Federation
government, Consul Chatfield, in Guatemala City, urged him on in these
designs, which he pursued by advancing the claims of the Mosquito king.
British territorial expansion southward, in the direction of the Mosquito
Shore, began in 1838 with British seizure of Roatan, the main island of the
Bay Islands. MacDonald directed this operation after an appeal by Cayman
Islanders who had recently come to settle and whose right to be there was
contested by the Honduran government. Taking advantage of the breakup
of the Central American Federation, which was occurring at this time,
MacDonald's move proved to be acceptable in London. The British government paid no attention to the issue or claim of sovereignty by weak and
protesting Honduras.

By 1840 MacDonald was involved, as a self-appointed adviser to the king, in the administration of the Shore. Still, this intervention in Mosquitia, with its implications of a protectorate, did not have the sanction of the British Colonial Office. However, the headstrong superintendent soon forced the issue. With the Federation dissolved, the independent state of Nicaragua, wishing to exert what it considered its legitimate territorial rights on the Mosquito Shore, sent a commandant to the small port at the mouth of the San Juan River, called by the Nicaraguans San Juan del Norte. In 1841, declaring that the Nicaraguans had occupied part of the Mosquito king's domain, MacDonald arrived at the port, with King Robert Charles Frederick, in a ship that flew the Mosquito and British flags. He demanded Nicaraguan recognition of the Mosquito king's jurisdiction over the port, which was refused, whereupon MacDonald's group kidnaped the comman-dant, took him up the coast, and released him, apparently to teach Nic-aragua a lesson. (At the time, Britain had several outstanding claims against Central America, resulting from various debts and damage to property of British residents and commercial interests. The "claims weapon" had al-ready been used by Chatfield to pressure the Central Americans in whatever imperial designs he entertained in Britain's behalf. MacDonald also used it as a pretext for his action, unauthorized by the British government.)

The "lesson" had several significant results. It brought loud protests from the secretary-general of the Nicaraguan government over British usurpa-tions of its sovereignty, and aroused not only Nicaragua's Central America neighbors but also the United States, which was beginning to take interest (at first, commercial) in the isthmus. The Nicaraguan government de-manded that Britain desist from further unauthorized actions on the Mos-quito Shore, but the demands seemed only to stiffen the British government's stand on the controversy and to strengthen the hand of those who advocated return of their countrymen to the Mosquito Shore in an official way. There had been for some time a conflict of views on this matter between the Colonial Office and the Foreign Office. King Robert Charles Frederick's death in 1842 and the danger to British subjects that his absence seemed to indicate in the face of the Nicaraguan threat were further stim-ulus to play a more active role in Mosquito affairs. Also, the MacDonald incident had played a role in a revival of unionism in Central America, and with the first of these ultimately unsuccessful attempts—a pact between Nicaragua, Honduras, and El Salvador early in 1842—the threat upon the Shore appeared even greater.

The strategic importance of the Shore, and particularly the mouth of the San Juan, had not been overlooked by the British. Indeed, one of the first canal surveys of Nicaragua after independence was by an Englishman, John Baily. It became very clear during the 1840s that control of at least the Atlantic terminus of any canal and, if possible, the likely Pacific terminus as well, to prevent such control from passing to other powers (via Nicaragua), was a paramount objective for the world's greatest trading country. Finally, giving in to MacDonald's and Chatfield's recommendations, the British government authorized a blockade of Atlantic ports, ostensibly to force payment of delinquent claims. Costa Rica, Honduras, and Guatemala acquiesced, but Nicaragua did not, and the blockade of San Juan del Norte went into effect. Only when Guatemala agreed to guarantee Nicaragua's share of the claims did the British navy withdraw, a few months later. By this time, however, it was clear that the British government was willing to give official sanction to an assertive policy on the Mosquito Shore. The next step was formal acceptance of a protectorate in 1843 and, shortly afterward, assignment of a resident British representative, Patrick Walker.

During the entire period of commercial domination in Central America and revival of influence on the Mosquito Shore, British foreign policy was dominated by Henry John Temple, third Viscount Palmerston. With the exception of five years, Lord Palmerston was foreign secretary from 1830 to 1852, and thereafter became prime minister (twice). The thirty-year period of continuous high office, characterized by the distinctive stamp of this man, has aptly been called the Age of Palmerston. Greatly influenced by Canning, his predecessor and mentor, he always pursued an independent policy, not bound by any party or faction. Judging questions on their merits, he was thus unpredictable, but implicit in his foreign policy was his determination to uphold the interests and honor of Great Britain in all parts of the world. This was not new, but his interventionist methods were. They were often so forthright and blustery, so neglectful of the subtleties of established practices of diplomacy, that they were sometimes interpreted as belligerent, jingoistic, high handed, and unduly meddlesome. Offensive abroad, the policies did not escape criticism by his fellow statesmen at home, and even on occasion by the queen, but they were popular with the British public. The people liked Palmerston's bold assertiveness, and considered him not only a champion of British prestige but also of justice. His strong-willed independence of action and seeming devil-may-care attitude were attractive. Nevertheless, even his opponents were forced to admit that though he believed fervently in Britain's supremacy and saw no need to court other governments, he knew more about foreign countries and foreign affairs than most public men of his age.

Palmerston believed in making shows of force whenever British interests or prestige were involved, expecting they would suffice. Although these shows were manifested mainly in important affairs concerned with Europe, the Middle East, and Asia, it is characteristic of Palmerston that he was as ready to apply them against small powers as against great, and, in his view, "a British subject, in whatever land he may be, shall feel confident that the watchful eye and strong arm of England will protect him against injustice and wrong."[12] Hence the policy did not exclude Central America. Palmerston's clear, bold, blunt, and logical dispatches to the region made this obvious, and his representatives on the scene, such as MacDonald and Chatfield, followed the policy with vigor, though often to excess. At times, it was also characteristic of Palmerston, here and elsewhere, to show restraint and be conciliatory when it appeared that longer-range British interests could be better served thereby.

Internal politics in Central America after Morazán's fall and during the British revival of influence in the 1840s was marked by several movements to reunite the states. The unionist sentiment was stronger in the so-called central states, Nicaragua, Honduras, and El Salvador, while Guatemala and Costa Rica were more reluctant, preferring governments under their own control. As noted, British encroachment was an important stimulus in most of these unionist plans, particularly for the central states; Guatemala and Costa Rica had closer relations with Britain, through Chatfield. However, the deep divisions between Liberals and Conservatives, in addition to the conflicting personal and political aims of *caudillos* in the various states, did not allow any of these movements to succeed. Also, Chatfield discouraged any unionist plans which threatened Britain's hegemony on the isthmus, particularly later in the decade, when it appeared that the United States might support the movements.

In Nicaragua, movements toward unification during the 1840s had been overshadowed by the regional feud between the cities of León and Granada. In the post-Morazán period, Nicaragua had been the only state of the dissolved Federation to retain a Liberal-controlled government, in which the real power resided in army chiefs rather than heads of state. However, it was under constant threat from the Conservative-controlled governments of its neighbors. Finally, in 1845, the Nicaraguan Conservatives obtained armed assistance from Honduras and El Salvador and overthrew the Liberal government in León. They devastated the capital and massacred many of its inhabitants. Thereafter, with a new military leader installed by the Conservatives and the seat of power back in Granada, the conflict continued, with outbreaks of violence occurring regularly throughout the state.

In these conditions of virtual anarchy, it is little wonder that Nicaragua was easy prey to British advances. Chatfield, in his attempt to counter Nicaraguan protests regarding the Mosquito Shore, brought new demands for settlement of claims. When the country again refused to come to terms, the British employed a second blockade at San Juan del Norte (in 1844) and Nicaragua capitulated. A mission, representing the newly formed confederation of Chinandega Pact countries and headed by Francisco Castellón, an eminent Nicaraguan Liberal leader, was dispatched to Europe after this most recent humiliation.

Up to that time, Central Americans had blamed Chatfield personally for much of the British problem. Besides the wide displeasure provoked by his use of the "claims weapon" for what were considered imperialistic motives, Federation proponents accused him of plotting with Conservatives against the unionist movements. One objective of the mission, therefore, was to present grievances to Lord Aberdeen in London, who had in 1841 taken over from Palmerston as foreign secretary. Aberdeen had not been fully sympathetic with the methods of Chatfield, whom on occasion he had reprimanded, but he received the mission coldly and refused to recognize a confederation government that did not represent all five of the states. The mission learned that Chatfield would not be recalled (as it wished) and would be supported by the Foreign Office in general policy matters, regardless of his questionable techniques. Chatfield's position became even more secure when Lord Palmerston returned as foreign secretary the following year. With all doubt removed that Chatfield's policy was Britain's policy, further impetus was given to the unionist movement in Central America, and it became more closely linked than ever with the British threat.

3   British Occupation
           and American Reaction,
           1844–1850

With the protectorate established and
the British in control of the Mosquito Shore north of San Juan del Norte,
another plan to colonize evolved in 1844 after a crop failure in Prussia that
year. There was no official Prussian-government sponsorship or authorization, but Prince Charles had a personal interest in the proposed ventures.
He had been in communication with a group of English traders who had
informed him that they possessed a tract of land near Cape Gracias a Dios
which would be suitable for colonization and that they would like to sell it.
They claimed to have received the land as grants from the now-deceased
King Robert Charles Frederick; but if such "grants" were ever made, it is
likely that the transactions occurred while the king was intoxicated.[1] Like
MacGregor, these Englishmen hoped to capitalize on European land hunger
by selling off land for which they had paid nothing. Nevertheless, Prince
Charles was sufficiently convinced that he personally paid the expenses of a
commission to the Mosquito Shore to investigate the lands in question. The
commission members (with the English promoter who acted as guide, one
Mr. Willett) were Patrick Walker's fellow passengers aboard the ship that
took him to his new post at Bluefields in July of 1844. Although Walker was
impressed with the character of the commissioners, he suspected the validity of the property rights and the probity of Willett and his friends. In any
case, the commissioners returned to Prussia with a favorable report, and
Prince Charles continued to support the colonization project of a Königsberg company.

After concluding an agreement to purchase the Mosquito Shore tract and
after vigorous recruitment, including newspaper notices aimed at enticing
colonists to Central America, the company dispatched a ship, the *Friesch*,
with 107 emigrants in the spring of 1846. While it was en route, the authorities of the Mosquito kingdom (the Council of State) and Patrick Walker

52

informed Prince Charles that the grants were not valid and that their "recipients" therefore had no authority to sell the land. However, not wishing to discourage Prussian colonization, the council offered to sell land for the purpose, under generous conditions, but with the important provision that sovereignty be reserved to the Mosquito kingdom.

After a voyage of five months (during six weeks of which their ship was detained by adverse winds), the emigrants reached Bluefields on September 27, 1846. It was a discouraged and destitute group who told Walker that they had been induced to emigrate under false pretenses by Königsberg recruiters and had not been told *where* in Central America they were being taken. After depositing his human cargo, the German master of the vessel resigned his responsibility and sailed away under cover of darkness, leaving scores of unpaid accounts and taking one of the emigrant's daughters with him. To Walker, the unfortunate arrivals appeared to be "without one exception . . . a most orderly, quiet and industrious people," and he thought they might prove to be "a great acquisition to this place."[2] In any case, since they were almost completely without resources, Walker felt he had no alternative but to offer them temporary asylum in Bluefields, where they remained until 1849 (some dying and others dispersing). Meeting their needs, meanwhile, was no easy task.

Walker sent men to the Rama keys and to Monkey Point to induce the Rama Indians to supply vegetables and manatee meat with which to feed the Prussians. (This indicates the poor state of agriculture and Mosquito Indian food production in the Bluefields area.) Fortunately, two American vessels soon arrived in the port and some pork and flour were obtained. Walker expected that the Prussian government would reimburse these expenses. He could not feed the immigrants indefinitely from his provisions, and after a while they had to fall back upon whatever food the natives could provide, however deficient in quantity and nutritional value. Beyond this, it was food to which they were completely unaccustomed.

Housing was another problem. No accommodations were available in separate houses, and the immigrants had to be quartered all together in whatever makeshift shelter could be arranged. Temporarily, the women and children were lodged in the courthouse and the men in the schoolhouse. Walker generously provided his dining room to serve as the school, and quartered the schoolmaster in his home.

The weather took a turn for the worse in that fall of 1846. After an unusual dry spell, it rained almost incessantly. Many of the immigrants were ill, and two houses were rented for use as infirmaries. Walker thought much of the illness was caused by the extreme dampness as well as the lack of nutritious food, accompanied by general disregard of his advice on tropical living. He wrote:

> All my entreaties were of no avail in urging them to guard against the effect of the climate both in person and diet—but all that I could say would not induce man, woman or child to abstain from loading their stomachs with unripe Guava apples and with vegetables to which they were unaccustomed and ignorant of the method of dressing. During the whole day they would expose themselves to the sun without a covering on their heads and when steaming with perspiration they threw themselves into the water. In clearing the forest for locations for their houses, the men, full of health and strength, were so anxious to make a show, that instead of acting on my advice, in fact even orders, of taking the cool of the morning and evening for labor till they got climatised, they would work through the heat of the day. The infallible consequence of these inconsiderate acts had been as I foretold to them, sickness and death—already ten have been consigned to the tomb and I am afraid two or three more I can supply them with, and in reality all my servants are now hospital attendants.[3]

Their British hosts and benefactors expected that within a reasonable time the immigrants would be installed in houses of their own and find employment, so that the expense of feeding and caring for them could be terminated. But they were ill, and continual rain prevented the construction of houses according to schedule. Nevertheless, Walker took advantage of good days to push ahead with the building program, employing Creole laborers, and he was optimistic that before much longer all the immigrants would be settled and able to assume responsibility for their own lives.

Walker spent much of his time acting as "regent" for the young son of Robert Charles Frederick, who had succeeded him. This function, of course, was tantamount to being in control of the protectorate. In preparing for the coronation of the new king, an event not yet scheduled, he wrote to Lord Aberdeen, the foreign minister, in 1845:

> I sent for the Regalia of the kingdom from Wanks River, where it has been deposited by the King. I received a sort of crown formed of silver gilt and studded with crystal ornaments. . . . I have sent it to Jamaica to be cleaned and repaired, but as it is, in my humble opinion, unworthy of its destiny, I have most respectfully to suggest for your Lordship's consideration, the propriety of Government presenting the young King with a new crown and adding thereto a scepter and sword.[4]

It all seemed very familiar, to have the British officials, with their ceremonial ways (which the Mosquitos aped and enjoyed), back on the Shore.

Walker, moreover, seemed to believe it important to have the trappings of position and rank not only for the Mosquito kings but also for the British "ambassadors" to the "kingdom." He felt he could be far more effective in his post if he were knighted, because "in the altering circumstances of the country I could compass a great deal more than I have already achieved if I was visited by a mark of favor from the Crown."[5] The crown never granted this favor, but the request showed a good knowledge of Mosquito values of the day (besides opportunism). Although some of these colonial methods might seem ludicrous, even comical, as viewed today, the British considered them effective ways of dealing with the Mosquitos and maintaining control.

The year 1846 seems to mark the first serious British concern with a U.S. threat to their position in Central America. The Mexican War had started, and to Chatfield and the British this could mean that the "Manifest Destiny" of the United States extended southward beyond Mexico. Certainly, the challenge to the British control of interoceanic routes seemed manifest when the United States concluded the Bidlack Treaty with New Granada (which had advanced claims to parts of the Mosquito Shore) regarding Panama transit rights. Chatfield, increasingly, voiced the importance of Britain's gaining control of San Juan del Norte and certain strategic Pacific ports, such as those in the Gulf of Fonseca, to thwart any designs the Americans might have on the Nicaraguan interoceanic route. Of course, preoccupation with the Mexican War prevented U.S. intervention elsewhere, but the British seemed to detect signs that, with the conclusion of that war, one way or another, they would confront the United States in Central America. Accordingly, in 1847 Lord Palmerston announced that the Mosquito kingdom, and thus the British protectorate, extended from Cape Gracias a Dios to the mouth of the San Juan River. He instructed Chatfield to inform Nicaragua of these limits and that the British government would not be indifferent to encroachments into Mosquito territory. The intent to occupy this part of the Shore seemed clear.

Nicaragua was at the time extremely weak and disordered, and the most recent confederation plans, those of Sonsonate and Nacaome, had produced no results for a united front. The new Conservative military leader of Nicaragua, Trinidad Muñoz, who had taken power after the revolution of 1845, had failed to bring unity to the country and succeeded only in keeping it in factional turmoil. (Later, he alienated even the Conservatives who brought him to power, when his vacillating policy led to conciliatory moves toward the Liberal camp, including transfer of the capital back to León.)

After several months of dispute between the British and Nicaraguans over which flag should fly over San Juan del Norte, outright hostilities began there in early 1848. Consul-General Walker of Bluefields, with the young Mosquito king, sailed into the port in January and, with a Bluefields militia and sailors from an accompanying British warship, occupied the town. The Nicaraguan authorities were able to put up little resistance, and were driven to an upriver fort. When British officials were installed in their place, the ships returned to Bluefields.

Apparently, the British were confident that they would remain at San Juan del Norte. They renamed the port Greytown, in honor of Sir Charles Grey, governor of Jamaica, a change which was approved by the Foreign Office the following November. They did not find the prize initially appealing. There were but two public buildings: wooden, with thatch roofs, consisting of two stories. The ground floors were used as warehouses and the second floors as living quarters for the customs collector and visiting British officials. The private houses were crude, temporary structures. According to the British, "Everything in fact has to be done. There is not a convertible building in the place." They found that Greytown was not a healthy place, as others would depict it later. Malaria must have been a problem, particularly during the drier season, when land breezes blew mosquitos (the cause of the disease was not known at the time) from stagnant pools inland. Also, sanitation was poor, and the people resisted British regulations for fencing in animals, which customarily were allowed to roam freely in search of food. As viewed by the British occupation authorities, "the shutting up of one class of animals, pigs, is of extreme importance, for they breed and deposit everywhere."[6] There was a great abundance of fleas, which attacked the feet and were bothersome pests, as well as carriers of disease.

However, one week later—word of San Juan del Norte's capture having reached Granada—a Nicaraguan army force retook the town and removed the acting governor, George Hodgson, a native of Bluefields and of Mosquito origin, and the British captain of the port, Commander Little, as prisoners. It was not long before the British warship was back. The protest of its commander, Ryder, to the Nicaraguan military chief in Granada is worthy of John Bull's sternest ultimatums, and in receiving it the Nicaraguans, if not altogether intimidated, must have felt themselves among the great powers, capable of bringing down the wrath of both the Britannic and Mosquitian majesties:

> I take this opportunity of informing you that I shall hasten to report to the Militia and Naval authorities at Jamaica this set of willful aggressions on the

part of the Nicaraguan Government and which I have little doubt will be considered by them as a declaration of war against the Queen of England and the King of Mosquitia.

I am still in hopes that Colonel Salas has acted without orders from you or his government. Should this be the case I recommend you as the *only* means of averting the vengeance of their Britannic and Mosquitian majesty to visit this port *without a days delay—to rehoist the flag of this Mosquitian majesty and to reinstate in their positions the Captain of the Port, Captain Little, and the Governor, Major Hodgson, and to write a letter by the English packet which will call there on the 25th of this month*, to the Governor of Jamaica, informing him that these steps have been taken and that Colonel Salas' conduct will be severely punished by the Government of Nicaragua.

In the mean time I beg to inform you that in the name of "Her Britannic Majesty" I hold you *personally* responsible for the safety and good treatment of Capt. Little and Major Hodgson.[7]

The Nicaraguan reoccupation was brief. They were driven out a second time (in February) by a sizable British force dispatched from Jamaica, and this action proved decisive. For the first time since 1780, a British expeditionary force ascended the San Juan River. First, it attacked the fort at the confluence of the Sarapiqui River, containing Colonel Salas' troops, causing them to flee upriver. The British force then destroyed the fort, after which it proceeded up the San Juan and captured Fort San Carlos on the lake. In early March, the Nicaraguans capitulated and signed a treaty accepting the *de facto* British occupation of San Juan del Norte, relinquishing their customs collections at the port, and freeing the two prisoners they had taken. Nicaragua made it clear, however, that it did not consider its sovereignty rights to the Mosquito Shore in any way renounced, despite British occupation of the whole of it.

Up to this time the United States had paid little attention to Central America and the growing British influence there since independence. There had been the beginnings of commercial interest, but it was minor. There had been no stable diplomatic representation in the region, and most of the time Frederick Chatfield, because of his assiduous promotion of British interests, enjoyed free rein and little competition. Through more than two decades, the most significant North American contact was probably the trip that John Lloyd Stephens made in 1839 as President Van Buren's emissary to Central America at the height of its civil war, and as the Federation was disintegrating. Already an eminent archaeologist, Stephens combined this interest with diplomacy and later wrote an illuminating book, *Incidents of Travel in Central America, Chiapas, and Yucatan* (published in 1841 and reprinted by Rutgers University Press in 1949). The book stimulated interest in Central America among Americans and contained much information about the countries, their conditions, and their politics; but Stephens, as diplomat, was unable to establish meaningful relationships between the countries and the United States. He spent much of his time searching for a legitimate Central American government to which he could properly present his credentials, but found there was none: only two warring factions, unionists and secessionists. And chaos.

By 1848, the United States had reason to be aroused by British activities on the San Juan. It was in this year that the Oregon Territory was created and that the treaty with Mexico was signed, ending the war and resulting in U.S. acquisition of California. Gold had been discovered there, and a gold rush was imminent. The control of an isthmian crossing to reach these new territories of settlement now appeared critical, and it looked as if Great Britain was posed to monopolize the San Juan–Lake Nicaragua interoceanic route, which was even then considered a prime canal site. With the war over and the United States free to direct its attentions elsewhere, and with American rights in Panama apparently assured, the British felt all the more that they should maintain seaward control of the Nicaraguan route. This resolve was manifested in the activities of Chatfield, thereafter aimed primarily at checkmating greater influence of the United States in Central America. The expansionist tendencies of the United States, exemplified by the Mexican War and the following territorial annexations, led to British distrust. There were suspicions that the lands acquired from Mexico might be only the beginning and would not satisfy American territorial ambitions.[8]

The Nicaraguan government increasingly looked to the United States for assistance against British "encroachment," but Palmerston, in the summer of 1849, informed Nicaragua's ambassador, Francisco Castellón, of Britain's refusal to recognize any of that country's Mosquito claims (on the basis of inheritance from Spain) and of Britain's firm intention to hold on to its protectorate. According to Castellón, the British foreign secretary made it clear that this policy would prevail despite any intervention by the United States, saying: "We have been disposed to treat the United States with some degree of consideration, but in reference to this question, it is a matter of total indifference to Her Majesty's Government what she may say or do."[9] In just a few months, however, this confrontational policy changed to a conciliatory one.

Meanwhile, the British were quietly consolidating their position on the

Mosquito Shore. Consul-General Walker had been drowned in the upriver excursion against the Nicaraguans in February 1848 and been replaced in Bluefields by William D. Christie. The Prussian immigrants were still there and still a considerable burden; the courthouse was still filled with sick people who had to be fed and cared for. Thus there was ample cause for desperation as Christie reached the point where he could hardly manage. No assistance, material or moral, was forthcoming from the Foreign Office in London.

The Mosquito government extended loans to the Prussians for the purpose of supplying the ill people among them with food and medicine. The consul, his predecessor's widow, and the local British doctor (James Green) had also advanced money to them and were very concerned about reimbursement, perhaps because the immigrants seemed to consider the funds and the land assigned to them as gifts. In any event, they were in no position to repay, and attempts to collect from the Prussian and British governments were unsuccessful. It was the attitude of the benefactors that the Prussians themselves should eventually make some sort of return for all the help that had been given them in money and effort, and that they were liable to make payment for the land. Partly for this reason, there was no overwhelming wish to see them migrate elsewhere, before settling these debts or assigning their lands to others who would be responsible. In Europe, meanwhile, the plight of the Prussian immigrants did not escape notice; in fact, it affected Britain's hopes for more colonization along the Mosquito Coast. Of course, excuses were offered by persistent advocates of such colonization: the Prussians had arrived under unfortunate circumstances, after a voyage that took much longer than expected, and were not only destitute but exhausted when they reached Bluefields; some were already ill, moreover, and others had little resistance to diseases.

Bluefields in 1848 was very isolated. Its inadequate harbor could receive only small boats, of less than 12 feet draft, because of the sandbar across its entrance. Larger vessels had to anchor outside the harbor. In short, it was not a good port for shipping mahogany. As a result, cutting in the area was very limited, and there was no trade with the interior, so that Greytown received most of the ships from the outside world. The prime minister of Britain was entreated to extend the monthly services of the Royal West India Mail Steam Packet Company to include a call at Bluefields, in addition to Jamaica and Greytown. The only connection with the outside was by canoe, and official correspondence had to meet the steamers at Greytown. Bluefields-bound travelers had to hire canoes for the trip, which took three or four days since the wind was almost always contrary. Once in a while, a trading vessel came into Bluefields harbor from Jamaica, but this was irregular and uncertain.

Bluefields, nevertheless, had always been considered by the British as the best site for permanent settlement; it was selected as the place of residence for the consular agents of the period and as the "court" for the Mosquito king. Although the climate was healthier at Bluefields than at Greytown, there were many complaints about Bluefields' lack of skilled artisans, as well as the "lazy and apathetic" African and Creole inhabitants, "content to live on plantains"; the bush closing in on the small settlement, with no labor to clear it; the lack of regular supplies; and extremely high prices.[10] A few costly barrels of flour were bought from American traders by the Creole population, but other than this, their subsistence foods were yams, plantains, coconuts, and manioc. A considerable quantity of American flour was imported into the Central American countries through San Juan del Norte, but most of this was in transit to cities beyond the Mosquito Coast. So limited was food production in and around Bluefields that even the British consul's meals were monotonous. (He breakfasted on sugar and chocolate, with either rice or plantains. The meat at dinner was usually pork or turtle, or occasionally manatee, with rice or yams.)

Most believed that conditions could be improved only by a regular, monthly steamer service between Bluefields and Jamaica, and connections, via the San Juan, with the Pacific side of Nicaragua. Only by lessening its isolation could the town be made more attractive to settlers. However, the shipping company was not willing to make these changes, recommended by Christie, on the grounds that taking time from its Chagres and Greytown schedules to call at Bluefields would disrupt its postal service and thus damage its public service function. It was also reluctant because of the unsheltered, open-coast anchorage at Bluefields.

Upon taking his post at Bluefields, Christie expressed his disdain of the so-called Mosquito Council of State in writing to Palmerston, and gave this characterization of one of its members:

> Mr. Alexander Hodgson, one of a large family of natural children of Colonel Hodgson, the former Superintendent [Robert the Younger], by an African woman—his appearance is quite that of an African—he can sign his name but can write nothing else, and, when called on to append his signature to a document in the Council, it takes him five minutes to do so.[11]

However, he found them all, including the king, very pliable; they never opened their mouths in the meetings. Christie was expected to propose everything, and everything he proposed was assented to immediately. He was quick to perceive, nevertheless, that despite the council members' ignorance and lack of any real role in governing, their fellows were impressed by their office and this could be used on behalf of the British. Still, it was Christie's view that the council should be dispensed with and that the British should deal only through the king. If the council were disbanded—quietly, so as not to upset the Mosquitos—the real power structure would remain unchanged.

The young king, thought to be about 16 years old, was educated and spoke and wrote English well. Up to then, he had been subservient to his British tutors and overlords, even to the extent of asking for small favors, such as money to buy dresses for his sisters. But Christie was concerned for the future: the king was "very acute and observant," his ancestors had been men "of violent passions," and reports were that, as a youth, he had "often shown great waywardness" when his pleasures had been interfered with. Christie went a step further in his letter to Palmerston, after appraising the danger of a less docile king: if it suited the policy of England, "he might easily be shelved now: it may be much more difficult hereafter."[12] Even so, there was still vacillation, arising from the fear that, without the king, British power over the native population would be lessened. The desire of the British to manipulate the king meant understanding his childish reactions and whims, and responding in the proper manner so as to keep him satisfied, yet accomplishing British objectives. As Christie noted:

> The King is very sensible of neglect and he is quick in observing it. I have often seen his countenance change at a thoughtless word when strangers have supposed him indifferent to what was being said. This treatment makes him sullen and sometimes vindictive and he does not soon forget it. He is apt to show violent passion when contradicted, but if he is reasoned with, his passion soon gives way and not infrequently he will voluntarily express regret for having shown temper. I have seen him sullen and timid when spoken to authoritatively and in a harsh manner and he can then show himself capable of giving a good deal of trouble. I have heard the term "Indian cunning" applied to this state of temper, when probably the want of management in the mode of correction is the chief fault. I have never known the King to resent proper correction.
> . . . The King has strong feelings of respect for English authority and is flattered and much gratified by any mark of regard shown to him by English people. If treated with candour he is confiding and I have many proofs of his feelings toward us being esteem as well as respect.[13]

Lawlessness became worse when the Mosquito council was disbanded, allegedly due to the lack of native authority and stability. Some British residents reported that the Indians now felt they could do anything and not be held responsible or punished for it—from violent crimes to breaking contracts for goods or labor. Intoxication was part of the problem. Drinking parties on the native drink, *mushla*, were frequent, particularly from September to Christmas, and maiming and shooting often accompanied these parties. Anarchy sometimes prevailed, with the Indians saying that *all* of them were kings. Cultivation of crops was neglected, except for cassava, from which *mushla* was made.

Soon after his arrival on the Mosquito Shore, Christie became absorbed with the possibilities that Costa Rica might offer for the British; he perceived the important role that this country, without an Atlantic port, might play in Greytown's trade. However, if substantial trade were to be diverted to Greytown, it would be necessary for the Costa Rican government to construct a road from San José to the Sarapiqui River, a tributary of the lower San Juan. Christie was so interested in this possibility that he went to San José in the fall of 1848 to investigate the route, and wrote a vivid account to Palmerston of the difficulties he encountered.

It was clear that little use of the route could be made without improvements. The trip required four days by river, battling the currents of both the San Juan and the Sarapiqui, even though the distance was only 60 miles. But the road from the Sarapiqui to Alajuela, described as "only a path cleared in a way through a dense forest, over which mules can pick their way slowly, and it passes over very steep mountains," took another four days.[14] The entire route was almost devoid of human settlement; even the military post at the junction of the two rivers was deserted, with no vestige of its fortifications after the British attack earlier in the year. Once past the rude customs station, where there was a handful of persons (the first he had seen), Christie found only five habitations (all "wretched"), but he was enthralled with the change that occurred as he approached Alajuela:

> The plantations of maize and sugar and coffee are numerous: numbers of fine cattle are grazing: and my today's ride from Alajuela to San Jose has been through a perfect garden; it has more the appearance of England not only than anything I have seen since I left home, but also than anything I have seen on the continent.[15]

These favorable impressions of the temperate plateau country, so different from the Shore, prompted Christie to suggest in his letter to Palmerston the possibility of extending the British protectorate south of the San

Juan and opening these lands for British settlement.[16] There is no indication, however, that this proposal was ever considered seriously in London.
Outright colonial ambitions in Central America, aimed at the acquisition of
territory beyond what was needed to secure a prospective interoceanic
route, did not fit in with Palmerston's policy objectives. In fact, he rebuffed
Christie's suggestion, made about the same time, that the protectorate on
the Shore be converted to a crown colony: "I have to state that H. M. Govt.
have no wish at present to increase the number of Colonial possessions of the
British Crown and that their desire is to assist the Mosquito state in its
advance towards civilization, and to secure it against aggression and encroachment on the part of the neighboring Spanish Republics."[17] It seemed
there was little desire to add to the suspicions already aroused in Central
America and the United States about Britain's intentions.

At Christie's urging, however, the British government encouraged the
Costa Ricans to build the Sarapiqui road—to no avail. The idea met opposition within Costa Rica: from Liberal politicians, fearful of British influence
in their country, and from interests that favored a road to the Pacific port of
Punta Arenas. The Nicaraguan government, opposed to any Costa Rican
involvement on the San Juan, especially a downriver trade over which it
would have no control, was pleased that the road was never built. So were
other Central American governments, suspicious of any British–Costa
Rican commercial liaison which would strengthen Britain's hold in the
region.

By 1849 the surviving Prussian immigrants had begun to disperse from
the Bluefields area. Some went to Greytown, as they had been encouraged
to do, because of its demand for labor, but others went to parts unknown.
Although there was no significant or lasting settlement impact in the Bluefields region or, indeed, along the Mosquito Shore, the British had admired
the Prussians' perseverance and industriousness. After more than two years
of battling illness and attempting to become accustomed to tropical living,
many had managed to build houses of their own and to construct a good
road through the part of Bluefields they inhabited, though they never became fully self-supporting.

Despite the experience with the Prussians at Bluefields, the British and
Mosquito authorities were not altogether discouraged about further German colonization, provided it could be carried out in a carefully planned
manner, with preparation. They negotiated with various German interests
as late as 1849, and got to the point of designating "favorable" areas for

farming and mahogany-cutting projects, and quoting prices. However, when political implications entered the picture, the British attitude cooled. When the later schemes included conditions for protection by the Prussian government, Christie and Palmerston perceived ominous overtones. They were very much against the Prussians' being separate from other Mosquito Coast residents and not subject to the local laws. They saw this as almost a transfer of sovereignty of part of the Shore to Prussia. Thwarting what was feared might be a beginning of German colonial expansion on the American continent, they made it clear that no colonization could be effected except under the full authority of the Mosquito government, itself a British protectorate. The failure of the first attempt and this assertion of British control over who would settle on the Mosquito Shore ended German colonization overtures. If it had been successful, one historian notes, Germany's first overseas colony might have been here instead of Africa, forty years later.[18]

The Anglo-Prussian negotiations, which lasted about three years, had a lasting influence of great significance, however. In 1846, soon after the 107 Prussian immigrants reached the Shore, German Moravians approached the British about setting up missions there. The need of the immigrants for religious services and indoctrination in their own language was one stimulus for this request, but the Shore, with its native population, was also considered a suitable field for missionary endeavor. Palmerston instructed Walker and Christie to assist in every way in this venture, so that the first missionaries, who arrived in 1849, were welcomed by the British, who granted them tracts of land. After the immigrants dispersed, the missionaries remained and turned their full attention to the Indians. This was the beginning of a degree of stability along the Shore, which, with the later arrival of American Moravian missionaries and medical personnel, continued to modern times. In health and education, the Moravians proved to be a vital force, providing essential services for the native population that the Nicaraguan government generally neglected.

Greytown was very undeveloped, but the British saw promise here, particularly if more Costa Rican trade could be diverted that way. The major problem would be labor for future development. Although land had been purchased and buildings were planned, there was only one carpenter in the town, and the only available labor was Nicaraguan boatmen while their *bongos* were temporarily in the river port. This source of labor was very undependable, at best. Resident Nicaraguan labor had fled, and returnees, if detected, were detained by the Nicaraguan government; it kept a close check on all boat traffic downriver, as well as lists of the boatmen to see that none of them remained in Greytown. The situation regarding building materials, their transport, and labor was such that the British considered obtaining prefabricated buildings from the United States (as a U.S. transit company did later). As at Bluefields, construction was very poor, and the British were concerned with improving the existing structures as well as expanding. The *best* houses, built of boards and thatched with palm, deteriorated rapidly in the wet climate; and insects, though they did not seem to be a personal problem for the settlers, accelerated the deterioration, so that houses were in need of continual repair.

The taking over of Greytown by the British had an adverse effect upon food supplies for the town. The Nicaraguan government cut off all commercial contacts with the interior, whence all of Greytown's meat, vegetables, and fruits had come. The town was in a precarious position: it had to rely solely upon provisions brought by ship from abroad. The British were hopeful that a military garrison, established at the port, could be provisioned with agricultural produce grown in the vicinity. They expected that settlers would be able to raise plantains and yams, which could be sold cheaply, and that these could be supplemented by fish and turtle caught by native fishermen. However, this self-sustaining function never materialized throughout the town's entire history of occupation.

It was obvious that much would have to be done before Greytown could be the port the British envisioned. It had been hoped that its economic situation might be improved by providing it with American shipping connections—for example, by having the New York–Panama service call en route, thus providing faster service to Britain and to Europe as well. Late in 1848 the British were anticipating a stream of American traffic, via Greytown, to California, but they knew that the port was physically deteriorating. The entrance was obstructed by bars and islands, formed by river deposits. They also saw the problem of low water in the river during the dry season, as well as the great difficulty of river navigation (even by small boats). The port needed everything: dredging, a wharf, buildings. There were no building materials in the vicinity and no transportation to bring them in from a distance. The nearest building stone was at Machuca Rapids and Monkey Point.

Revenue for the Mosquito protectorate came principally from customs and harbor dues at Greytown, and it could not be substantial without greater economic development of the Shore, which was thwarted (in part) by insufficient labor. The fees on mahogany cutting, potentially a source of increased revenue, had been difficult to collect, due to the dispersal of this operation. Most of the cutting was north of Cape Gracias a Dios, and almost nothing could be collected from that remote region. South of the cape, most operations were minor, with little capital, and thus a source of few and meager receipts.

The mahogany trade of the Shore had other disadvantages as well. The native population was not accustomed to wage labor, and costly apprenticeships would be necessary. It was difficult to induce ships to detour from their regular trading routes for mahogany cargos along this little-known stretch of coast, and if they did, their rates were much higher. Also, prices for mahogany had fallen as a result of overproduction, and wood of finer quality could be gotten from Cuba at less cost through the use of slave labor. In addition to the higher freight and labor costs were the costs occasioned by the necessity to import almost all supplies, with duties more than twice as high as those levied in Belize.

All the while, the mahogany cutters had their troubles with the Indians and they appealed to the British for assistance. They complained of having made advances to Indians for labor services that were not provided, then not being repaid. Also, the cutters suffered much plunder and violence at the hands of the Indians. Finally, the "Indian problem" became so deleterious to the important mainstay of mahogany exploitation that Christie proposed sending a British representative from the protectorate agency to investigate the scattered sites north of Bluefields, and possibly have the Mosquito king go along to exert his influence upon his subjects. The plan was for the agency to prepare a speech that the king would deliver (in Mosquitian) to as many assembled Indians as possible at various stopovers. In the speech, the king would tell the Indians that they would incur his displeasure, and be dealt with harshly, unless they ceased their harassment of the mahogany cutters, plundering, and violation of labor contracts. Christie planned to have copies of the king's speech distributed widely so as to reach those natives who could not hear it firsthand. However, the agency seat was transferred from Bluefields to Greytown early in 1849, because of the latter's better shipping connections, and the plan appears to have been forgotten. In any case, it was never authorized. Greytown was even farther from areas of mahogany exploitation, as well as major Indian groups, and British surveillance and control of outlying parts of the Shore was not easy because of scarce personnel and transport. The mahogany industry was left to handle its own problems, as revenues from it dwindled.

At Greytown, Christie set himself up as the sole authority in what he viewed more as a colony under British administration than a protectorate with a degree of Mosquito control and influence. He contended that the move to Greytown was not to his personal advantage: it was "a more dis-agreeable residence than Bluefields," there was no medical man there, and Dr. Green's services as secretary were no longer available.[19] All supplies had to be brought in from Jamaica, the United States, or Britain, and they were costly because freight costs were high. With vessels calling infrequently, it was necessary to get large quantities of supplies at a time; therefore much was wasted by spoilage in the damp climate. Also, housing in Greytown was still a problem: its two public buildings were in such a decayed, insect-ridden state that Christie expected them to be blown down by the coming northers. The thatch required repair at regular intervals; a new customs house was needed, as well as a courthouse and a prison; and Christie so recommended. There was a serious shortage of residential housing, and privies were nonexistent, but all who had received parcels of land were required to build one by the end of the year, modeled after the sample agency-built privy (which had "a chimney thirty feet high to carry effluvia above the houses" and "a box to prevent the water, which is everywhere within four feet of the surface, from being spoilt").[20]

To help the labor problem, the policemen—brought from Jamaica—were chosen for their knowledge of different trades and they doubled as work-men. Two carpenters, also from Jamaica, were put to work building a police station (the first new construction), assisted by a few prisoners.

After a brief residence in Greytown, Christie qualified his previous state-ments about its healthful qualities:

> Persons who have lived here for some time and W. Shepherd at the head of them, call the place healthy; and trusting to their testimony I have in a previous dispatch spoken of the general healthiness of the place. I cannot say that my ten weeks' experience of the place is favorable to their view. There is, I have not doubt, a malaria proceeding from a lagoon immediately behind the site of the town. The constant irritation of the *chigoes* produces illness, and they have been known to cause death. I suspect it requires some time for a person to get acclimatized: and then he may live here for many years without illness.[21]

Thus began a series of ambiguities and conflicting statements about healthfulness at Greytown which was to continue for decades. Perhaps Christie was one of the realistic observers, and he may have been correct in assigning such an important role to acclimatization, for it appeared to be true that those who were able to survive and who remained in the place lived long lives.

Despite its shortcomings, the British promoted Greytown during these days as a place for immigrants, who were encouraged to go there rather than to other parts of the Shore. Its prospects seemed promising in view of California-bound Americans, soon expected to be passing through in large numbers, and the addition of U.S. shipping connections to the monthly services to and from Jamaica and England. As for agricultural settlement: although admitting that the black-sand soils in the vicinity of Greytown were not adapted to crops ("which do not thrive here"), advocates of colonization emphasized the richer valley soils upriver.[22]

Christie was so preoccupied with problems of labor and provisions on the Shore and particularly at Greytown that he made a trip to Jamaica, hoping to arrange for a "supply" of convict labor. Governor Grey, moreover, supported the idea. Another objective of Christie's mission was to encourage emigration by planters, mechanics, and laborers from Jamaica to the Shore. Finally, he hoped to find peasant farmers who would go to Greytown and superintend cultivation with the prospect of supplying the town with provisions. He even believed that if Jamaican farmers were installed, there might be surpluses for export.

To proponents of convict labor for the Shore, the idea was logical. The Shore needed the people and the labor; the West Indies had the convicts, and would be glad to relieve their prisons by sending them elsewhere, but needed a way of transporting them. Another advantage was the fact that prisoners received excellent training in various trades at the Jamaica penitentiary: brickmaking, lime burning, carpentry, tailoring, and gardening. (The prisoners themselves had constructed all the buildings of the penitentiary.) Also, there was the possibility that the Jamaica legislature would support the prisoners in their new Mosquito home with grants equal to their cost in the Jamaica penitentiary. The British government, however, was not willing to use its colonial funds to transport prisoners to the Mosquito Shore from West Indian islands or for the additional military forces to control the convicts.

The proposal, in short, did not win the enthusiasm of the British authorities at home; and Palmerston thought it "impossible to entertain a proposition for establishing a British convict settlement in a territory which is not British."[23] This view is especially notable because Americans were accusing Palmerston of having imperialistic designs upon the Mosquito Shore, and already considering it to be a British colony of sorts.

The assumption that Britain had territorial ambitions in Central America, to assure itself exclusive control of interoceanic routes, led to countermeasures by the United States after the end of the Mexican War. Except for the war, these measures might have been taken earlier, for President James K. Polk was concerned as early as 1846, when the treaty with New Granada gained Panama transit rights for the United States. By 1848, as his administration was ending, the British occupation of San Juan del Norte (Greytown) and Chatfield's activities seemed to indicate that territorial acquisition was part of British policy. In response, the U.S. State Department dispatched Elijah Hise, during the Polk administration, then Ephraim George Squier, during the Zachary Taylor administration, on fact-finding missions to Central America. These missions were aimed at countering British inroads, encouraging united resistance by the republics, and promoting U.S. commercial interests, especially with regard to the interoceanic route (the private American Atlantic and Pacific Ship Canal Company was at that time seeking a concession from Nicaragua). Once on the scene, both diplomats had become alarmed about British intentions and were inclined to proceed on their own initiative, beyond their governments' instructions. Hise, who arrived in Guatemala City as U.S. chargé d'affaires late in 1848, immediately recommended intervention by the United States or, at least, a show of force under the principles of the Monroe Doctrine. Almost in desperation, he wrote to Secretary of State James Buchanan in February 1849:

> Can it be possible that the United States will permit England to play out the Game she has Commenced in this part of North America, which will result in her Colonizing this Magnificent Country of Central America to Monopolise its Commerce and Either to Make herself, or prevent altogether the Making of a Canal through Nicaragua?[24]

Without express authority from the State Department, Hise diligently pursued negotiations for a treaty with Nicaragua, which he and the Nicaraguan chargé d'affaires in Guatemala signed in June of 1849. Under its sweeping terms, Nicaragua ceded to the United States or to any company— in this case, the Compania de Tránsito de Nicaragua, headed by an American, David J. Brown (later absorbed by Cornelius Vanderbilt's American Atlantic and Pacific Ship Canal Company)—exclusive rights to construct a canal, railroads, and transit roads across the isthmus. In addition, it granted access to all public lands necessary for the traverse and the right to fortify the route, as well as free passage of people and goods, without restrictions or duties. In return, the United States pledged to support Nicaragua in the exercise of its sovereignty over all its territory.

Negotiations for the Hise treaty and its signing had actually taken place after Hise's official replacement by Squier, in the previous April. Arriving in León from Greytown to take up his assignment in late June, Squier was greatly perturbed when he heard of the Hise treaty. He informed the Nicaraguan government that since Hise had not been empowered to enter into the agreement and since he had done so *after* the appointment of Squier, his successor, the treaty should be treated as unofficial. He also complained to John Clayton, the new secretary of state, about the matter. Meanwhile, in June, Hise had departed from Guatemala and, upon arrival in Washington, presented his treaty to the government and recommended its ratification. In León, Squier, who found many provisions of the Hise treaty objectionable—especially the U.S. pledge to guarantee the territorial integrity of the whole of Nicaragua—pursued negotiations for an alternative treaty. This was signed, along with the American Atlantic and Pacific Ship Canal Company's contract, in September of 1849. It confirmed some of the provisions of the earlier agreement and bound both nations to protect the concession of the AAPSCC in pursuance of its operations. However, while the United States would guarantee the sovereignty of Nicaragua over the *route*, Squier's agreement did not contain a guarantee to ensure the territorial integrity of the *whole* of Nicaragua. Provisions for exclusivity were only partial. There was a stipulation that the rights and privileges conceded to the United States or its citizens not be granted to any other nation unless it should "first enter into the same treaty stipulations for the defense and protection of the proposed great interoceanic canal."[25] Some exclusiveness was nevertheless provided in that the company awarded the concession be always composed of American citizens, who must own the majority of its stock, and that, in the event of noncompliance, the concession be granted to another American company.

These two treaties were assertive and even defiant compacts, clearly expressing the apprehensive and anti-British stands of their diplomat-authors. But the Costa Rican and Guatemalan governments, more friendly to Britain, opposed them. In Washington, the Whig administration, under Taylor, was less defiant, and Clayton had started negotiations with Great Britain as early as October of 1849. Squier was so informed, and as it turned out, neither his nor Hise's treaty was ratified. Despite the failure of this attempt at a formal political alliance between the United States and Nicaragua, the Hise-Squier treaty negotiations had assisted in the conclusion of private-company contracts for opening a transit route.

Squier remained in Central America until June of 1850 as a roving U.S. diplomatic representative. Throughout his stay, he was acutely suspicious of Great Britain's design, particularly as it related to Costa Rica. He was convinced that the two countries wanted a treaty which would place Costa Rica under British protection and thus back up Costa Rican claims to the south bank of the San Juan River and the southern shore of Lake Nicaragua. He feared that this would strengthen Britain's exclusive control of the inter-oceanic route—her obvious objective, in his opinion. He wrote numerous letters to Secretary of State Clayton about the "British-Costa Rican conspiracy" and aggressively promoted U.S. countermoves in Nicaragua, Honduras, and El Salvador.

Frederick Chatfield, who had been promoting British interests in Central America for many years, finally had a shrewd competitor. Having originally favored the cause of the Federation, but unsuccessful—amid the instability—in negotiating a trade agreement with it, he later adopted the policy of courting the individual states as more promising for British hegemony than revived attempts at union. He employed all manner of intrigue to promote British ascendancy, and was not disinclined to meddle in internal political affairs or to make policy decisions on his own, without consulting his government. As noted, his methods had brought him enemies among Liberals in the various countries, who accused him of being a major disruptive force in the struggle to revive the union. All of this tended to strengthen the position of the United States. President Polk's policy, continued under the Taylor administration, was to encourage reunion of the Central American states as offering the best bulwark against the British, and Squier's efforts were so directed.

By nature, Squier was a true counterpart of Chatfield: indefatigable, aggressive, and willing to employ whatever means he considered necessary, even to the point of excess and exaggeration. Both diplomats worked persistently to establish spheres of influence for their respective countries. When Chatfield saw the apparent progress Squier was making in winning over the three "center" countries to the U.S. side (by late September 1849 Squier had signed another treaty with Honduras), he became more fearful of U.S. intentions and made his own countermoves. One of these was in the Gulf of Fonseca, considered then as the best Pacific terminus for a projected canal. Tigre Island, strategically located in that gulf and belonging to Honduras, was seized by British forces—directed by Chatfield—on October 16, 1849. Honduras had been notified that if certain outstanding British claims against the country were not settled, a lien would be placed upon the island. Palmerston, however, was opposed to this unorthodox method of satisfying claims. Meanwhile, Squier had anticipated Chatfield's move and had secured from the friendly government of Honduras a temporary cession of the island to the United States. With no support from his government for this latest aggressive action (rather, he received a reprimand for it) and a possible confrontation with the United States in the offing, Chatfield retreated and the British Caribbean fleet commander ordered restoration of the island to Honduras (after a brief occupation). Nevertheless, the incident exemplified, in a very overt way, the clash for control of the isthmus. It inflamed public opinion in the United States, further alienated U.S.-British relations, and united Nicaragua, Honduras, and El Salvador as never before.

By the time of the Tigre affair, however, Clayton had started negotiations with Great Britain, aimed at settling the Nicaragua dispute. Thereafter, he advised Squier to show restraint and not to exceed his instructions. In November of 1849 he wrote that he had no reason to believe that Great Britain was on the verge of concluding a treaty with Costa Rica, and that while U.S.-British negotiations were proceeding, Squier should "carefully avoid all discussions or exhibitions which can possibly tend, by irritating the British agents in Central America, to embarrass our negotiations with the British Ministry."[26] Yet Squier and Britain's overly zealous Chatfield remained archantagonists during the following months in a personal struggle for dominance in the isthmus by their respective countries. Each exemplified, to an extreme, the fears and suspicions that the United States and Britain had entertained toward the other with regard to intentions in an area now recognized as strategically critical.

Squier's activities as a diplomat are perhaps obscured by his renown as the author of several books on Central America, based upon his travels and experiences there. Besides their great volume of factual information on archaeology, history, physical geography, people, customs, and transport routes, there are, of course, anti-British tirades. Many of these he directed at the so-called Mosquito kingdom, which he had been charged particularly to investigate. His expressions of contempt for the British usurpers, the Mosquito puppets, and the unjustified protectorate are profuse, as might be expected. Bancroft wrote that he "espouses the Central American side with so much warmth as to awaken a suspicion that his judgment may have been warped by his patriotism."[27]

Although he wrote extensively about Mosquitia, Squier did not have firsthand acquaintance with all parts of the Shore. One place that he *did* visit, however, was San Juan del Norte, and his impressions of that port under British control are hardly complimentary. He described it as centered around a small fort built of logs and "manned by a commandant who wore his shirt outside of his pantaloons, at the head of a dozen soldiers who wore no shirts at all." There were few amenities. The houses were palm thatched, with sides of rough boards or cane matting plastered with mud. Furniture was elemental: the hammock was a central item, with a few rough chairs and a table. There was neither church nor school in the place. Ordinarily, most of the inhabitants were unoccupied—in their hammocks or enjoying their guitar music and dancing. Occasionally, when a rare vessel was in port, they worked a few hours loading and unloading. Rum was a major import.[28]

> We caught also occasional glimpses of the domestic economy of the inhabi-
> tants, and could not help admiring the perfect equality and general good
> understanding which existed between the pigs, babies, dogs, cats and chick-
> ens. They lay down together in millennial confidence, and the pigs gravely
> took pieces of tortillas away from the babies, and the babies as gravely took
> other pieces away from the pigs.[29]

As the decade ended, Chatfield still busied himself with trying to consolidate Britain's position in Central America. He went to Greytown intent upon providing increased naval protection for the Mosquito king, improving the town's police force, and strengthening the municipal government.

Christie, for his part, had come to believe that the policy of a British-protected Mosquito kingdom was not the most suitable for dealing with the natives, and he communicated this view to Palmerston. He considered it a sham to look upon the Mosquito people as capable of governing themselves—to any degree. To deal with "barbarous, aboriginal tribes," he felt that outright British control, including military, was necessary. He further thought that a great deal of the opposition of neighboring Spanish countries toward Britain was due to their view that a Mosquito kingdom composed of savages, having national rights to which they should defer, was ridiculous. In his view, this "kingdom" could never expect recognition from these countries or from the United States. He favored return to the direct control that Britain had exercised until 1787, in which the Indians were "cared for" but had no power, and harmless coronations were held for their "king." Only then, in his view, would the Shore become secure and appealing for substantial, lasting colonization.[30]

But the influence of these underlings on a matter that now affected overall

Anglo-American relations was waning. At a higher level, in both the United States and Great Britain, conciliatory voices were heard. Although it appeared from events in Central America that the two countries were headed toward a dangerous confrontation, the desire to avoid it and, if possible, negotiate a peaceful settlement was not lacking in Washington and London. For President Taylor, an explosive sectional conflict over slavery in the newly acquired Mexican territories had developed, and the danger of civil war loomed. Palmerston was meeting increasing opposition, from the press and within his government, over the aggressive policy, as expressed by Chatfield, in Central America. Provocation of America was not popular at home.[31] This was one reason why the foreign secretary was not always receptive of Chatfield's and Christie's recommendations.

Basic throughout the controversy, apparently, had been a misunderstanding by each country, at the highest policy level, of the other's true motives with regard to the Nicaraguan interoceanic route. Each suspected the other of wishing to gain exclusive control of the route. The first approach had been for each country to prevent this through the contentious, even threatening and bellicose, activities of the two diplomatic adversaries on the scene. While this was in progress, however, Secretary of State Clayton (as noted) had initiated a movement toward negotiations with the British through the American ambassador in London, not knowing where they might lead. There was no retreat from the basic objective to protect U.S. interests in Central America, and there was a contingency plan to revert to pressure if the negotiations failed. However, after talks with Palmerston and his Foreign Office began, late in 1849, it seemed that the actions of each country in Central America had been basically defensive and aimed at preventing the other from monopolistic control there, not at establishing its own. With this mutual disavowal of self-interested colonial or territorial ambitions, the confrontational policy ended and the way became open to a peaceful solution. Both countries agreed that their best interests would be served by an interoceanic route, open to all, in a Central America free of the internal dissension encouraged in the past.

This new understanding became the basis for the Clayton-Bulwer Treaty, signed in April 1850. The treaty provided that neither country would seek to acquire exclusive control over the interoceanic route. Also, the pact included provisions for no fortifications, no colonization, no territorial dominion over Central American areas adjacent to interoceanic routes, no alliances with states or people with the purpose of securing special rights or advantages, and free-port status for Greytown. After its ratification, later in 1850, the treaty remained in force for the next fifty years, during which time neither country attempted to gain unilateral control of interoceanic routes, thus eliminating this source of conflict.

(Even *after* the signing of the treaty, Clayton still felt it necessary to restrain the confrontational tendencies of Squier. "Kindness and conciliation are most earnestly recommended by me to you," he wrote. "Let nothing be done to irritate the British Government . . . let there be no exultation on our side at the expense of British pride, or sensibility . . . deal gently and kindly in all your intercourse both with British subjects and British agents."[32] In the same dispatch, after thanking him for his services, Clayton recalled the controversial diplomat to the United States.)

Having used the Mosquito claim to eastern Nicaragua, and even San Juan del Norte (Greytown), as the basis for its occupation and protectorate, Britain nevertheless found itself with a commitment to the Mosquito people and their leaders from which it could not easily withdraw. Her long-standing and determined proclamation of Mosquito sovereignty, despite the signing of the Clayton-Bulwer Treaty, plagued British–United States–Central American relations for many years to come.

4   The Coming of the
                                Americans, 1850–1860

When the Clayton-Bulwer Treaty was signed, Americans had already been crossing the Central American isthmus en route to California for well over a year. The gold rush was under way. The Panama route, which attracted most of the transients, had the advantage of a head start. Fairly frequent and regular steamship service had been established there by American companies, even prior to the gold rush, to carry the mails to and from the Oregon Territory. Though hardly prepared to handle the hordes that were passing through Panama in 1849, the companies welcomed the additional passenger revenues and prospered. There were hardships, overcrowding, and delays, but during 1849 and 1850 this route was the most reliable and least arduous way of reaching the West Coast of the United States.

Although the Nicaraguan route was used by some transients during these years, this traffic was little more than a trickle. The first "gold rush ship" left New York for Nicaragua in February 1849, bearing 130 passengers, some of whom, after disembarking at Greytown, required six months to reach San Francisco.[1] For these early transients it was not easy. Ships from New York were infrequent and irregular, and there were no organized transport facilities for the river and lake journey in Nicaragua, or the overland trip from the lake to the Pacific. Transients were mostly on their own after they reached Greytown, obtaining whatever conveyances they could (usually at exorbitant prices) and living off the land. Upon reaching the Pacific coast, they often had to wait long periods for infrequent and unscheduled vessels to carry them to California. At least initially upon arrival, however, some who had chosen this route were pleased. One passenger had these impressions of Greytown (which Americans continued to call San Juan del Norte):

I never was more surprised than at my first view of this place. I had expected it would be like Chagres, a collection of huts on some low, marshy point, and utterly destitute of everything like beauty or interest; but I found it one of the prettiest and most charming little places it was ever my happiness to fall into. As we came in it looked just like a picture. The little bay with its three or four islands, skirted by a fine beach, on the outside of which a heavy surf was rolling, while within all was calm and still; the steep, thatch-roofed cane houses clustered together at its head relieving the dense forest behind; and the dimly seen summits of the far-off mountains of Nicaragua, made to me one of the most beautiful landscapes that I have ever beheld.[2]

Idyllic though this scene appeared from the sea, the port settlement had not progressed beyond thatched huts. The only substantial building in those early days, when California-bound Americans were passing through, was the customs house and residence for the Mosquito and British officials, in the middle of the grass-covered central square. All other buildings were the flimsy houses of residents, mostly constructed of cane poles and thatch. There was not a hotel of any sort to accommodate the transients, who found whatever shelter they could for their sometimes lengthy stays. Some of the first groups used a converted warehouse.

San Juan de Nicaragua ("Greytown") in 1849 (*Harper's Monthly Magazine*, vol. 10, no. 55, December 1854)

Greytown was similarly ill equipped to handle the large numbers of boisterous adventurers by its dearth of places of amusement, consisting in the early days of no more than small bars. Law and order thus became an immediate problem, due to the widespread drinking and marauding in a small, isolated town with few things to do and walled in by jungle on all sides. There were no more than two policemen to handle the situation. It is no wonder that the British consul considered a police station, with jail, of first priority and yearned for more immigrants from Jamaica, from whom additional policemen might be recruited.

Most of the first groups of Americans headed for California used *bongos* and canoes to travel up the San Juan. The *bongo*, a huge dugout made from the trunk of a single tree, was particularly well adapted to river transport, for it drew only two to three feet of water even when fully loaded. It usually

Going up the San Juan in a *bongo* (*The Century Magazine*, vol. 42, no. 6, October 1891)

carried around fifty persons, with a crew of naked Indian oarsmen (numbering between ten and twenty), and most often carried cargo as well as passengers. Roughly a third of the boat was decked, on which a shed or cabin was erected as protection from the rain. The *bongos* stopped at night and a meal would be cooked for the passengers and crew.[3] They were slow, crowded, and uncomfortable.

After leaving the Caribbean coast, the early transient saw only a few riverside settlements, which, like Greytown, produced little food. El Castillo, the village at the moldering Fort Inmaculada Concepción, and San Carlos were the largest settlements, but they were inhabited by only a few soldiers and their families. Each had known better days in the eighteenth century, when the military function was more significant. Since then, the San Juan had fallen into disuse as a waterway.

While these haphazard conditions existed for early transit via Nicaragua, plans were under way to make the route a serious competitor of Panama. Cornelius Vanderbilt of New York had entered the picture. At age 44, he was a self-made millionaire of humble beginnings who had captained his own boat in New York harbor as a youth and gone on to become a shipping magnate, controlling steamboat lines throughout the United States. Commodore Vanderbilt, as he came to be called, was an iron-willed entrepreneur who made his own decisions and with tremendous energy and unwavering resolve implemented them, usually with utmost success. When the need for interoceanic transport across Central America arose in 1849, he saw it as a lucrative and challenging business opportunity—the biggest yet—and he was interested. Other capitalists already were in control of the Panama route; so he looked to Nicaragua. From the beginning, he perceived its advantages: the shorter distance it offered for the trip from New York to San Francisco and its river-and-lake waterway, traversing most of the isthmus. He conceived a plan, more grandiose than that for Panama, involving a canal, steamship service on both oceans, and transit facilities (while his canal was being built) across Nicaragua. The latter would consist of regular boat service up and down the San Juan River and across Lake Nicaragua, and carriage transport across the narrow neck of land between the lake and the Pacific.

From the spring of 1849 to the summer of 1851, Vanderbilt worked to implement his plan. A contract of concession was obtained by Squier in behalf of Vanderbilt's American Atlantic and Pacific Ship Canal Company, providing not only for canal-construction rights but also for the transit service. A survey of the route was made and specifications were drawn for a canal. Navigational improvements on the San Juan were accomplished. Oceangoing steamships and steamboats for the river and lake were constructed. At first there appeared to be no problem with the British and Mosquito authorities at Greytown. When the Clayton-Bulwer Treaty was signed, early in 1850, joint support of the United States and Great Britain for Vanderbilt's projects was forthcoming, and as the time approached for opening the transit route, the greatest problem was the San Juan rapids. (It was only with much difficulty that the new lake steamer was gotten past the last and most formidable rapids, El Castillo.) When the route was opened in July 1851, Vanderbilt was a passenger on his new steamship from New

York, carrying 100 California-bound transients. Transfer to the new river steamer proceeded as scheduled at Greytown, and when the steamer reached Machuca Rapids and had difficulty passing over, Vanderbilt took the helm and steered the vessel through under full steam. Using *bongos* and mules for parts of the journey, the passengers reached the Pacific three days later and awaited arrival of the companion steamship for the San Francisco run. During the rest of 1851, almost 2,000 passengers were attracted to the Nicaragua route, thenceforward served on a regular bimonthly schedule, and in 1852 the number reached more than 10,000, almost half of Panama's total.[4]

Meanwhile, though the terms of the Clayton-Bulwer Treaty seemed, to the United States, to forbid it, Britain maintained its protectorate over the Mosquito Shore. Unfortunately, the treaty's language allowed for quite different interpretations by the signatory governments, although this was not realized until after ratification. The critical difference was that the British did not view the treaty's provisions as retroactive and, therefore, affecting their previous arrangements in Central America, such as their Mosquito protectorate and occupation of the Bay Islands. Moreover, they refused to concede that their Mosquitia protectorate constituted assumption or exercise of "dominion," the word used in the treaty. On the other hand, the U.S. Senate's ratification had been based upon the understanding that the British would withdraw from all areas except Belize, which was specifically excluded. When they did not, the treaty was condemned in Washington—the first of many attacks on the unpopular treaty (which would continue for the rest of the century, for different reasons). For the next four years, the unresolved matter led to further confrontations between the two countries at Greytown.

Even as the Clayton-Bulwer Treaty was being signed, Christie had proposed that a new consular residence be built in Greytown, indicating that he expected the British to remain there. Unlike the situation in other, large cities of Central America, where spacious old houses, built by Spaniards, were available for rent to foreign officials, there was no appropriate residence in Greytown. Christie proposed an elegant mansion, in keeping with both the British colonial tradition and his own desire for full colonial status in Mosquitia. (If it had been built, it would have been in striking contrast to other buildings in Greytown, all of which were constructed of wood, and the *only* masonry construction at any time, besides the marble portions of the Pellas Hotel later in the century.) A noted British architect in Jamaica submitted plans, which called for a two-story structure with open towers at either end. All building materials would be shipped from Jamaica, and the estimate (£3,000) covered such things as brick, lime, cement, tile (for floors), flagstone, cast iron pillars, lead sheets for the roof, hardwood-frame windows, pitch pine flooring, and all carpentry.[5] (For such a house, with all materials and workmen brought in, it was not a bad price, even for the time.) There is no evidence that any of this progressed beyond the architect's plans, however. Christie, soon afterwards, began to absent himself for long periods in England, and eventually received a new post in Switzerland. The agency at Greytown was downgraded to a consulate, and Dr. Green, who often was acting British representative in Christie's absences, was appointed consul.

During the months immediately following the treaty's signing, the British had continued to watch over their interests in Greytown, as Americans passed through, to and from California, and as Vanderbilt prepared to open his transit service. Ships arrived from Jamaica, to lie at anchor in the harbor. Naval commanders, not happy with their assignments, complained that their men contracted fever and that half to four-fifths of them were incapacitated at any one time; they considered Greytown not worth the price. In November 1850, Vice Admiral McDonald, in charge, urged that the Admiralty in London "find means less injurious to the Naval Service for the protection of this worthless and unhealthy place."[6] Later, from Jamaica, came this report of Lord Dundonald:

> If it is the intention of H. M's governt that a ship of War shall be permanently stationed at Greytown, my successor will find that impossible. Unless their Lordships will augment the very small force on the Station by two sloops or small steam vessels, at present the ships sent there have to remain for months in that fatal climate, there being no other vessels to relieve them.
>
> I beg to call their Lordships' most serious attention to the fact, that not only are the vessels sent to Greytown speedily incapacitated from the performance of any useful service there, but on their relief months are required before they can be efficient for any other duty, by reason of the deteriorated state of their crews.[7]

Beyond this, it seemed clear to naval officers on the spot that continuing to hold Greytown with men-of-war would inevitably result in clashes with the United States. This impression was gained from transient Americans who voiced the American interpretation of the recent treaty as calling for British withdrawal and ending the protectorate.

Ironically, the British naval units stationed in Greytown were called upon for assistance by hundreds of Americans, returning from California, who found themselves stranded without sufficient food or shelter because no ship arrived to take them home. There were some 800 additional persons in a place "incapable of containing very few more than the residents." The British consul, Dr. Green, noted that under these circumstances, and "taking into consideration the dreadful state of the weather (it raining almost incessantly), I have no hesitation in saying that they must either die with fever or from starvation."[8] However, the British vessels in port complied with a request for beef and pork, even though their crews were short.

There was nothing to be gotten from the area; no cattle could be procured at any price, and only salt meat was available. The British ships transported 500 Americans to Chagres, at $15 a head. But the problem of food in Greytown was not over, for more Americans were coming into the town than were able to get transport out.

When Vanderbilt's Accessory Transit Company began its service in the summer of 1851, Greytown underwent a rapid transformation. The forest receded and two wide streets, parallel to the shoreline, replaced the single, narrow one. The thatched huts became less conspicuous, as many American-type structures, wooden frame buildings, with verandas, appeared. They were grouped around the central square. Few features recognizable from previous years remained. The new St. Charles Hotel was a landmark, which Squier later described as

> a gaunt edifice of pine boards, framed in the United States, and brought out bodily, as it were—a huge tinder-box of two stories. . . . Within was a bar and row of bottles, and plenty of people in check-shirts and straw-hats, with quick, intelligent eyes, ready of speech and swift in action.[9]

Near the original government building, new foreign consulates were established; they were raised on foundations, well above the ground, and painted white, with green shutters and shingle roofs.

Foreigners, now a sizable proportion of the increasing population and including a majority of Americans, dominated the newly introduced business establishments. In response to the entertainment needs of the hordes passing through, there were bowling alleys, billiard parlors, gambling houses, and, of course, more bars. Since most food was imported, some of the important, new businesses were grocery mercantile stores. The town, no longer so distinctively a British-Mosquito outpost, was becoming more and more Americanized through the influences of transients and settlers. The American consul encouraged residents to abide by the laws of the

San Juan de Nicaragua ("Greytown") in 1853 (*Harper's Monthly Magazine*, vol. 10, no. 55, December 1854)

governing power, Britain, but this was a pragmatic policy that in no way diminished the official stand of the United States that Britain had no rights, through a Mosquito protectorate or otherwise, to the Shore. Of course, there was no recognition of a Mosquito king. Nevertheless, even under British authority, most Americans felt more fortunate living here than in Chagres, Panama, renowned as a "hellhole."

King Street, Greytown, looking south, 1853 (*Harper's Monthly Magazine*, vol. 10, no. 55, December 1854)

Soon, however, conflict developed between the city authorities and the transit company. Since it had been established as a free port by the British government, in accordance with provisions of the Clayton-Bulwer Treaty, Greytown could collect no duties on transit company cargo. It thus found

King Street, Greytown, looking north, 1853 (*Harper's Monthly Magazine*, vol. 10, no. 55, December 1854)

itself without sufficient revenues at a time when municipal costs were mounting due to rapid growth. The town had quickly become unruly, with waves of boisterous American transients, and an adequate police force could not be maintained without a source of funds. When the city authorities decided to institute a small charge to cover harbor expenses, Vanderbilt not only refused to pay these charges for his vessels, claiming this was a violation of the treaty and Palmerston's promise, but considered his installations across the bay as outside the jurisdiction of Greytown and within Costa Rican territory. (Subsequently, the Costa Ricans agreed with this interpretation and repeatedly harassed transit operations there.) The outcome was that the Greytown authorities, in late 1851, appealed to a British warship, which fired upon one of Vanderbilt's ships, the *Prometheus*, forcing it to pay the harbor fee.

The "Prometheus Affair" inflamed American public opinion, exposing the fragility of the Clayton-Bulwer Treaty, and extremely hostile editorials appeared in U.S. newspapers. For a time it seemed that not only was the treaty in danger of abrogation but that the two countries might go to war. This "gunboat diplomacy" would not be tolerated by the United States— quite apart from the matter of the harbor dues and whether they were justified. If the latter was not a clear violation of the Clayton-Bulwer Treaty, as Vanderbilt claimed, firing upon a U.S. vessel certainly was, and the apology demanded from the British was ultimately forthcoming. The British Foreign Office stated that the action was unauthorized, which reflected the changing British policy regarding Central America: Britain's relations with the United States should not be sacrificed for any interests she might have in this corner of the world. Particularly, it seemed to some British officials, there should be no involvement in quarrels between private citizens of Greytown (increasing numbers of whom were Americans) and the transit company; it was not worth the price diplomatically. Besides the feeling at home, there is little doubt that Britain's attitude was affected by the loud American outcry, the furor of which apparently had not been anticipated.

Meanwhile, during 1851, there was renewed Liberal–Conservative strife within Nicaragua and in Central America as a whole. A new Conservative uprising, aided by forces from Honduras, overthrew the Nicaraguan military chief, Trinidad Muñoz, and transferred the seat of government from León to Managua (later to become the permanent, compromise capital). The latest attempt at union by the "central" states, the National Representation of Central America (Representación Nacional), began to falter almost as soon as it was inaugurated. Formed to give unity in foreign policy, the federation failed to gain recognition from either Britain or the United States. The new American minister to Nicaragua, John Kerr, reported that the government did not have popular support, was ineffective, and unable to deal with conditions in the states, particularly Nicaragua. Kerr was frustrated by not finding any authority to which he could properly present his credentials; likewise, his Nicaraguan counterpart in Washington complained that there was no government *he* could properly represent.

Guatemala's Rafael Carrera remained a steadfast opponent of all forms of unionism, and Chatfield, until his recall in 1852, encouraged this stand. Hoping to remove this obstacle, an army of Liberal unionists, supported by the Representación Nacional, invaded Guatemala, but Carrera defeated it in the decisive Battle of San José la Arada in February 1851. Thereafter, both the Liberal threat to his power and the Representación Nacional government disintegrated. A pro-British government was then in control in El Salvador, and the new leader in Nicaragua, Fruto Chamorro (a Conservative, who had formerly supported unionism), wanted his country to pursue an independent course. Both countries defected from the Representación Nacional and refused to send delegates to Tegucigalpa, the new federation capital. Only Honduras remained loyal. Its president, José Trindad Cabañas, attempted to regain El Salvador's and Nicaragua's support, and failing in this, invaded Guatemala again, on his own, in 1853. After another defeat by Carrera, the Representación Nacional cause was indeed lost and there was a resurgence of Conservative power all over Central America, with Carrera recognized as supreme leader.

The *Prometheus* incident, peacefully resolved, appears to have been a watershed in British-American relations regarding Mosquitia. Thereafter, with Palmerston's resignation as foreign minister and Chatfield's recall, the British government's position for the remainder of the decade was clearly headed toward diplomatic settlement. But settlement was still several years away. The protectorate remained and the conflict between the mostly Creole Greytown municipal governing body and the American transit company persisted. Nevertheless, transportation steadily improved at Greytown. The transit company assembled two river steamers in the harbor and put them into service. Besides the fortnightly service to and from New York, there was now frequent steamer service to New Orleans.

The days of stranded transients, depending upon irregular and unreliable British mail vessels, were coming to an end. In the early years of transit operations, however, there had not been enough river steamers to accommodate the increasing numbers of passengers. There were no rooms or berths for most of them, and often, when the boats anchored for the night, no room even to lie down. At times of abundant rain, the "walk" around the rapids could be arduous, requiring almost a full day to struggle through deep mud with baggage. During periods of low water, boats could be stuck on sandbanks for days, and often the transit company had to use *bongos*, in combination with its steamers, to get passengers up and down the river.

Despite the rapid changes, Greytown was incapable of handling the immense influx of transients. Provisions of meat, both fresh and salt, as well as groceries, were in short supply and prices were double those in England. Since the beginning of British occupation, the Nicaraguan government had not allowed food from the interior to pass down the river. Rents became exorbitant due to the lack of hotels and housing, and servants' wages steeply climbed—if servants could be obtained at all. The British consul's salary covered only about half of his expenditures, he claimed, for besides the high cost of his own expenses he had to accommodate (at the consulate) numerous government officials passing through.[10] Besides being on the California route, Greytown was then the point of entry for several Central American states. With an insufficient number of boarding houses and hotels, which were constantly filled with Americans en route to or from California, it was impossible for such officials to be put up elsewhere.

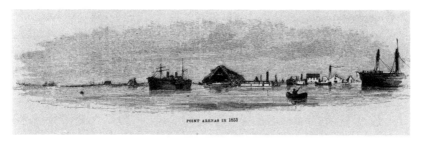

Point Arenas in 1853 (*Harper's Monthly Magazine*, vol. 10, no. 55, December 1854)

Some of Greytown's upsurge was short lived. The transit company had originally used the narrow, sandy spit across the bay from the town and next to the ocean as a utility base for housing its workers. Unfortunately for many of Greytown's businesses, the company subseqently made this spit (Punta Arenas) more and more self-sufficient. Its convenience for the company's operations was obvious, but eventually passengers no longer had to pass through Greytown at all; they could transfer to their ships and boats at Punta Arenas, after arrival from the interior or from the United States. Nor did transit company personnel need to trade in Greytown, since all of their needs could be met in the company store at Punta Arenas. Vice Admiral Seymour, in Jamaica, received this description of the problem from James Wilson, one of the visiting British representatives in Greytown:

> As the steamers frequently bring 400 or 500 passengers at a time, the money disbursed by them during their stay at Grey Town amounted to a considerable sum, and I imagine was the main source of the prosperity of the town— the American transit company, now in possession of Punta Arenas, have managed later to cut off this source by establishing Hotels or Barracks. . . . they monopolize the whole of the money spent by the large migratory population during their stay at this point of the route, and not a dollar of it finds its way to Grey Town, the consequence is that the Town has fallen off as rapidly as it sprung up, and upwards of one half of the settlers are said to have left within the last twelve months.[11]

This loss of business by Greytown enterprises, so soon after their flourishing, caused further bad relations and ultimately led to crisis.

By spring of 1854 there had been many incidents of animosity, including theft of company property and destruction of some of its buildings, after an ultimatum from Greytown authorities for removal of Punta Arenas installations went unheeded. No agreement was ever reached for relocating the transit company's facilities at Greytown: each side had held fast to provisions and qualifications not acceptable to the other. At the height of this conflict, Solon Borland, the U.S. minister to Nicaragua, arrived in Greytown as a passenger on one of the river steamers. As a witness to and a participant in the conflict, Borland brought the matter to a high level of international politics. He had offered protection to an American river-steamer captain when a Greytown law-enforcement squad attempted to arrest him for the murder of a native, insisting they had no authority to do so. This infuriated a mob which followed Borland to the U.S. consul's home with the intent of arresting him for interfering in their execution of justice. Borland reminded the townspeople and police of his diplomatic immunity, but they told him this meant nothing and a broken bottle was hurled at him, from which he suffered a slight wound. Thus Borland, extremely protective of U.S. interests in Central America and highly suspicious of British aims, was disposed to think the worst of Greytown's populace and administrators (most of whom were Jamaicans), and he reported their "bad character" to his superiors: "I am unable to regard them in any other light than as pirates and outlaws."[12] Naturally, at the hands of such people, he felt he had been insulted, and so did his government in Washington.

For this "insult" to its minister and for the theft and destruction of property at Punta Arenas, the official reaction of the United States was that the people of Greytown, and especially the authorities there, should be held accountable. The transit company was delighted when the warship *Cyane* was dispatched to force reparations and apologies, and made no secret of the fact that it hoped the outcome would be company control of Greytown. Although there is no indication that the *Cyane* was sent with any violent solution in mind, much discretion was conceded to the commander to do what he thought proper under the circumstances. Upon the arrival of the warship, on July 11, 1854, the U.S. consul communicated the demands of his government to the city authorities, who found them unacceptable. Commander Hollins issued this proclamation to the people of Greytown the following day:

Proclamation

To all men to whom these presents shall come, or whom they may concern;
Know ye, that whereas certain gross outrages have at sundry times been perpetrated by the "authorities" (so called) and people of San Juan del Norte [Greytown], upon the persons and property of American Citizens at that place and vicinity and whereas a serious insult and indignity has been offered to the United States in the conduct of the said "authorities" and people towards Mr. Borland, U.S. Minister to Central America, for which outrages

and insult no indemnity has been given and no satisfactory reply returned to
demands already made.

Now therefore, I, George A. Hollins, Commander of the United States
ship of war Cyane, and by virtue of my instructions from the U.S. Government at Washington do hereby solemnly proclaim and declare that if the
demand for satisfaction in the matters above named, specified in the letter of
Mr. Fabens, U.S. Commercial Agent, dated 11th inst, are not forthwith
complied with I shall at 9 a.m. of tomorrow 13th inst proceed to bombard the
town of San Juan del Norte aforesaid. . . .[13]

Despite protests from the British, Hollins made preparations to carry out
this "violent solution" on schedule if he did not receive a favorable reply. It
was not forthcoming. The American commander gave ample time for the
evacuation of some British subjects and a few Americans, mostly women
and children, while others removed themselves to the forest. Intermittent
bombardment of the town followed, and finally, with the remaining buildings set ablaze, it was totally destroyed.

Disapproval of this act came from all quarters: the residents of Greytown,
including the Americans; the U.S. Congress; the American public and
press; the British. The fact was that it hurt Americans who lived, and
worked, and had businesses in Greytown as much as any others, and it was
seen as unnecessary. The U.S. consular agent, J. W. Fabens, wrote afterward:

Public sentiment was unequivocally American. The British influence which
formerly existed there and on this "Isthmus" had been gradually expelled and
superseded by our own. But the public feeling has been so exasperated by the
Arbitrary, unwise and improvident conduct of the Commander of the Cyane
that I verily believe that had it not been for the strong personal regard entertained for the incumbent of this office that this Agency would have been
destroyed and its incumbent accomodated [sic] with a Coat of Tar and Feathers
by Americans—his own countrymen.[14]

British residents and those of other nationalities felt very bitter and filed
damage claims with the U.S. consulate. They also appealed to Queen
Victoria against this act which had reduced "to a heap of ruins all the
property and valuable merchandise without compassion and respecting
neither flags nor the laws of nations," in the following terms:

Your petitioners, therefore, humbly beg Your Majesty, as protector of this
Coast, to demand reparation of this grievous wrong; and that they may be less
liable to a similar attempt in future, entreat and most earnestly supplicate

Your Majesty to extend to them a kind and protecting hand, receiving them under Your Majesty's immediate care and protection, and incorporating them into the Colonies of Your Majesty's Kingdom, thus sheltering them within the folds of the British Flag.[15]

But this petition reflected the frustrating problem that had brought the "lesson" of the bombardment: the continuing presence of Britain in Greytown, which negotiations, proceeding between Washington and London, had as yet failed to settle. As one historian notes, the real lesson of the bombardment—though some officials believed it could have been learned without such drastic measures—"was meant for the British government rather than the citizens of Greytown."[16] Achieved at a heavy cost for Greytown, it was a price the Monroe Doctrine–adhering Pierce administration was evidently willing to pay for making its Mosquito policy known in no uncertain terms. The danger of civil war in the United States had faded for the time, so that the new Democratic government was willing to be much more aggressive about the British protectorate in Nicaragua. Even prior to the bombardment, President Pierce had strongly protested, as a violation of both the Monroe Doctrine and the Clayton-Bulwer Treaty, the 1852 British proclamation of colony status for the Bay Islands.

Greytown's physical aspect following the bombardment must have dismayed California-bound Americans and returnees. They saw a town which, already suffering economically, had been forced to start over—from ashes. Although rebuilding began immediately after the bombardment and continued through 1855, there was no recoupment of previous advances. This showed up in the town's physical aspect and in its economic life, which retrogressed. Among the crude abodes were but a few frame buildings, all constructed in a very rough manner with cheap lumber, without ceilings or interior finishing. These were generally multiple-unit housing accommodations. Most of the housing, however, consisted of single-unit thatched huts, seemingly thrown together in a haphazard mixture of boards and reeds, with crude outbuildings for cooking, which was done on the bare ground. Their occupants were Jamaican blacks, Mosquito Indians, and a few Nicaraguans from the interior. The somewhat-better-constructed buildings were warehouses, retail stores, hotels, drinking and gambling houses, and brothels. There was neither church nor schoolhouse. As had always been the case, agriculture was almost nonexistent, and even home gardens were extremely rare.

The chaos into which Greytown had descended made life precarious, or at least uncomfortable, particularly for Americans. Another American minister, John Wheeler, who was compelled to spend time in the town assisting in collecting claims information after the bombardment, described the conditions early in 1855:

> Your Department has been advised that there is no authority at this place to which I can apply, or appeal for redress for the past, or protection for the future.
>
> A large portion of this community is composed of men of the most lawless character; without any visible means of living; whose taste and temper delight in scenes of tumult, crime, and blood. Daily, at this place within my hearing, are outrages committed; and my repose is broken by their bacchanalian orgies "making night hideous". I rejoice that I have completed here the matters to which you directed my attention; (aiding Mr. Fabens in collecting testimony;) and that I go, in the first Steamer, to the Interior. Nothing but a sense of duty, and instructions from your Department, could compel me to remain two more such months here; for there has not been a hour that the safety of myself and family has not been jeopardized.[17]

Vanderbilt's ultimate project, the transisthmian canal through Nicaragua, had been dropped one year after the opening of the transit route, when he was unable to raise the necessary capital in the United States and England. But even though his rivals (former business associates) had gained control of the Accessory Transit Company and been forced to compete with an opposing Vanderbilt operation in Panama, the Nicaragua operation had become a financial success by 1855. It was functioning more efficiently, with better equipment and faster and more comfortable service, than ever. However, after 1855 a decline set in. A flood diverted some waters of the San Juan to the Colorado distributary that year, making the lower river less navigable and bringing greater silting problems to Greytown's harbor. In 1855, too, the newly built Panama Railway opened, heralding a new era of competition. Finally, an American adventurer, William Walker, arrived in Nicaragua with a band of filibusters in June of 1855. That same summer, Vanderbilt, who had vowed to "ruin" his rivals, was regaining control of the transit company through buying up its stock. These latter two forces would eventually clash along the San Juan, with damaging consequences for the route's progress.

In 1854 the well-meaning and competent Conservative leader, Fruto Chamorro, who had been head of the Confederation of Central America (Chinandega Pact), was chief of state in Nicaragua and was attempting to bring order to the country. However, having failed to gain cooperation from the Liberals in a moderate approach, his government began to pursue order by adopting severe measures against the Liberals in their stronghold of León. This resulted in a Liberal revolt led by Francisco Castellón, who in friendlier times had been a colleague of Chamorro in unification movements and head of the Confederation mission to Europe in 1845. At first the Liberals made advances in this new civil war, expelling government forces from León and attacking Granada. But at the same time, Carrera, who had consolidated his absolute power in Guatemala (he had been appointed president for life), sent assistance to the Conservatives. Suffering a serious setback, the Liberals soon found themselves under siege in León.

At this critical juncture an American opportunist, Byron Cole, who had traveled the transit route in the days of the gold rush, happened on the scene with an offer to engage American mercenaries, or filibusters, to assist the Liberals. Engaged in mining ventures in Honduras (whose government was also assisting the León forces in their struggle), he saw additional business opportunities with a victory of the anti-British Liberals in Nicaragua. Moreover, he knew just the man to head the mercenary expedition: William Walker, a San Francisco acquaintance with recent experience leading a filibustering expedition into Mexico. The Liberals proved willing to extend land grants to the Americans in return for this foreign support, and concluded a contract with Walker, through Cole as intermediary. The contract was made in the guise of a "colonization grant" in order not to violate U.S. neutrality laws. Walker set about organizing his expedition in California, and in June of 1855 arrived in Nicaragua with a band of fifty-six men, a number that was greatly expanded thereafter by recruiting in the United States and among American transients along the Nicaragua route.

William Walker's background does not seem to have prepared him for the fame and power that would be his in Nicaragua. A Tennessean, he had a rather strict and fundamentalist upbringing, but his obvious intelligence led him to unusual educational achievements at a young age. He appeared to have difficulty, however, in deciding upon a career. After obtaining a medical degree and then studying law, he failed to practice either profession for very long and became a journalist in New Orleans. As editor of a New Orleans newspaper while still in his twenties, he was idealistic and often controversial, adopting an antislavery position—sharply in conflict with his later identification by Southerners with the idea of Nicaragua as a proslavery haven. Still searching for a cause, he emigrated to California, via Panama, during the early days of the gold rush. His first three years in California were spent writing for a San Francisco newspaper, during which time he seems to have become a radical proponent of Manifest Destiny—to the extent of feeling that it was his personal destiny to "spread" American democracy and economic interests, by invasion if need be. From idealistic journalist he became a dedicated man of action, with grandiose plans and no small ambition for personal power and glory. Although he was by nature shy and reticent, these traits were deceptive. When aroused, he could show a quite different personality. His first attempt at filibustering (with a band of forty-five men) was in Lower California and Sonora, where he proposed to set up territories, under the U.S. protection, for the colonization of Americans. Although this plan collapsed (but not before Walker proclaimed himself "president" of the "independent state" of Lower California) due to U.S. interference and insufficient reinforcements and supplies, it gave him valuable experience for the Nicaragua adventure. Moreover, it gained him supporters in the United States who were similarly inclined toward radical Manifest Destiny, and mercenary forces to obtain it.

Initially suffering reverses, Walker's small band was augmented by native forces and was able to seize Granada by surprise attack only five months after he arrived in Nicaragua. Although the Conservative forces were mostly intact, the government, fearing for the safety of families held hostage, agreed to a settlement. Very quickly, Walker was in virtual control of the country. As he desired, a coalition government was formed, with Conservatives occupying the offices of president and secretary of war, but Walker was the real force, as commander in chief of the army (which was then mainly composed of his Americans). This government soon fell apart, as the Conservative members defected, sought help from neighboring Conservative-controlled states, then mounted a countermovement. Walker ordered the exile or execution of some Conservative leaders for treason during this period, and it soon became clear that his real objective was a political takeover of the country, for his own purposes.

However, Walker retained his charismatic hold on his American followers in Nicaragua. He was able to maintain iron discipline and, at the same time, command extreme personal devotion. He also attracted much support from the public in the United States, and even internationally; his exploits were considered by some to be of heroic proportions. The problem of the British protectorate was still outstanding, and Walker's control in western Nicaragua was satisfying to many Americans on this account. Particularly, as time went on, he gained the support of many proslavery Southerners in the United States, who saw in the Tennessean's takeover of Nicaragua the possibility of its annexation as another slave-holding state. By his statements and actions, Walker encouraged and exploited these views; there is little indication that he intended, however, to sacrifice his dreams of personal empire-building in Central America to the ambitions of slave-holders. [18] Furthermore, the composition of his army (which grew to over 2,000 American recruits) showed no strong ideological or sectional inclination. His men came from all parts of the country and seemed to be attracted mainly by a desire for adventure and personal profits. Some were escaping troubles back in the States; many of them, though not all, were impoverished drifters, degenerates, and renegades (an element which some cities in the United States appeared happy to be rid of); others had occupations and trades, but thought they might "improve" themselves in Nicaragua. [19]

Initially, President Franklin Pierce and Secretary of State William Marcy opposed Walker's exploits in Nicaragua and his recruiting in the United States. In any case, the efforts to uphold neutrality laws and prevent recruits and expeditions from reaching Nicaragua were not greatly effective. To complicate matters, the U.S. minister to Nicaragua, John Wheeler, a North Carolinian, was staunchly pro-Walker, even to the point of exceeding his authority. Censured by his superiors in Washington for his early recognition of the Walker-supported puppet government of Nicaragua without instructions to do so, Wheeler later recognized Walker as president of that country, again against instructions.

This dramatic period of Nicaraguan history—about which much has been written—had an important but indirect link with the Mosquito Coast. Until 1857, the San Juan River and Greytown were not parts of the battleground in the Filibuster War. Thus it was to a relatively quiet Greytown that another group of would-be filibusters, under another leader, came during the summer of 1855. Henry L. Kinney, of Pennsylvania, and a group of American investors had purchased the bogus concessions assigned in wholesale fashion, by inebriated King Robert Charles Frederick, to former residents of the Shore. The British government had denied the validity of these claims when the protectorate was established, but the papers had nevertheless gotten into European hands and been sold. Kinney organized an expedition in New York for the avowed purpose of colonization in Mosquitia—but it was suspected that the real intent was akin to that of Walker: to put Manifest Destiny into practice through armed filibustering.

Although opposed by the transit company and detained by U.S. authorities as a violation of neutrality laws, the expedition, much reduced in number, reached Greytown after several mishaps. It arrived when the port was struggling to revive after the bombardment, when most of the American residents were demoralized. Hence it was most welcome, and later when Kinney's group proved a catalyst in rebuilding the town, its popularity mounted. At the time, there was almost no government in Greytown, and the establishment of *some* authority and order seemed essential. The citizenry was much impressed by the self-styled "Colonel" Kinney, and in a convention of townspeople unanimously chose him "Civil and Military Governor of the City and Territory of Greytown," in September of 1855. Expectations were that he and his government, composed of colonist friends, could remedy the problems that plagued the town: poor order, inadequate revenues, and difficulties with the transit company.

But this private attempt to expand American influence at the mouth of the San Juan was unsuccessful. Although he had grandiose designs not unlike those of Gregor MacGregor and William Walker, Kinney did not receive the support he had expected from the parent company, formed in the United States. No new colonists and no provisions arrived. The British government did not recognize Kinney's appointment as governor or his American council, and his followers soon went their separate ways. Most of them were American, and not only aware of Walker's successful operations in the interior but persuaded of the justice of his cause, joined his forces. Kinney, holding to his dream of heading a state in eastern Nicaragua, sent a letter with the defectors to General Walker, offering his recognition of Walker as commander-in-chief of the army of Nicaragua in exchange for Walker's recognition of him as governor of the Mosquito Territory. Walker's reply was immediate, and left no doubt as to how he viewed interlopers: "Tell Mr. Kinney, or Colonel Kinney, or Governor Kinney, or by whatever name he styles himself, that if he interferes with the Territory of Nicaragua, and I can lay my hands on him, I will most assuredly hang him."[20] This quickly put an end to Kinney's enterprise. In disappointment, he resigned and later went to Granada, where Walker issued an order for his expulsion.

Walker made it clear from the beginning that, far from sharing the spoils with other American adventurers or assigning "spheres of influence," it was his intention to claim and hold intact for Nicaragua her entire territory, coast to coast, repudiating all "Mosquito claims," "Sambo grants," "British protectorates," "Kinney kingdoms," etc. He confirmed this intention in his instructions to John Heiss, his emissary to Washington and London, regarding the U.S.–British Mosquito controversy.[21] Had he lived and managed to retain his power in Nicaragua, that country's incorporation of the Mosquito Shore (or "reincorporation," as the Nicaraguans perceived it) as part of its national territory might not have waited four more decades.

Central to Walker's military campaign, conducted mainly in western Nicaragua, was control of the transit route. Upon it depended the transport of scores of additional filibuster recruits from the United States during the two years of fighting, and much of Nicaragua's revenues came from customs collected at the inland lake-river port of San Carlos. Vanderbilt's opponents in the transit company struggle for power in 1855, New York agent Charles Morgan and San Francisco agent Cornelius Garrison, consequently saw in Walker a possible ally. After initial Walker victories over Conservative forces in western Nicaragua and harassment of transit company operations on the Pacific side, the Morgan-Garrison interests concluded an agreement with the filibuster leader in early 1856. In return for financial support of his attempts to gain control of the Nicaraguan government and with assurances of free transportation of recruits, Walker secured revocation of the transit company's charter and obtained a new one, assigned to Garrison and Morgan. (Earlier, he had considered cancellation of the charter for his own purposes, on the grounds that the company had not settled debts owed the Nicaraguan government, according to the provisions of its concession.)

With scores of Americans passing up and down the San Juan in the years 1852–1856, significant settlement developed at various points to sell merchandise to the travelers: mainly liquor and food but also other needs. Prices were extremely high for all goods and services (such as were available). One traveler wrote in his diary in 1855: "There is also a few houses whose tenants live by fleecing those who travel this way."[22] The places chosen for these enterprises and settlements were the "wooding" stations, where the steamboats (but not the *bongos*, which carried many of the passengers) had to stop, and the rapids, where passengers disembarked and often waited several hours. At certain wooding stations, American and German families carved farms out of the tropical forest—probably the only real farming near Greytown. Along the river and on islands within it, the soil was fertile alluvium, derived from volcanic materials, and tropical crops and some crops introduced from the United States were produced on a small scale.

El Castillo, a rapids settlement, experienced a revival; it began with vendors in tents, who sold food and liquor to Americans, and the town's population grew to about 200 permanent residents, with several new and substantial structures, such as hotels, stores, and restaurants. A traveler wrote in 1856: "American enterprise and industry have built a tramroad around the rapids, and at their head a large and commodious warehouse, and one or two frame hotels have sprung up on the spot, and enlivened the scene and made it look somewhat like home."[23] El Castillo had an advantage

Town and fort, El Castillo, 1853 (*Harper's Monthly Magazine*, vol. 10, no. 55, December 1854)

over other settlements in that disembarkation and portage were necessary throughout the year, not just in the dry season. Since passengers usually stopped here, the hotels were generally filled, especially the clapboard-thatch "El Castillo", which had two stories (a bar–dining room downstairs and sleeping quarters upstairs). Of course, many El Castillo residences quickly became "hotels," "bars," "restaurants," or "shops"—or a combination—as soon as a boat came in.

Ironically, the improvement of transit operations by 1855 did not prove advantageous for the river settlements. Their businesses had depended upon a certain crudity in the transport system. In the early years, no food was served on the river boats; passengers had to provide their own provisions or be at the mercy of riverbank sellers. By mid-decade there were better boats, with more services aboard; the trips were faster, more efficient, and there were fewer delays at fewer stopover points. Boats that could carry 1,000 or more passengers had been added to the fleet. They had rows of double bunks on the upper deck (with no segregation of sexes) and galleys for cooking and serving meals. Most portages, except the one at El Castillo, had been eliminated—and even there, passengers no longer had to make the long walk. Baggage was transferred around the rapids by tramcars.

By the spring of 1856, Walker's support in the United States was growing. Through his agents in Washington, he continually emphasized the British danger and gained allies within the government. Public and press outcry developed against the administration's anti-Walker, anti-filibustering policy, accompanied by endorsement of Walker by leaders within Pierce's own Democratic party, so that the president, finally in May, made the decision to recognize Walker's minister to the United States. Because the interoceanic route was involved, it appeared vital to have diplomatic relations with the *de facto* government of Nicaragua. Also, the United States wanted to settle the Mosquito controversy with Britain, and there was the possibility that U.S. recognition of the Walker government might persuade the British government to abide by the U.S. interpretation of the Clayton-Bulwer Treaty.

Simultaneously, however, and less than a year after his arrival, Walker's problems in Nicaragua were mounting. His actions, which appeared to be directed to conquest of the entire isthmus, had thoroughly aroused the other Central American states. Costa Rica declared war in March, and soon the Conservative-controlled governments of Guatemala, Honduras, and El Salvador became engaged against the American invaders. Costa Rica was especially concerned because of her border controversy with Nicaragua over rights along the transit route, potentially a canal route. Urged on and supported by the British, and opposed to Walker's intervention from the start, a Costa Rican army invaded southwestern Nicaragua that spring. Although a devastating cholera epidemic aborted its offensive, the other Central American states carried on the fighting. In June, increasingly besieged and losing supporters in his coalition government, Walker arranged an election, from which he emerged as president of Nicaragua.

The friendly posture of the U.S. government toward Walker did not last long. After he lost the Democratic nomination for president, in June of 1856, Pierce no longer needed to make concessions to pro-Walker elements, either in his party or among the general public. Furthermore, in the summer of 1856, it appeared that Great Britain might consent to some agreement on the conflicting British–U.S. interpretations of the Clayton-Bulwer Treaty regarding Mosquitia. The Pierce administration therefore returned to its earlier opposition to the filibusters and refused to receive President Walker's most recent emissary to Washington, and it was in response to this setback that Walker started his most concerted campaign to woo Southerner support in the United States. In the fall of 1856 he annulled the laws prohibiting slavery in Nicaragua, at the same time promulgating a law which would permit large land grants to American immigrants and their families, and a score of offices was set up in the South to propagandize his new policy of free land with no restrictions upon slavery. Although these actions stimulated support among Southerners and more recruits flocked to Nicaragua, it was too late to help Walker.

After the defeat by the allied Central American army at Granada in the fall of 1856, Walker's forces retreated to Rivas, along the Pacific end of the transit route, where he awaited the arrival of new recruits to carry on and to regain the offensive. This proved to be the beginning of the last phase of the war—the San Juan campaign—and the beginning of the end for Walker.

Vanderbilt at this point was ready to make his move. After closing the transit route, only to see it reopened by Garrison and Morgan, he had successfully encouraged the Central American countries to unite against Walker, and now he was able to bring Costa Rica into the war a second time. His plan was to use the Costa Rican army, under the direction of one of his American agents, to gain control of the river and the lake. In the first step, the Costa Ricans captured transit company steamers at Greytown. Using them to transport the troops back up the river, where at one point additional Costa Rican soldiers were taken aboard, they quickly captured two more river steamers and the pair of lake steamers. Next, they easily overwhelmed the filibuster garrisons at San Carlos and other points along the river. With the river and the lake neutralized, the expedition proceeded to Greytown once again (with passengers from California who were aboard one of the lake steamers). The Vanderbilt–Costa Rican force accomplished all this in less than two weeks, in late December 1856 and early January 1857. Walker's forces were now cut off from assistance via the Atlantic, and Garrison and Morgan were out of business on the river.

For the following three months, Garrison-Morgan steamers continued to bring recruits to Greytown and Walker's supporters made many attempts to reach him, isolated at Rivas and badly in need of reinforcements. Soon the recruits were less than dedicated to, and sometimes unaware of, the Walker cause. His agents were openly recruiting, in violation of U.S. government policy against the filibuster action, in every quarter, indiscriminately in the streets in many instances. Though attracted by the misleading advertisements, slanted toward colonization, there were some who refused to fight when they found out what was required of them upon arrival in Greytown. The methods of dealing with such cases are vividly described in the following deposition of one Henry Foster, a 21-year-old drifter, made after his rescue by the British:

> In Broadway, New York, I saw a flag, and on the flag were the words "Free farms, free emigration, by steam to Nicaragua". I went into the office, and the clerk asked me if I wished to go to Nicaragua? I said yes. On the 24th of January 1857, I went to the office and took my ticket to go in the steamer "Tennessee". I embarked on board the Tennessee for Nicaragua, and all things went on smoothly until the arrival of that vessel at Greytown, and I was turned over to the steamer Texas on the morning of the 8th of February. The morning of the 9th the uniform of General Walker was served out, which I refused, because nothing had been said in New York about bearing arms. Nothing new was said until this morning, when the river steam boat came alongside the "Texas" and took on arms and ammunition. A part of men (sic) then went on the river steam boat, and I with others went forward. One of Walker's Captains who had charge of the volunteers for him came to me and ordered me into the boat, and I told him I would not go. He then drew a revolver . . . and said if I did not go into the boat, he would shoot me. I resisted against going, upon which he drew his pistol and said he would shoot me, or else I must jump overboard. I prepared myself to jump overboard, but seeing a boat from the man-of-war manned and come round to the stern of the "Texas", I went into the Port Guard and told the English officer that I was a British subject and compelled to take up arms against my will, and that it was a sly way of slavery. The crew of the Texas abused me and the other men, until the Man-of-war's boat came back in about half an hour afterwards when I was allowed to go into her.[24]

The filibusters tried to recapture the river boats at Greytown, but British port authorities prevented such actions as had occurred on the *Tennessee*.

Although they opposed Walker, the British refrained from taking an active part in the struggle; they were nevertheless determined to suppress violence and to protect the lives of British and American residents. In this policing action, they, in effect, aided the Vanderbilt–Costa Rican cause by preventing countermoves.

Eventually, some filibuster forces were able to proceed upriver by using old, repaired steamers still in their possession, but meeting many mishaps and incapable of dislodging the defenders of the river fortifications, they turned back. (A few even tried to reach Walker by way of Panama.) With information of the river retreat, Garrison and Morgan ceased to send steamers, and no new recruits arrived in Nicaragua thereafter. All the while, desertions from the filibuster army mounted, particularly among recent arrivals, because of disillusionment and demoralization. Defections were also encouraged by a proclamation of the Vanderbilt–Costa Rican authorities, offering free passage back to the United States to all who would desert.

Walker, waiting with his men at Rivas in early April, had not seen a lake steamer for three months. He was unaware of their seizure in January and that the river had been captured. When the enemy arrived in force on one of the captured steamers, he still hoped that his Greytown forces would bring assistance. Meanwhile, the allied armies of hostile Nicaraguans and of the other Central American states were brought together in uncommon unity upon the news of the San Juan's capture. Inspired, they advanced upon Rivas with renewed vigor. After a series of attacks, lasting through April, the position of Walker's forces became untenable.

The major problem for the filibusters, disease, continued to deplete their ranks, and as men took advantage of the offer of free passage home, desertions increased daily. Then Walker received the news that the Greytown filibusters, upon whose assistance he had pinned his hopes, had returned to the United States. A U.S. naval vessel came into San Juan del Sur for the avowed purpose of protecting the lives and property of American citizens, but its commander also acted as mediator in the closing days of the war, attempting to persuade the filibusters that theirs was a lost cause. On May 1, 1857, William Walker surrendered and he and his officers were escorted from Nicaragua on the U.S. warship. The remainder of his army, much depleted, soon followed.

Even after this, Walker was unable to relinquish his dream of conquest. The acclaim he received in such cities as Washington, New Orleans, and his home town of Nashville showed that he still had supporters in the United

States. Encouraged by this, he planned a reconquest of Nicaragua, and this time, as he traveled from city to city in the South, seeking financial support and recruits, he vigorously proclaimed his dedication to the proslavery cause, almost as if he had been a life-long adherent. Using the proslavery stance as a means to his ends, he gained support for another expedition, which set out from Mobile, Alabama, in November of 1857 and arrived at the mouth of the San Juan some two weeks later. It was Walker's first trip to Greytown.

After setting up base camp at deserted Punta Arenas and dispatching a force upriver, it looked for a while that the filibusters would recapture the San Juan. By December, an upriver force had taken the Castillo fort and several river steamers, while meeting little resistance. But this time the U.S. navy played a direct role, with British support. With the river blockaded, an overwhelming force of marines attacked Walker's camp, forced him to surrender in short order, and returned him to the United States. However, his seizure by naval commander Hiram Paulding worked to Walker's advantage: it created massive protest in the South, where the legality of U.S. intervention against the filibusters on Nicaraguan soil was vehemently contested. Even President James Buchanan recognized the unsound legal basis, but he defended Paulding's action. This alienated Southern Democrats, who accused Buchanan of being a traitor to the slavery-expansion cause. The controversy over the legality of Walker's seizure finally reached Congress, where a months-long debate raged during 1858, with ever-increasing sectional and pro- and antislavery overtones. The growing tension between North and South became personified in Walker, who took full advantage of the publicity and cultivated the role assigned to him, adapting it to his own designs. He again traveled through the South, where he attracted many influential adherents who contributed financial support for a return expedition to Nicaragua. In May 1858, when his trial for violating neutrality laws was held in New Orleans, he was in a sympathetic setting and emerged a free man. A lawyer himself, he had addressed the jury in his own behalf. His appeal to Southern interests, in addition to his substantial public following, had again proved persuasive, this time in the courtroom.

Six months later, Walker dispatched a shipload of followers on another expedition from Mobile, intending to follow later and join his fellow filibusters in Honduras. However, the ship was wrecked off Belize, before reaching its destination, and the British returned the men to the United States.

After this failure, Walker's popularity in the South began to diminish.

Despite his loss of support and extreme difficulties in further recruiting, he made yet another attempt to return to Central America in the spring of 1860, which proved to be his final undoing. Hoping to join with Honduran Liberals, then in revolt, and possibly seize control of the country, he led an expedition to Trujillo, where he met British resistance in the form of marines from the Bay Islands. After a month, they trapped Walker and his forces in a swamp. The British then delivered the wounded filibuster leader to Honduran government forces, who executed him by firing squad. He was only 36.

Walker's final turning to Honduras lends credence to the view that his ultimate objective was a personal Central American empire and that he would not have been satisfied simply with Nicaragua. The fears of the neighboring states, which brought them together in common action against him, were justifiable. After half a decade, the threat was over in Central America. In the United States, meanwhile, the Civil War was looming. Regardless of his motives, Walker had played a role in polarizing the developing sectional conflicts which led to that war in his native country.[25]

According to some interpreters of the Walker period, of all that "the grey-eyed man of destiny" is remembered for, the most significant result of his actions was the closing of the interoceanic route at a crucial time, when it had been doing well.[26] After the seizure of the river steamers in January 1857, in the final phases of the Filibuster War, the route remained closed for the remainder of the decade. Vanderbilt had his revenge and turned to other business ventures. The gold rush had subsided and a railway had been constructed across the Panama isthmus, which greatly enhanced that route's competitive advantage.

The British held their protectorate during the late 1850s but paid little attention to it. In Bluefields, George Augustus Frederick, the reigning Mosquito king, under tutelage of the British, was a vast improvement over some of his predecessors in terms of education and culture, even though his role was less significant. He had been educated in Jamaica, spoke English perfectly, and was well read. (Not only had he read Shakespeare, Byron, and Scott, he could quote from their works.) While there had been an era of better British feeling for Americans after the *Prometheus* affair (despite some setbacks because of the bombardment and Walker), the Mosquito king expressed the old Chatfield views. Sir Bedford Pim described his meeting with the king while visiting Bluefields, following the Walker period. Receiving in white jacket, waistcoat, and trousers and wearing a felt hat, the king had roundly denounced Americans, informing his visitors that his earlier admiration had turned to contempt for these intruders, for whom "no tricks are too mean or cowardly . . . to practice to gain their ends."[27] What he considered humiliating depictions of him and his kingdom in American-authored books especially offended him. He called Squier's accounts of the Mosquito Coast a "pack of lies."[28]

With the transient traffic gone, even at Punta Arenas, Greytown deteriorated even further. Many American residents departed, disposing of their possessions even though it meant much sacrifice. Lots that had been held in expectation of increasing value became worthless. Departing residents even dismantled and took away some of the buildings. Of the few remaining buildings, several ceased to be occupied, and grass grew in the largely deserted streets. The few churches and schools, rebuilt after the bombardment, ceased to function. This was the first of Greytown's "ghost" periods, as the town became more isolated. The U.S. consul, B. Squire Cottrell, reported that

> the expense of *living* at this place is not only far greater than at any other port on either Coast of Central America, or at Aspinwall, but is at least *double* that of any town or city in the United States. None but the commonest merchandise, provisions, etc. are sold here, nor is there anything cultivated worth mentioning. . . .
>
> Houses—so called out of compliment for they would hardly pass for respectable cattle sheds at the North, with the exception of half a dozen which are occupied by their owners—are scarce, and the rents are enormous.[29]

While the transit route remained closed, the United States and Great Britain headed toward settlement of the Mosquito controversy in the latter part of the decade. After a critical period in 1856, when it seemed that hostilities between the two countries might erupt over British refusal to consider her Mosquito occupancy in violation of the Clayton-Bulwer Treaty, a breakthrough appeared as the Pierce administration ended. There was much pressure in Britain, after the Crimean War, to come to a settlement with the United States over Central America. So many Britons had come to believe that retention of the Bay Islands and the Mosquito protectorate was unjustifiable that the government recognized it could muster little public support for war with the United States over such issues. Far more important for Britain, according to industrial interests, was its substantial trade with the United States, especially in cotton.[30] It was in this conciliatory climate that George M. Dallas, the U.S. ambassador to Britain, began negotiations with Lord Clarendon, the foreign secretary, in the summer of 1856. During these discussions, Britain reached an agreement with the government of Honduras that made the Bay Islands a free state, under Honduran sovereignty. Dallas did not feel that this posed a problem in his negotiations; even though the arrangement seemed designed to protect British settlers already on the islands, he saw no reasons for U.S. opposition, if it was agreeable to Honduras.

He concluded his agreement with the British within three months, with the Dallas-Clarendon treaty, which provided for withdrawal of the British protectorate in Mosquitia, and the boundaries for a Mosquito reservation (under the sovereignty of Nicaragua), within which the Indians would have self-government, and for Greytown to become a free city with a free port. Under its terms, the provisions of the recently completed British-Honduran agreement regarding the Bay Islands were confirmed. It also set the boundary or limits of Belize as those at the time of the signing of the Clayton-Bulwer Treaty, by agreement between Britain and Guatemala. Finally, it gave Costa Rica certain rights to the use of Greytown harbor and the San Juan River, and its boundary dispute with Nicaragua was to be referred to the British and American governments for arbitration.

Although President Pierce approved the treaty and commended it to the Congress, it was not well received by Buchanan, the succeeding president, or by his secretary of state, or the Senate. The basis for their opposition was the arrangement regarding the Bay Islands. The separate Anglo-Honduran treaty, which the Dallas-Clarendon agreement incorporated, calling for the islands to become a free state under the sovereignty of Honduras, had yet to be ratified by that country. If it were ratified, it would mean, in the U.S. view, establishment of an "independent" state within Honduran territory which would nevertheless remain subject to British influence and control. If it were rejected, it would mean Britain's retention of the islands. So, either way, the administration and the Senate were not prepared to accept the treaty. They made changes in it and sent it back for British consideration. After many exchanges, lasting several months, the matter was closed when word came that Honduras had rejected its separate Bay Islands treaty. The government had been under pressure from its Central American neighbors to do so because of fears that, if the Bay Islands were a free state, Honduras would be unable to protect them from incursion by filibusters. Significantly, all of these negotiations were conducted during the final months of the Walker conflict. Although the Dallas-Clarendon treaty was not ratified by the United States, it was a step toward eventual settlement.

Having failed to reach an agreement with Britain, the Buchanan administration seemed inclined to abrogation of the Clayton-Bulwer Treaty on the grounds of British violation. There was strong support for this in Congress, where the treaty had become ever more unpopular after almost a decade of frustration with regard to the conflicting interpretation of its terms. To avert this, the British tried a different approach: concluding treaties individually with Nicaragua, Honduras, and Guatemala, which they hoped would be agreeable with the United States. The British sent a special mission to the countries for this purpose in 1857, but internal problems, involving Walker's efforts to return, the Nicaraguan–Costa Rican conflict over the San Juan, and frustrated negotiations over new canal-route concessions, delayed progress until 1860. Meanwhile, the U.S. government had decided against abrogation of the treaty, as an alternative which would prolong tensions, and it had come to view the British mission to the Central American countries as the best method of settling the long controversy.

In January of 1860, two months after signing a treaty with Honduras for the unconditional return of the Bay Islands, Great Britain and Nicaragua signed the Treaty of Managua, closely corresponding to the Dallas-Clarendon agreement. Article 1 provided that Britain would relinquish its protectorate over the Mosquito territory, including Greytown, and recognize Nicaraguan sovereignty. Succeeding articles provided for establishment of Greytown as a free port; establishment of a specific portion of the Mosquito territory as a reservation for the Mosquitos, in which they would enjoy self-government under the sovereignty of Nicaragua and receive monetary compensation (an "annuity") from the Nicaraguan government for ten years; the alternative that the Mosquito reservation could incorporate itself into the republic of Nicaragua, when and if agreed upon by the inhabitants; confirmation of all *bona fide* land grants made since 1848 by the Mosquito authorities (within certain bounds) beyond the limits of the reservation (such grants being restricted as to size).

With this, official British occupancy of the Mosquito Shore ended and the U.S. interpretation of the Clayton-Bulwer Treaty prevailed. However, the problems did not end: the restrictions upon the United States with regard to unilateral control of a canal route became less and less tolerable. Nor did the Treaty of Managua prove entirely satisfactory to the Nicaraguan government during the remainder of the century. Seeds of future trouble were sown by Britain's *quid pro quo* terms in the treaty, particularly those for Mosquito self-government and extraterritorial status for the reservation—within which British influence markedly remained, as well as some British residents.

5   The San Juan in
Quieter Times,
1860–1885

After 1860, the United States paid little attention to Central America for a while. The country was preoccupied with its Civil War, and the signing of the Treaty of Managua had settled the issue of British territorial expansion in Central America. There were still many critics of the Clayton-Bulwer Treaty, for its provisions restricted expansionist aims of the United States in a strategic region and did not allow exclusive U.S. control of interoceanic routes. However, with the crisis at home, the United States was not ready to press for advantages in these respects. The practical consequences of the treaty's obstacles, furthermore, did not become apparent for many years.

In Nicaragua, a long period of stability was beginning, for the first time in its history. With Walker's defeat in 1857, it appeared that Conservative–Liberal strife would continue; armies of both factions were under arms, and neither faction seemed willing for the other to assume control of the government. However, a potential threat from Costa Rica brought them together. The Costa Rican army had remained in Nicaragua after the Walker defeat, hoping, by its occupation of parts of the San Juan Valley, to bolster Costa Rica's territorial claims along this prospective canal route. After ruling jointly for a while, the leader of the Liberals consented to establishment of a Conservative government under a moderate, Tomas Martínez. A new constitution, adopted in 1858, declared Nicaragua a republic. Martínez became the constitutionally elected president, and the capital was permanently established at Managua. An era of cooperation between Conservatives and Liberals was ushered in.

Meanwhile, as a result of Walker's attempts to return to Central America, Costa Rica withdrew her armies from Nicaragua and the two countries drew closer together, attempting to settle their differences. Their moderate and progressive Conservative presidents negotiated the disputed western boundary, and became the leaders of a new Costa Rican–Nicaraguan bid to unite Central America (which, like earlier confederation plans, failed). The Martínez administration of the late 1850s and early 1860s (he held two terms), however, marked a turning point in Nicaraguan politics. It began a long period of Conservative rule, lasting thirty years, in which, in orderly succession, presidents were elected to four-year terms with peaceful transition of power and little turmoil.

Also about 1860 a shift of commerce from Caribbean to Pacific ports began with completion of the Panama Railway. Although the Pacific ports were not ideal, lacking deep-water anchorages, they were nearer the most productive parts of Central America, and now, via the railway across Panama, the Atlantic was more easily accessible. Even Belize, the major Caribbean port and entrepôt for Central America, experienced a severe decrease in its volume of trade, from which it would never recover. For Greytown, then, it was not simply the closure of the transit route that made its prospects discouraging.[1]

Nevertheless, there were many attempts to reopen the Nicaraguan route after 1857. Until 1862, only one of these proceeded beyond the planning stage and resulted in sailings. Prematurely, without waiting for final ratification by Nicaragua of a provisional contract, the American Atlantic and Pacific Ship Canal Company prepared to reopen the route in 1858, and its steamship departed New York in November of that year. Meanwhile, the Nicaraguan government was negotiating a contract with another company, and when the steamship arrived at Greytown, Nicaraguan authorities did not allow for its passengers (suspected of being filibusters) to cross the isthmus. At the same time, the master of the steamship, sent around Cape Horn to transport the passengers to San Francisco, ran out of funds en route and had to borrow money to continue the voyage. The creditor appropriated the vessel upon its arrival in Panama and ordered it to proceed to California, without stopping in Nicaragua. The steamship company then transported the passengers from Greytown to Panama, and some of them proceeded to San Francisco via the competitive Mail Line, while others, not having the additional fare, returned to New York on the same steamship which had brought them.[2]

The Central American Transit Company, successor to Vanderbilt's American Atlantic and Pacific Ship Canal Company (under a different directorship), obtained a concession from the Nicaraguan government and reopened the route in 1862. In July of that year, company personnel arrived in Greytown, took possession of the old transit company property at Punta

Arenas, and began operations. A ship was in harbor, unloading lumber and machinery, and several workers were putting up buildings. Along the river, woodcutters were at work, stacking fuel to feed the steamboats that were expected again to ply the river. The following November, for the first time in five years, Americans passed up and down the San Juan.

A commercial downturn had afflicted Greytown for several years. On the eve of the route's reopening, the American consul reported that the amount of business was so small that it was hardly possible to make a report.[3] So it must have seemed like old times when the *America*, first of the ocean steamers, arrived from New York, loaded with 560 passengers headed for California. Two days later, about the same number of passengers, arriving in Greytown from California, boarded the vessel for the return trip.[4]

The service got off to a slow start, however. For almost two years it was inefficient and irregular, attracting few passengers. The company did not have its own ocean steamers, and had to rely upon those of another steamship line. These steamers were subject to removal for Panama service when it appeared that, because of local transit conditions or disputes with the Nicaraguan government, profits were threatened. In the first months, insufficient equipment (only one river steamer, one lake steamer, and a few carriages on the transit road) caused lengthy crossings. From the beginning, the company had problems with the financially pressed Nicaraguan government, which at this time was attempting to extract as much revenue as possible from its interoceanic route. After a few months, the Nicaraguans cancelled the company's charter, on grounds that to some, appeared unjustifiable. They demanded more money, which the company had to pay in order to resume operations.

Meanwhile, the Nicaraguan government was becoming adamant about some of the financial provisions of the Treaty of Managua. George Augustus Frederick, the former Mosquito king who became chief and president of the Mosquito reservation, died in 1864, and Nicaragua refused to continue payments of the annuity to his successor, who, it was claimed, did not really represent the Mosquito Indians. The Nicaraguan position was that the new chief had been elected by the so-called Creoles of the Shore, of mixed foreign and Indian blood, without the knowledge of the Managua government, and that these pro-British inhabitants were attempting to exert the same influence as they had under the protectorate.

Natural calamities, too, befell parts of the Mosquito Shore during the early 1860s, slowing the recovery that might have been expected as a result of resumed transit operations. In the summer of 1863 an earthquake raised the bar at the entrance to Greytown's harbor, making it less accessible from the open sea and encouraging silting. In October of 1865, one of the worst hurricanes ever to strike the region destroyed much of Bluefields. Part of the Mosquito king's house and the Moravian mission building survived, but the storm swept away less sturdy outlying Moravian churches and mission houses, in addition to the natives' houses. According to reports, the entire coast, from Monkey Point to north of Bluefields—plantations and wilderness alike—was a wide wasteland, a mass of jumbled debris. The offshore keys were even more vulnerable. A coconut plantation on one of them completely disappeared, as well as its American proprietor, his family, and workmen, as the islet was covered by 5 feet of ocean.[5]

It was not until the summer of 1864 that the Central American Transit Company was able to institute a regular service through Nicaragua, more or less comparable with the service during the 1850s. After negotiating a new contract with the government and meeting its financial terms, the company made many improvements. With the purchase of its own steamship, it could assure a regular sailing schedule. It provided an adequate number of river and lake steamers, capable of accommodating sizable numbers of passengers, with efficiency and speed. Further improvements were the resurfacing of the transit road and many more carriages. However, although the number of passengers greatly increased, it never approached the volume of the earlier 1850s venture and was, at its peak, no more than about a quarter of the number who used the Panama route.[6]

It was during the Central American Transit Company operations that navigation problems became a serious impediment, though silting in the lower river, near its entrance to the harbor, was already a problem. The latter had been noted as early as 1840, when observers reported that even *bongos* at times ran aground and were "obliged to be dragged by main force through temporary channels."[7] As more and more water was diverted to the Colorado distributary during later years, the silting continued, until, by the 1860s, not only the lower river but Greytown harbor was affected. Undoubtedly, volcanic sand, brought into the San Juan by the San Carlos, clogged the lower river and aided in shifting more of its discharge into the Colorado distributary. Thereafter, since there was less washout of sediment by the San Juan current, the sea deposited sand across the narrow harbor entrance. Soon after its arrival, the company made a valiant effort to improve the harbor by sinking several hulks at the many distributaries where the San Juan emptied into the bay. The objective was to confine the water to a single channel and increase its depth at the sea entrance, but it produced no noticeable results. For almost a year, it was deep enough that the normal operations of river steamers—the meeting of ocean steamers at Punta Arenas on the opposite side of Greytown harbor—could be carried on; but by 1863, shallowness over the bar kept ships out of the harbor and forced them to anchor outside.

In 1867 the problems of the shallow Greytown–Punta Arenas harbor and the lower river were acute. This was the peak year of passenger traffic—despite the inconvenience of transfer from ships in the open sea to lighters, before embarkation on the river boats. But conditions *inside* the bar were becoming so bad that Greytown was no longer on either a flowing river or the open sea, but in a marshy lagoon. Rushes and marsh grass grew in front of the town, and boats had to follow meandering channels through the maze. Dredging was not a promising possibility, in view of the small quantities of water that emptied into the river at this point. Nor was diversion of the Colorado branch possible, due to Costa Rica's control of it.

At first, the company thought that Greytown might have to be abandoned as the Atlantic terminus. It seized upon a plan of Sir Bedford Pim to build a railroad from the deep-water port of Monkey Point to Lake Nicaragua. Pim had obtained a land grant from the previous Mosquito king with this in mind. With such a railroad, passengers could bypass the river altogether, and steamers could be in readiness when they reached the lake. Much time could be saved by this arrangement, enabling competition with the Panama Railway. After receiving encouragement from the Nicaraguan government, then from the company, Pim had opened a road along the projected route. However (perhaps because of the anticipated cost of the project), the company lost interest in this approach and opted for dredging, as a kind of holding action for its San Juan transit system. But this also promised to be very expensive. With concessions by the Nicaraguan government in its contract (which presumably would allow it to meet the heavy costs of dredging), the company started work in the summer of 1867, but Nicaragua soon reneged on the agreement and granted another canal-rights concession, along the San Juan, to German interests. The United States intervened successfully in having this concession defeated in the Nicaraguan congress, as in conflict with the rights of the Central American Transit Company; but the action was unusual. From the time of his arrival in 1863, the U.S. minister to Nicaragua, Andrew Dickinson, had championed the cause of the company against what he considered Nicaraguan harassment for gain. His repeated requests for more active U.S. government intervention in the company's behalf had mostly met with indifference by Secretary of State William Seward. Central American affairs simply were not dominant or urgent in Washington during this period.

In the early months of 1868, company relations with the Nicaraguan government reached the breaking point. The price exacted for retaining its concession had put the enterprise in financial trouble, and much more expense would be necessary if Greytown harbor was to be restored. With its course clearly set—to gain additional revenue from a new grant—it was only a matter of time before the Nicaraguan government again cancelled the company's charter (in April), on the grounds of noncompletion of a railroad from Lake Nicaragua to the Pacific. This proved to be the decisive blow. The company's steamers and carriages carried the last transients across the Nicaragua route during that month, after which the company discontinued the service for good. (Nicaragua later seized some of the company's boats as payment of alleged debts.) Despite the Nicaraguan government's hand in the demise, it would have soon happened anyhow, for one year later the transcontinental railroad across the United States was completed and there was no further need for Americans to use either Nicaragua or Panama to reach their West Coast.

During the final months of company operations, a passenger who made the crossing was one Daniel Cleveland, and a remarkably detailed account of conditions at that time is given in his diary.[8] He found Greytown— revived because of transit company activities of past years, but with its harbor deteriorating—a place of some eighty or ninety palm-thatched huts, in addition to foreigners' houses and company facilities. The population was about 500. A new wharf, constructed only a few months previously, was already in a "state of ruin," due to climatic conditions. Swampy land lay all around. Despite this, the town appeared "remarkably healthy and free from fevers and other epidemics."

The appraisal of Greytown's potentialities by this traveler was on the dismal side, and in this he was unusually perceptive. He thought that the chances of an interoceanic canal were small and that when there was no longer the transit business, the town would "sink into insignificance," that "the only possible Atlantic terminus is now one of the poorest on the whole coast." Whatever the reasons for this gloomy outlook by an outsider, just passing through, few others would predict the rest of the century so correctly. The difficulty of navigating the winding channels of the lower San Juan was described. The river boat went aground several times, but the shouting American mate each time incited the "listless looking" Indian crew into action to free it with their long poles. The 59-mile trip from Greytown to Castillo required about twenty hours when river conditions were good; when the water was low, it could take two to three days. The remaining 29 miles from Castillo to San Carlos required about eight hours.

A typical journey by boat up the river for a traveler of the period was presented in the diary. Eating arrangements were picnic fashion, with plates, cups and saucers, knives, forks, sliced bread, and cold meats obtained from a table in the stern, and passengers, upon returning to their benches to eat, were served hot tea, which attendants brought in a large tin pot. There was no cooking on board; the food for the entire trip was prepared before departure from Greytown. Cleveland did not describe refrigeration methods, but presumably river water was the only means of cooling. In any case, there were no complaints about the quality of the food on this run.

Nights along the river were unexpectedly cool, and overcoats had to be donned when "cold wind" swept through the boat. The rains and humidity made it seem cooler than it really was (light showers fell every hour), and the normal nighttime chilling of the wet tropics was enhanced by the fact that the San Juan was a corridor for the trade winds. Throughout the trip, nevertheless, the Indian crew, accustomed to the conditions, slept on the open deck in their flimsy cotton clothing.

Also in the diary are descriptions of life along the river in the widely scattered habitations. The boat stopped at the hut of a German and his family, in a clearing on the Costa Rican side of the river. They all seemed "unhealthy, sallow, thin, and listless." For Americans, this seemed in great contrast to the physical setting, which had the aspect of an idyllic tropical paradise. Orange trees, banana plants, and other tropical fruits surrounded the house, and there were even European flowers as a nostalgic touch. Nevertheless, the scene was rather sad, as it was clear that the immigrants had hardly found a Utopia—if that is what they had sought—but only a difficult and isolated existence on the brink of poverty.

The boat passed many *bongos*, which carried most of the freight to and from the interior. These were large, carrying up to 20 tons, and were manned by crews of ten, dipping their poles in time as they chanted. The absolute nakedness of these natives always seemed jarring to the sensibilities of American travelers along the river, but, making a note of it, this observer was less conservative and felt that, under the circumstances, perhaps there was no impropriety, the natives being "clad in the fashionable forest costume of the country." The difficulty of getting their loaded *bongos* upstream, against the current, taxed the native crews to the limit: one of the Indians always had to follow along the river bank, attaching and reattaching a long rope to trees up ahead; the boat crew would then pull on this rope, thus moving the boat gradually forward.

Bongos, however, had the advantage of maneuverability, which the river boats lacked. They were especially suited to continuous transport of freight during the dry season, when it was necessary for river boats to be unloaded below each rapids and their cargo and passengers transferred by land to boats above. On this particular journey, because the river was high, the river boat was able to make it through the Machuca rapids. But at the Castillo rapids, ten miles upstream, such was not the case. The freight was transferred to a waiting river boat by cars on rails, then pulled by mules, with natives pushing. As the transfer took twelve hours, the passengers had time to observe the town of Castillo, at the foot of the hill on which the fort was situated. It was the only settlement of any size, then as now, between Greytown and San Carlos. It consisted of about thirty huts in a single line, constructed of "poles or canes," bound together by vines, and thatched with palm. There were a few small stores, restaurants, and lodging houses, of which at least the fronts were of boards; inside, for the most part, the floors were dirt. The houses reminded the traveler of well-ventilated chicken coops, close together and without yards. There were no gardens or signs of agricultural endeavors in or around the town; all of its food and other needs had to be brought in via the river from outside.

Castillo's activity increased when a boatload of Americans arrived—the town arose from its lethargy according to the transit company schedule. Suddenly, this being one of those times, every house became a store or restaurant, or "almost anything else," to bring in a little cash. Eager vendors brought out their small stock of liquor bottles, home-made cigars, hammocks, and strange concoctions of food. On shelves above the crude bars were a few articles of merchandise and engraved calabashes, as well as crude earthenware cups and saucers. Foods were displayed on a table that was covered with a clean cotton cloth: bread made from California wheat flour, bananas, chicken cooked in several styles. Milk was an expensive luxury, due to the fact that its sole source was a few scrawny cows, each producing only a pint per milking. Two or three cigar-smoking native girls served the American customers, and brought coffee at the end of the meal, while the men and old women hugged the background and watched the free spending in happy anticipation. The diary gives this account:

The men and old women know that their sex and wrinkles are not attractive, so they remain in the background while the señoritas do the honors of the house, which consist in making as much money as possible. They send out their handsomest young women, because they know by experience that Californians have a keen eye to good looks. If a traveller passing near a door glances in, one of the damsels will remove the cigarro from her lips for a moment and accost him somewhat as follows: "How you do, California? You hungry? Come in my house. I got plenty good things; Coffee, chocolate, chicken and chickenny soup, señor. I got whiskey too, and every kind of drink. Come in, señor".

And she looks at him out of her dark long lashed eyes as sweetly and bewitchingly as she can. "California" will probably hesitate a moment, then look into those eyes and go in, and Juanita will be happy while she is inducing him to eat and drink, and beguiling him out of as much money as he will spend.

Americans concluded that almost anything was for sale, including pet animals and birds, as the inhabitants had to subsist until the next boat arrived. In general, transients were impressed with the meals they received, and particularly with the low prices (a 60-cent bill for six) and the home-grown coffee, brewed in the fireplace. Such satisfactions overcame the dirt floors and crude surroundings. Sanitation was very poor, but this did not seem to bother the travelers. They noted the distended bellies of children, but apparently failed to relate this to sanitary conditions, observing that "when they are grown they look as slim as anybody."

While this group was in Castillo, another river boat, carrying steerage passengers to the lake, arrived. It disembarked its passengers and the boatmen forced it through the rapids; then the passengers reembarked and the boat departed. The women merchants became extremely upset by this and berated the transit company for not allowing the boatload of potential customers to remain. With all of their food and coffee prepared, and cigars and *aguardiente* (an alcoholic beverage made from sugar cane) bought for resale, who would now pay for it? They blamed the government, and even the president, for not forcing the company to stop its boats long enough for the passengers to buy from the locals—or to compensate the native vendors for their losses.

Castillo quickly declined once Americans stopped traveling up the river. Thomas Belt, the English naturalist and veteran of many expeditions to remote regions of the world to study the flora, fauna, and people, also came here, and was not impressed: "The first view of Castillo is the only pleasant recollection I have carried away of the place. The single street is narrow, dirty, and rugged, and when the shades of evening begin to creep up, swarms of mosquitoes issue forth to buzz and bite."⁹

Despite the loss of the transit trade, the town, like Greytown, clung on. Because the only road around the rapids went through the town of Castillo, the customs house remained, to control river commerce. Also, the town was a center of india rubber collection, which was becoming important. It became a place for outfitting the collectors, supplying them with canoes and provisions, and a departure point for the deep forests of the Atlantic slope— up the tributaries of the San Juan. It was also the place to which collectors, after months in the jungle, brought their rubber to the merchants who had financed and dispatched them (though some never returned). There was no reliable labor force. Recruitment of collectors was difficult in the sparsely populated area, the system the collectors (mostly Indian) had to endure was slavelike, and work in the forest was arduous.

Nicaragua was probably one of the first countries to be involved in rubber production, a major trade commodity that was handled by the Greytown port after 1860. Prior to 1858, the prevailing opinion was that the india rubber trees (*Castilloa elastica*, indigenous to the tropical forest in Nicaragua) were useless. However, teams were sent out by American rubber companies to investigate the possibilities, the first shipment (sent to New York in 1858) demonstrated its worth, and a small boom was on. Once it became known that a profusion of the right types of trees grew in the Nicaraguan tropical forest, the merchants of Greytown sent natives to gather the latex. This trade continued for many years, then diminished as the Brazilian rubber boom intensified, but these early rubber merchants made small fortunes. Much of the india rubber that was shipped out of Greytown originated in Costa Rica and came down the San Carlos River, tributary to the San Juan. As this river entered below Castillo and Greytown was a free port, the Nicaraguans were unable to collect their export tax.

Besides india rubber, Greytown's exports consisted of more or less exotic products, such as coffee, skins, hides, indigo, and dyewood; but never in large quantities. Imports from the United States were mainly lumber and foodstuffs such as flour and bacon. They were generally insignificant, compared with imports from Britain, which were mainly manufactured articles. Although the few Americans in Greytown were largely engaged in trading enterprises and had become quite successful, there was little economic basis for any significant expansion of the American colony. A probably realistic appraisal of conditions came from a U.S. consul in 1872, who reported:

Nations dealing with this country ought not to expect too much from her, as by examining her area only so much is found to be valuable. . . . This country is divided between water, swamps and arable. The lakes occupy a large share, there being several. Then comes this eastern coast up to the lake, embracing about one third, devoted to almost impenetrable swamps. The producing portion is therefore beyond and round the lake, and only a certain portion of that is valuable, as many mountains exist.[10]

This consul, who had never been in Nicaragua before, was newly arrived in Greytown (he did not remain long before submitting his resignation), and although all of his geographical facts were not correct, his impressions were acute. His report regarding the climate's limitations upon agriculture was not encouraging, but it was more accurate than most: "Were the soil arable and fertile along the coast, no cropping could be successfully done. Nor is any attempted in Nicaragua on this line, until the lake country is reached."[11] The isolation of Greytown was very apparent in 1872. The new consul resigned because he could not manage his business affairs in the United States, as he had hoped, by correspondence. His letters either did not arrive or arrived only after two or three months, via Panama. The harbor was silted in and surrounded by swamps, which made the malaria problem greater than ever. In his final letter, the consul commented upon the town's deteriorated physical, social, and economic environment:

This place is sickly; it is a marsh; the inhabitants are half-civilized and consequently no society; two little churches and no priests. The United States have scarcely enough trade at this place to justify an officer's attention or stay in its dismal locality.

I have to say, that B. Squire Cottrell my predecessor, owns here a house, store-house and lot where he lived. This seems to have tied him here for so long; together with the deaths of his wife and her brother who lie here buried.

Though here for a shorter time than I wished, I trust my service may have been useful to the Government.[12]

Even the acclimatization of a long-term resident, such as Cottrell, had not prevented his breakdown earlier, as this letter from Dr. Green, physician and British consul at Greytown (and long resident there), certifies: "B. Squire Cottrell, Consul of the United States of America, resident of the Port, is suffering from general bodily debility the result of a long residence under the debilitating influence of the climate of this Coast and that a change to a healthier climate is absolutely necessary to his recovery."[13]

Despite the difficulties of using the lower river and the harbor, Greytown remained Nicaragua's Atlantic port, and had a limited function. This kept it alive from 1870 to 1889, when nothing was being done about a canal. The steamboat concession on the San Juan River (including Lake Nicaragua) had a varied history after the transit operations of the 1860s. In 1870 the government awarded a twenty-five-year concession for exclusive rights of navigation to J. E. Hollenbeck, an American. During the following seven years there was enough trade and passenger exchange for Hollenbeck to keep five steamboats in service between Greytown and Granada, and for the latter port to enlarge its lakeside terminal facilities.

No large seagoing vessels had been able to enter Greytown harbor since the early 1860s. The vessels which now came infrequently usually would not send their boats ashore because of the rough and dangerous sea to be crossed to reach the channel into the harbor. Ships' captains also feared the uncertain conditions of the channel. They ordinarily dispatched the mail in a canoe manned by Mosquito natives, long recognized (from the days of piracy) as the only ones competent for this kind of demanding seamanship. (Consular records frequently reported drownings of unaccustomed for-eigners who made the attempt.) At times of high seas, the mail pouches and other movable items had to be fastened securely to the canoes to prevent loss in case of their capsizing or swamping, an ever-present danger in riding the waves that crashed over the outer bar. Iron steam lighters came alongside the vessels to receive freight and passengers, which also was a hazardous opera-tion, particularly in bad weather. Many times, in transfer by derrick from the deck of the ship, cargo would be damaged or lost.

The lighter arrangement for handling freight in the years following the closing of the harbor was quite inadequate. In 1872 the equipment consisted of a small tugboat, carrying 200 or 300 sacks of coffee at a load, drawing 3 to 4 feet, and going about 12 miles per trip to reach ships anchored beyond the bar.[14] Not infrequently, the iron lighters were thrown against the ships, damaging them considerably. Sea conditions sometimes forced ships to pull up anchor and leave, with half of the cargo destined for Greytown still on board, and return to Colón, thus delaying delivery for months.

Channel conditions varied with the seasons. The vagaries of the river, its volume and force, caused not only the characteristics and course of the channel to change, but also its location. The sand of the San Juan and that of the sea, coming together, formed a shifting bar, which at times was subject to substantial displacement within a single day. Instead of one channel, two and even three might form through the bar, so that width and depth changed accordingly. The fear was ever present that conditions might get so bad that steamer traffic on the river would cease altogether and that *bongos* would again be the only form of transport to and from the Pacific. Few doubted that a return to this primitive form of transport, not able to handle much cargo and particularly not coffee, because of the problem of keeping it dry, would sound the absolute death knell of Greytown. Already, much freight was diverted via Corinto and the Panama route, which in the days of the transit company was the less desirable route on the basis of time and cost.

Official U.S. interest in Nicaragua had diminished when it became no longer useful as a transit route, but it revived in 1872, when President Grant ordered a new survey of isthmian canal routes. The report of the commission, headed by Admiral Daniel Ammen, a friend of the president, recommended construction of a canal through Nicaragua, to be internationalized and thus in conformity with provisions of the Clayton-Bulwer Treaty. However, British support for the plan was not forthcoming, and difficulties ensued in negotiations with Nicaragua and Costa Rica, which were engaged in a boundary dispute. Thus the second Grant administration ended without much more than directing national attention again to this part of the world and recognition of the need for an isthmian canal, preferably in Nicaragua.

Thereafter, the canal policy of the United States tended more and more toward exclusive control, and was strengthened by the contention that the Clayton-Bulwer Treaty had been abrogated by Great Britain in its continuing influence in the Mosquito reservation. The government of the reservation had fallen into the hands of persons considered by Nicaragua to be nonrepresentative of the Mosquito people and who managed it to favor business and commercial interests, British and foreign, rather than the natives. There were controversies between the Managua and reservation authorities for almost twenty years, with the British joining protests against what it considered Nicaragua's violation of the Treaty of Managua: refusal to recognize the new Mosquito chief and to continue annuity payments to him, in addition to limitations imposed upon Mosquito autonomy.

It seemed that the authorities of the Mosquito reservation could still look to Britain, for moral support, at least, although more active and direct British influence would not come until later, in 1878, when the British and Nicaraguans agreed that the dispute over their treaty of 1860 be referred to Emperor Franz Joseph of Austria for arbitration. His decision, highly unfavorable to Nicaragua, proved to be a turning point, economically and politically, for the Mosquito Shore. It encouraged increased British and foreign influence in the reservation by restoring almost complete autonomy to the Mosquito authorities and by strictly limiting Nicaragua's sovereignty rights, as provided under the treaty. Not only did it call for continuation of the annuity but also for settlement of all the unpaid installments of previous years, with interest. More significantly, it provided that the government of Nicaragua not be entitled to grant concessions for the acquisition of natural products within the reservation; that this right be reserved to the Mosquito authorities alone. For the Nicaraguans, the arbitration decision was flagrantly biased and it made them more embittered over the Mosquitia issue and more determined to resist the abridgment of their territorial sovereignty. In this they were to have the support of the U.S. government, but not of the Americans who settled in the reservation during the next two decades, as a result of "banana developments" and resurgent canal interest.

The earliest trade in bananas to the United States had begun during the years following the Civil War. Carl Augustus Frank, who had been a steward on a Pacific Mail ship from New York to Panama, was the pioneer, planting one of the first Central American banana farms in Panama after having tested the receptiveness of the New York market for this relatively unknown tropical fruit. The success of Frank's venture by the early 1870s led Minor Keith, builder of Costa Rica's railway from San José to the Caribbean (almost twenty years under construction), to consider bananas as a source of much-needed freight revenue for the railroad. When completed, it would carry the coffee of the highlands, but meanwhile a crop was needed for the section being constructed through the tropical jungles of the Caribbean lowland. Keith planted bananas along the main line, and later along spur lines, in the hinterland of Limón. By the late 1870s the Costa Rican fruit was being marketed in New Orleans and New York, and in 1885 exports totaled more than half a million bunches.[15] Keith's interests soon extended to the Caribbean littoral beyond Costa Rica, and he established a chain of commissaries from Belize southward. An advantage of the commissary business was that its supplies could fill some of the otherwise empty cargo space in banana ships on the return trip from U.S. ports. One of the commissaries was at Bluefields, and banana farms were begun in the Escondido Valley as an adjunct to this business, with the fruit shipped out as a supplement to the cargos from Limón on vessels chartered by Keith. Many of the bananas in this early trade came from individual native producers. Meanwhile, an itinerant Caribbean coastal trader from New Orleans, Jacob Weinberger, had begun making calls at various ports, bartering a variety of manufactured items for bananas, coconuts, parrots, and whatever exotic products he could obtain, then selling them in the United States. One of the ports he visited was Bluefields, and it was there that he would center his operations as a pioneer in the banana business.

With these stimuli, and competing banana shipping and marketing companies from Boston, Philadelphia, and Baltimore as the U.S. market expanded, several American banana planters were attracted to the Bluefields area during the 1880s. Moreover, after the arbitration decision, the Mosquito reservation and Greytown (the free port) assumed practical independence from Nicaragua. This was additional encouragement for American settlement: investments were considered safe in a stable economy, now that its Anglicized cultural institutions were seemingly assured under British-backed autonomy. It is safe to say that the high level of Americanization during the next decade would not have occurred if immigrant planters had seen a threat of Nicaraguan control of the reservation.

Simultaneous with the banana developments was an improvement in river and lake transport services between Granada and Greytown. An enterprising 25-year-old Italian immigrant, Francisco Alfredo Pellas, who acquired the Hollenbeck concession in 1877, had enough confidence in the future of the San Juan route to expand the services substantially. Coffee from the volcanic uplands of western Nicaragua had become the leading commodity in Nicaragua's overseas trade, and its nonperishable nature made delays in ocean transit at silted-in Greytown tolerable; thus the San Juan was able to compete with Pacific coast outlets for a considerable share of the shipments. The railway from Granada, via Managua and León, to the port of Corinto was not built until the early 1880s. Moreover, the banana developments and talk of a canal created more Nicaraguan interest in the Mosquito Shore, leading to increased passenger traffic to and from the region. All of this encouraged Pellas to add more river steamboats, and in 1882 to order from a New York shipyard a new boat for the lake. With two decks and two steam engines, it had accommodations for 50 passengers—and was considered quite deluxe. This was the famous *Victoria*, the largest lake boat ever used. Proceeding up the river during the rainy season, it passed the rapids at Castillo with no mishaps and arrived amid great celebration at Granada.[16] (It remained in service on the lake for many decades and became a Nicaraguan institution.) Pellas became a wealthy pillar of Greytown society as he directed his successful transit operations during the 1880s. He owned the largest warehouses and built the most imposing residence the town had ever known.

But the Pellas developments did little to relieve the air of lethargy in Greytown. The number of transients increased during the early 1880s, but almost none arrived by sea. The economic impact of riverboat passengers was slight. Most were interested in acquiring banana lands in the Bluefields area and usually did not linger longer than necessary. The decaying port had no appeal. In 1881, as another U.S. consul was resigning, he was hardly able to write this letter—his hand shook so from weakness:

> Continued ill health together with urgent private business compel me to ask, most respectfully, for a leave of absence for the period of sixty days. The fever, so peculiar to this port, takes hold of me nearly every month— followed by great prostration in body and mind; and in order to regain strength and vitality, a change of air and food is occasionally necessary. Greytown is a very sickly place.[17]

Those who came via the river might have difficulty getting out, however much they wished to. The formerly thriving coastal trade between Greytown and points along the Shore, as far north as Cape Gracias a Dios, no longer existed. Communications between Bluefields and Greytown were worse than ever, as the consuls' complaints about mail would indicate. Other than one scheduled ship monthly between the two ports, there was only the chance coasting vessel.

Occasionally, lands along the San Juan River were considered for banana cultivation. A few planters, in scattered clearings along the river, were producing the fruit for local demand, and expected that they might eventually ship to the United States, once an efficient method of transport was realized. They hoped that fruit steamers of light draft would be able to proceed up the river, as they did the Escondido; but this never materialized, and Greytown failed to add the banana trade to its flimsy economic base. For many years the main income of the port was the fees charged ships to defray the expenses of maintaining navigational safety and policing the port. By the 1880s, however, the port's ruined condition and the lack of shipping, pilot, and lighter services made this income almost nonexistent, so that the expenses of the port had to be met mostly by resident commercial interests. An indication of how the function of Greytown had deteriorated is that the only officials who were maintained there were the governor-intendente, a secretary, a port surgeon, a postmaster, a police chief, and three policemen.[18]

Nevertheless, later in the decade, this sad and unattractive place would again draw scores of Americans, this time to begin construction of an interoceanic canal.

6   Toward a
                    Nicaraguan Canal,
                    1880–1893

                                        During the 1880s Nicaragua was in its
last decade of a thirty-year period of relatively peaceful and stable Conservative rule. Its presidents had come from a small, harmonious group of
Granada politicians who represented that city's most aristocratic families.
For the most part they were able men who, by arrangement, succeeded each
other in orderly fashion, with the full support of their associates. Intraparty
jealousies were few. The administrations were also marked by a moderate,
conciliatory policy toward Liberals, who for most of the period offered no
serious dissent, even though they yearned to return to power. In any event,
they profited from the maintenance of order, and saw some of their economic and social reforms adopted by the Conservative governments.

    Though uneventful in terms of traditional uprisings, the succession of
Conservative governments was eventful in bringing economic progress to
the country. Railways were built late in the period, linking Granada, Managua, León, and Corinto. Coffee culture was encouraged, and the crop
became a major pillar of the commercial-agricultural economy. There were
also improvements in education. Stability was a vital factor in the considerable achievements. While it was true that the peasants realized little benefit,
and that the achievements affected only a small part of the country (the
Pacific lake region and environs), these developments were critical
milestones in Nicaragua's evolution as a nation. Throughout most of the
thirty-year period there was also an attempt to cultivate friendly relations
with neighboring states, despite the fact that Liberal regimes came back into
power in those countries during the 1870s.

    Nevertheless, trouble was brewing for Conservative administrations of
the 1880s. Dissatisfaction was growing among Liberals over the long tenure
in power of this small political group, which had permitted no real freedom
of elections. The opposition drew support from an emerging middle class

with strong foreign ties, from the young, and from the lower classes. Conservative strength was clearly diminishing by the latter part of the decade, and Liberals awaited their opportunity. A destabilizing event occurred during the administration of President Adán Cárdenas in 1885, when the Guatemalan Liberal strongman, Justo Rufino Barrios (in power since 1873), appeared ready to force a union of the Central American states under his leadership. Fearful because of Barrios' previous interventions in Honduras and El Salvador on behalf of the Liberal cause, the Nicaragua government became alarmed over this prospect, and when Barrios marched against recalcitrant El Salvador to force its compliance with his grand plan, Nicaragua sent troops. Possibly serious consequences for Nicaragua's long prevailing Conservative power structure were averted, however, by Barrios' death on a Salvadoran battlefield. A few years of Conservative control of the government remained.

During the late 1860s and early 1870s in the United States, under the administrations of Presidents Johnson and Grant, there had been interest in an isthmian canal. Treaties had been signed with Colombia on a Panama site, and a survey commission, sent by Grant, recommended Nicaragua in 1876. Nothing developed from any of this, however. The Colombian treaties were not ratified, and no treaty emerged from negotiations with Nicaragua. The actions had been started too late in the administrations of the respective presidents, and hanging over them, in any case, were the troublesome restrictions of the Clayton-Bulwer Treaty. Congressional support—and even that of Grant's secretary of state, Hamilton Fish—was not strong.[1] It was only after Rutherford B. Hayes became president, in 1877, that events forced greater interest by the U.S. government.

In 1880, having secured a concession from Colombia, the private French company of Ferdinand de Lesseps was preparing to construct a canal through Panama. The American public became thoroughly aroused and the press expressed this hostility. In the ensuing years the U.S. government, this time with public backing, again began to consider a U.S.-built canal in Nicaragua, the Clayton-Bulwer Treaty notwithstanding. It was considered imperative to match not only the material achievement of the French but also the worldwide psychological impact. President Hayes made it clear, in a famous presidential message, that the aim of the United States was an isthmian canal under U.S. control.

Despite the fact that this policy was counter to provisions of the Clayton-Bulwer Treaty, it was continued after Hayes left the presidency, and the result was a treaty with Nicaragua signed by President Arthur's secretary of state, Frederick Frelinghuysen, in 1884. It provided that the United States would construct a canal, share its proceeds and management with Nicaragua, and guarantee Nicaragua's territorial integrity as well. Nicaragua would cede to the United States a strip of its territory along the projected San Juan route, as well as rights to use Lake Nicaragua. The treaty was ratified almost immediately by the Nicaraguan congress but was rejected by the U.S. Senate. Again, it had been presented during a lame-duck administration, this time of a president who had failed to receive the nomination of his own party. Even the defeated Republican candidate did not support the treaty.

The president-elect, Grover Cleveland, had different ideas about the obligation of the United States to adhere to the Clayton-Bulwer Treaty. He, with Senate leaders, was not prepared to support a treaty which would, in effect, be a unilateral abrogation of the agreement with Britain. Once in office, Cleveland withdrew the proposed treaty from congressional consideration. He believed that private enterprise should build the canal.

The groundwork was laid during the early 1880s for just such a private project. A naturalized Cuban immigrant and civil engineer (and later lieutenant commander in the U.S. Navy), Aniceto G. Menocal, had conducted isthmian canal surveys under Admiral Ammen in 1872 and, with him, had become an ardent proponent of the Nicaragua route. Attending an international congress on canal projects in Paris in 1879 and learning that the French company would begin construction in Panama in 1881, Menocal and Ammen were convinced that an alternative canal, by way of Nicaragua, should be constructed. Having gained the support of influential army and navy officers, as well as capitalists in the United States, they made their first contacts with the Nicaraguan government in 1880, which resulted in a concession for canal construction. Because of problems in accumulating the capital to begin the work, however, this concession lapsed in 1884. Two years later, Ammen and Menocal, with a number of other engineers and capitalists, including Charles P. Daily, Hiram Hitchcock, A. B. Cornell, and James Roosevelt, organized the Nicaragua Canal Association and obtained another concession from the Nicaraguan government.[2] The group received the exclusive right to excavate and operate a canal across Nicaraguan territory, and Nicaragua's congress quickly ratified the contract. Most of Nicaragua's neighbors in Central America supported the project, but Costa Rica was concerned about her riparian rights along the San Juan. However, this old controversy died down, for the time being, with President Cleveland's arbitration in 1888. The operating company, called the

Maritime Canal Company, with Aaron H. Palmer as president and Menocal as chief engineer, was incorporated under federal charter in early 1889. This time, sufficient capital had been obtained to begin the final surveys and actual construction.

As the American project got under way, having been stimulated by the developments in Panama, the French project was nearing collapse. Because of difficult and costly engineering problems, and disease taking a heavy toll among its work force, the de Lesseps company was bankrupt by 1888, having spent millions. Hundreds of thousands of French investors lost their money in the collapse. Due to these losses, it was conceivable, even likely, that there would be intervention in Panama by the French to recover something on the work already accomplished. Rumors of such action disturbed the U.S. government and stimulated congressional interest in the Nicaragua project, thereby encouraging its advocates. Also heartening was the apparent support of the incoming Benjamin Harrison administration. Interest seemed to die down, however, after it became apparent that there would be no French intervention in Panama. Hopes that the government would provide financial assistance, or at least a financial guarantee, to the Maritime Canal Company proved fruitless. Congress consistently resisted such entreaties, and the company had to proceed on its own.

The initial complement of personnel arrived in Greytown (Americans continued to call it San Juan del Norte) on December 9, 1887: six land parties, one hydrographic party, and two boring parties, numbering some forty-five engineers and rod-and-chain men, plus one hundred laborers.[3] Landing supplies and equipment at Greytown during the early period, before the breakwater was constructed and the harbor reopened, was extremely difficult. If not subject to lengthy transshipment from the mouth of the Colorado, all cargo had to be landed on the open, unprotected beach in front of the lagoon, while the vessels lay at anchor in the roadstead, 2 miles from land, exposed to buffeting winds, which usually had a velocity of 20 miles per hour. Many trips between ship and shore had to be made in lighters, through a violent surf. An additional problem was the swell, due to the continuous trade winds and the alongshore current, which kept the vessels broadside to the sea and gave them a tendency to roll. Many ships, unable to discharge, departed. This was very expensive, especially with costly cargo like coal.

The ship on which the surveying party arrived lay near the old entrance to the harbor, but the sandbar made it necessary to go down the coast quite a distance to gain entrance to the inner lagoon. From this point the party proceeded in a shallow-draft paddlewheel steamboat to the storehouse and wharf of Alfredo Pellas, who held the steamer concession on the San Juan River and the lake. Its initial headquarters was a large two-story house facing Plaza Victoria—an open space, several hundred feet square, bordered by coconut palms and mango trees. The engineers (most of whom stayed in the hotel) were agreeably surprised with the appearance of Greytown and pleased to learn from the local doctor that it was not the unhealthy place they had imagined. He described it as free of the childhood diseases so prevalent in the United States at the time (diphtheria, measles, scarlet fever)—a place where the dread Chagres fever of Panama (presumably yellow fever) did not exist, where persons who had come from Panama, completely broken down, had regained their health while stopping over.

In addition, agricultural production had become more pronounced during the 1880s. As a young man, long before his fame as the first to reach the North Pole, Robert E. Peary was chief engineer of the Maritime Canal Company surveying party. He observed that

> from Greytown to the San Carlos there are now many clearings along the rich bottom land of the river, the land about the mouth of nearly every tributary having been thus improved. Some of these clearings extend for a mile or more along the river, rich with plantain, bananas, oranges, limes, cacao, coffee, cane and vegetables . . .

and

> below the mouth of the Sarapiqui, and also at Ochoa below the San Carlos, and at Castillo, are large numbers of cattle, and as they gather at the river at night and morning, or feed over the hills during the day, they give a very pastoral air to those localities.[4]

Oranges and pineapples were particularly widespread, but much of the surplus went to waste rather than into trade. Coconuts, another important product of the Greytown vicinity, were widely used locally for cooking oil. One immense *cocal* (coconut plantation), about 7 miles north of Greytown, constituting a strip about 20 miles along the Caribbean shore, was estimated to have thousands of trees. (It has continued to modern times as Nicaragua's principal coconut plantation, furnishing most of its domestic requirements.)

Nevertheless, there were shortages in Greytown (beef supplies were insufficient and not of good quality), and in anticipation of much spending, merchants had raised their prices exorbitantly even for food staples. ("Just fancy, in this forsaken country, having to pay $1.50 for a poor little chicken

and 80 cents per dozen for eggs.")[5] Calls by steamers were few, and the
surveying party longed to receive mail more frequently. But with every
steamer came larger numbers of strangers, attracted by the revival occasioned by the survey. Most had an eye for the speculative. Since the arrival
of the survey party, property values had boomed.

The few Nicaraguan authorities and townspeople in the decaying port
were delighted with the activity and made every attempt to please the
Americans. Pomp was even displayed on occasion. In 1888, for a rare visit of
an American naval vessel (the *Boston*), the governor-intendente had the
American flag run up in lieu of the Nicaraguan flag and, hoping for a visit of
officers from the ship, ordered that Government House be thoroughly
tidied up and decorated. He kept a squad of soldiers in readiness, to present
arms when the American officers filed by. In new uniforms, donned only on
momentous occasions, the squad waited and perspired all day.[6] But there is
no indication that the Americans ever chose to come for a visit.

Using machinery purchased from the Panama company, after the failure
of its project, Menocal's company accomplished a great deal during the late
1880s. From the outset, however, the rainy season all but curtailed its
operations. Scores of Americans and Europeans, with no money, flocking in
at an inopportune time and expecting to be employed, found that little work
would be available for perhaps six months—not until drier weather returned. Disappointed and without means to sustain themselves, they tried
to get out of the country. Through newspapers, the company advised that
all prospective immigrants from the United States "stop at once, as there
will be no work for some time to come."[7]

For two years, the landing of supplies and equipment was extremely
difficult and tedious. The first big job was to open the silted harbor of
Greytown so that ships could enter it directly in support of construction
inland. Volcanic sands, brought from Costa Rica by San Juan tributaries,
had built a sand spit completely across the harbor entrance. As a solution,
the company determined to construct a breakwater or jetty 3,000 feet long,
at right angles to the shoreline, and to dredge a new entrance in its lee. The
sand could then accumulate harmlessly in the angle formed by the breakwater and the coast. The breakwater required exploitation of quarries approximately 10 miles inland and construction of a railroad to transport the
stone to the harbor. Soon, six dredges were operating in the harbor, all of
them brought up from Panama, and two large suction dredges were sent
from Charleston, South Carolina.

The company also accomplished a monumental job of forest clearing during these two years. For a distance of 10 miles back from the coast, the crews opened a swath almost 500 feet wide, preparatory to construction. Like a great avenue through the forest, it ended in a view of the distant mountains. This operation alone was mammoth (as anyone knows who has either tried or witnessed the back-breaking task of clearing a small patch of land for farming in the rainforest). Gigantic trees were felled and burned, as were the brush and undergrowth. There were no tractors or bulldozers, but much dynamite was used in removing stumps.

A telegraph line was of first priority, in order to establish contact with the interior and with overseas cables. The first 10 miles were through swampland, and the men who laid the line waded in water up to 4 feet deep. In some cases the water was so deep that the poles had to be attached to stumps rather than driven into the earth.

The preliminary surveys in the interior were extensive, slow, and costly (every step was preceded by the whack of a machete). Most of the travel between Greytown and the main camp at Ochoa, a distance of 30 miles, was overland—over hills so steep that travelers (carrying packs) had to pull themselves along by grabbing trees and plants, as the rain poured down, almost constantly, and made the slopes even muddier and more slippery. Some of the route was through swamps where "the men had to flounder along in water and mud waist deep."[8] They could use canoes only in a few localities, and only after the streams had been cleared of logs and other debris.

A great deal of initial reconnaissance attempted to find a route which would avoid a large ridge north of the river. Surveying parties examined the entire watershed, probing swamp and forest, following every meandering creek from its confluence with the projected canal to its source on the divide. After much time and effort, they found that the valley, low and flat, with many creeks and lagoons, could not provide a damsite for inundating the lower San Juan—and that there was no alternative to massive and costly rock-cutting through the ridge.

Once the line of the canal route was determined, engineering parties resumed the attack on the interior wilderness at their isolated camps. The pioneering zeal of the young engineers was praised by a *New York Times* correspondent who visited them:

It makes an honest American heart beat with pride to see how pluckily the American engineers stand the trials and privations, the isolation, and hard

work incidental to the pioneering now being done along the line of the Nicaraguan Canal. Some of these engineers are young men, mere youths, sons of
good families, accustomed to every luxury, unused to hard work of any description. These banged, perfumed, kid-gloves lads have shed their "trappings of civilization," donned flannel shirts, cowboy hats, coarse canvas
leggings, heavy boots, and rough trousers, girded on a machete, and cutting
their way through these virgin forests, dense with wiry undergrowth, they
wade all day, knee deep, waist deep and often back deep in swamps, running
levels, rod and chain, cheerful and contented, brave and energetic.[9]

The correspondent then gave an impressive list of these young engineers,
being initiated along the banks of the San Juan. Among them were the sons
of U.S. Adjutant General Kelton, Admiral Greer, Commodore Spicer
(U.S. Navy), General McAuley and Captain Pope (U.S. Marine Corps),
Major Woodward (U.S. Army), and Chief Engineer Menocal himself.

Excavation started in the fall of 1889, with two mammoth floating
dredges working side by side. Much ceremony marked the official breaking
of soil on that warm October day. Besides Chief Engineer Menocal were the
governor of San Juan del Norte, representing Nicaragua, the American,
British, and German consuls, and many other prominent personages.

Amid the booming of cannon, cheers of crowds of all nationalities, the clink-
ing of wineglasses, speeches and handshakings, dinners and receptions, services in the churches, and the jollity natural to a general holiday, at a given
word 100 American picks were driven into the Nicaraguan soil. 100 American
shovels followed suit, and then the trundling of American wheelbarrows told
that the soil was at least broken in the work upon the Nicaragua Canal.[10]

Under a large tree, refreshment stands were set up and the crowd milled
about, surrounded by carriages of all shapes and makes, and horses, mules,
and donkeys. After the speeches and the ground-breaking, almost the entire
crowd of spectators—men, women, and children—took shovels in hand to
participate in a small way. As they listened to the speeches, souvenir hunters
also gathered handkerchiefs full of earth, twigs from the large tree, and even
random stones and plants. The Panama Canal was not yet on the horizon for
Americans, and this was a great event. There was no reason to believe that
this would *not* be the long-awaited canal, that it would *not* be brought to
completion.

After retiring to Greytown, all the dignitaries and as many of the public
who could be accommodated—Americans, Spanish, and Indians—participated in a thanksgiving service in the Catholic church. In the organ loft,

musicians sang and chanted to the accompaniment of brass, silver, and stringed instruments. The altar was magnificently decorated. On the edge of all this, native laborers—barefooted, bareheaded, barebreasted or in shirt-sleeves—stood at the doors of the church, watching. After the Catholic service, the crowd moved across the plaza to the Protestant church for another service.

The festivities continued into the evening, with the whole town decorated for the occasion. It was also the occasion for many private celebrations, in which the British residents participated wholeheartedly. Their support for the venture seemed particularly to please the Americans.

Despite the festive start, only 1 mile of the canal had been excavated (280 feet wide by 17 feet deep) many months later—and the distance to be excavated between Greytown and the river was more than 15 miles. Moreover, only about 9 of the 15 miles were soft alluvial earth, which could be excavated rather easily by floating dredges. But by far the hardest work was through the ridge—a distance of only 3 miles but involving a deep cut through solid rock—and the railroad that was needed for this operation had to be built across swampland.

In the first 10 miles, only 4 miles of the railroad were built on solid ground. No earth for filling was available in the vicinity, and had to be transported from a distance by the railroad itself. There was no alternative to laying the track first and then build the embankment. Thus the first step was a heavy corduroy of logs, dragged and floated in, along the proposed line. When the ties and rails were in place, on top of the log base, railway cars brought sand and fill material, which they dumped along the way. In this manner, the roadbed was gradually raised as the rail line advanced. All of this work—6 miles in the swamp—was done without the aid of mechanical power other than locomotives, with the workers sometimes in water "up to the waist and armpits."[11]

The Maritime Canal Company was able to purchase much useful equipment from the defunct Panama company: several dredges, tugboats, many lighters, several launches, and many miscellaneous tools, spare parts, machine-shop equipment, engines, pumps, and the like. Upon arrival at Greytown, two of the dredges were put immediately on canal construction and another on the harbor deepening.

All the while, ships were calling, with much greater frequency, and anchoring beyond the bar. The experience of unloading was still harrowing, as described in this account:

Soon a tug came out, towing flats, or lighters, for our cargo. The sea was high: one minute a flat would be almost even with our decks, and the next fifteen or twenty feet below; one minute, thirty feet from the side, and the next, jamming into us with a tremendous crash, making the vessel tremble from bow to stern.

On the flats there were many men to receive the freight, but no one seemingly in command. When a package was hanging over the boat, yells to lower would go up from every one; the constant shifting of the boat would bring some of them under the package, and a wild scramble to get out of the way would begin; again, as it would be lowered, the flat would slide out from under, and all hands would yell to have the engine stopped. Sometimes, as the bale was lowered, the flat would go down at the same time, keeping the same distance between them; then a wave would suddenly lift it up against the bale with such force that one would think it must go through the bottom of the boat. . . .

Ladies, babies, and old people are lowered in the same way, tied in a chair, and one at a time. Two lines are tied to the chair to steady it, one held by a man on the steamer, one by a man in the float; the power is steam. But a man must climb, stay on board, or drown, and no one seems to care which.[12]

After a small portion of the breakwater was completed, the river began to cut a channel to the sea, shallow but useful for lighter traffic. Dredges deepened it, and eventually the channel provided more direct access to ships anchored beyond the bar. Although there were more interruptions of work, as additional shipments of pilings and lumber from the United States were awaited, now, when they *did* arrive, they could be unloaded near the job, rather than carried several miles down the bar to be discharged at what was previously the only inlet to the harbor.

The company suspended work on the breakwater after it had been extended to 1,000 feet. The small rock quarry, opened at Silico Lagoon (more than 10 miles away), had, as predicted, become exhausted before the work was finished. The plan had been to begin transporting rock from more distant sources in the eastern divide by this time, but difficult problems had been encountered for the railroad, and its construction had not kept pace. It never reached deeper than 11 miles into the interior. Unaccountably, work on the railroad had not begun ahead of the other projects, yet it was critical to all: from the harbor rehabilitation to construction of the canal itself.

Nevertheless, results from the 1,000 feet of breakwater seemed to be in accord with the predictions: where there had been a dry beach on the bar, a channel developed of sufficient depth to allow vessels of 12- to 15-feet draft to enter. This was due simply to reduced siltation and the increased force of the river. After further deepening by dredges, oceangoing ships were able to enter Greytown harbor for the first time in thirty years. (The year was 1891.)

Few vestiges of the Greytown of the gold rush still existed when the activities of the Maritime Canal Company revived the town around 1890. The original site had in part been washed away, and the old buildings, some abandoned and in an advanced state of dilapidation, had been replaced by others. About the only reminder of earlier days was an old fence, constructed of musket barrels stuck into the ground, a relic of the filibuster period.[13] Besides the few old structures were the new uniform buildings in the "company town" named America, constructed on an empty site 2 miles from the old town's center. Although the Mosquito Coast had a magnificent forest of pine, which was being exploited by U.S. companies (the *Bluefields Messenger* in 1894 regularly carried ads of the Wawa Saw Mill, "now prepared to fill all orders [for] superior yellow pine"),[14] local lumber was not used for the new buildings. Most of them were substantial "portable houses," built in the United States and sent to Nicaragua in sections— probably one of the first instances of prefabrication. All had corrugated galvanized iron roofs, such as the two-story chief engineer's headquarters, surrounded by a verandah; the officers' quarters and general offices of the company—also a two-story, with living quarters upstairs—a three-story building for officers' housing, whose lower floor was used as a warehouse— probably the largest portable building to that date (many freight cars were required for its transport in the United States). There was also an officers' mess hall. A tramway connected the important buildings and was extended to the old town. Housing for laborers consisted of temporary shelters, thatched with palm leaves. The cost of labor for these crude structures (there was little other cost) built for the company was several thousand dollars.

The new city included a two-story hospital, with double verandah, for officers; but according to most reports it was needed only infrequently, due to the outstanding healthiness of the personnel. Segregation was rigid, with separate hospital facilities for the laborers. Other integral parts of the complex were a blacksmith shop, machine shop, carpenter shop, canvas shop, and an explosives dump. Scattered about were small, palm-thatched huts that engineers erected for themselves, where they put up wire fences, planted gardens, and made comfortable and personalized abodes that were envied by the barracks inhabitants.

In addition to these facilities were more than a dozen large and small camps, scattered around the harbor, along the canal route, and along the telegraph and railway line. In the early phases, most of these camps were completely cut off from communication with the outside. They received, more or less regularly, supplies from the Greytown headquarters: beans, rice, plantains, beef, sometimes turtle, canned meats, bacon, eggs (for officers only), canned and fresh vegetables (when available), biscuits and flour, and rum. However, each camp also had a hunter whose duties were to bring in wild game.

The promoters intended their "America" to become a great new port and city. Lots would be sold at public auction to cover the cost of its construction. However, Greytown residents and property owners were little impressed and did not believe that it would ever realize such ambitions. This feeling may have resulted from a sense of pride, that Greytown could not be replaced, or possibly it was a realistic assessment, based upon Greytown's adverse circumstances.

The American entrepreneurs, proud that they were avoiding the errors of the French in Panama, emphasized health, plentiful good food, and efficiency. While the Panama company paid its laborers a wage and allowed them to fend for themselves and provide their own food, the Americans paid wages just as high and, in addition, provided food that was shipped from New York. Thus the view was that not only were the workers getting more wholesome nourishment, but their morale was boosted over that of the Panama workers. Better morale also resulted from the ability to purchase a variety of goods at cost—boots, shoes, clothing, cigars, tobacco. The company pointed with pride to its superior housing (the portable buildings), its health facilities, and its piped-in water supply, not only for the new town of company workers but also for Greytown.

Hardly any report by those engaged in canal surveys and construction in the late 1880s and early 1890s failed to mention, in glowing terms, the enjoyable climate and healthfulness of the place. (However, it must be taken into account that many such persons had an ax to grind or special interests to promote.)

In fact, propaganda for the Nicaragua canal underplayed the adverse climate around Greytown—to put it mildly. For example, in that portion of the Maritime Canal Company report describing climatic conditions in Nicaragua is the following: "The average rainfall, west of the lakes, for nine years, was about 64½ inches. On the Caribbean coast it is greater."[15] In fact, it is greater than most places on earth, and was *296 inches* that year. The climate was not comfortable for many visitors: "When at Greytown, I felt as if I were in a perpetual vapour bath, and found people everywhere using fans made from the palm leaf."[16]

The report of the canal company's first surveying party states:

> During the four months we remained in the country, of which more than three months were of constant, arduous work, exposure and privation, no officer of the party was ever affected by sickness due to climatic causes; and as for the natives attached to the party, their only ailments were due to bruises caused by want of protection for their feet or limbs. It may be proper to add that our work was confined to the uninhabited, and what is generally regarded as the most unhealthy portion of the country.
>
> . . . The only precaution observed was that the day's work was preceded by a cup of strong coffee and, when the work was concluded, it was followed by a bath and change of wet clothing for dry. After the evening meal, the men lay down in their dry clothing and slept, on the ground when on the march, or in their tents or thatched huts, on cots or cane beds when they were in camp, and this mode of life was endured day after day for months by them and by their successors. Yet, notwithstanding all this exposure, not only were there no deaths on the expedition, but there was not a single case of serious illness, and those who, at the expiration of their contract, returned to the United States, came back in better health and weight than when they went away. Of course, the men were well fed and sanitary rules were strictly enforced, but the results proved the natural salubrity of the climate.[17]

The annual report of the chief surgeon of the Nicaragua Canal Construction Company, submitted in 1891, praised the health care of the 2,000 men who were then employed: the furnishings and equipment of wards were similar to those of well-regulated hospitals in New York; a corps of nurses, under a competent head nurse, attended the patients day and night; there were several outpatient stations, an efficient sanitation inspection, quarantine service for incoming vessels, and a well-stocked pharmacy.[18]

The generally good health record of personnel should be attributed, in part, to the preventive advantages of the facilities, housing, and food. Some of it must also be attributed to the almost military discipline employed by the company. No liquor was sold on the company's premises, and the only source was Greytown, 2 miles away. To comply with the strict curfew, laborers had to be in their quarters each night at nine, and they were not allowed to leave them until working hours the next morning, except by special permission. In the field, these were the instructions to work crews:

> The daily routine will be as follows: Cooks must be called and hard tack served to the party so that all hands may be ready to start at 6:30 a.m. Coffee will be served to the officers of the parties in their mosquito bars [nets] before

rising. Work will be stopped at 4:30, when the engineers will return to camp after their day's work to take a small dose of spirits and then to remove working clothes immediately, take a thorough bath and rub down, and put on flannel sleeping suits, when dinner will be served them. It will be desirable to always pitch tents on the bank of a stream in some dry, level place. The ground will be bared of bush and trees and all precautions taken to insure a healthy location. [19]

Passing observers—and there were many during the period—cited "scientific" opinion to explain the "healthful" conditions of the region. Often they recognized the penetration of the trade winds, via the San Juan corridor, as a positive ingredient of the topographic-climatic environment. That the lower San Juan Valley received the effects of the trade winds is confirmed by the use of sails on *bongos*, going up the river as far as the Machuca rapids. [20] In exposed places, these fairly constant winds reduced the number of malaria-bearing mosquitoes, although, at the time, most thought that removal of "noxious exhalations" was responsible for the health-promoting effect.

Travelers also credited the sandy soils as an asset. The rapid absorption of rainwater, precluding formation of stagnant pools, was undoubtedly beneficial—again for reducing mosquito-borne diseases. Yellow fever was not a great menace at Greytown, as it was in Panama. Also, the sandy soil allowed residents to sink barrels into the ground to collect their drinking water, rather than use the river. Ground water was filtered naturally by the sand, thus aiding in the control of typhoid and other diseases.

The winds, a topography devoid of depressions, and the sandy soil cannot be ignored in any accurate appraisal of malarial tendencies in the tropics, and observers of the period rightly recognized their relevance, even if the relationships they inferred were not always correct.

Proponents of the Panama route, which had gained a bad reputation in terms of health because of the French experience, discounted the claims for Nicaragua, citing the facts that the Nicaragua experience had been brief, its works were not extensive, and comparatively few engineers and workers were assembled there. Also, the claims of naturally healthy conditions in Nicaragua seem at variance with the experience of many consuls, whose letters are likely to be more reliable than the reports of persons biased in favor of the Mosquito Shore because of special interests (colonization, trade, transit, the canal). Certainly many of them found that health was a major factor. However, most of the American consuls resided in Greytown only briefly, and requested transfer after initial bouts with illness. On the other hand, some foreign diplomatic agents such as the Britisher, W. D. Christie, lived on the Shore for long periods without serious impairment of health. Indeed, a handful of early British and American residents spent most of their lives in the region and lived there to an advanced age. It was obviously not a "disease-ridden graveyard," particularly after acclimatization and employment of reasonable sanitation and preventive measures.

Nevertheless, Mosquito Shore adherents exaggerated the healthfulness of the region though many in the United States remained unconvinced. New Orleans authorities showed their suspicion of conditions on the Shore, and in Nicaragua generally, by imposing a strict quarantine upon ships from that country, so that returning American residents were inclined to take ship to New York and avoid New Orleans altogether. Their reaction was twofold: there were no infectious diseases in Nicaragua to quarantine against, and New Orleans merchants were losing substantial business from Americans who would otherwise go there to purchase supplies.

Throughout the long canal controversy, adherents of Nicaragua refuted claims that their route was earthquake prone. In this, they displayed little knowledge of the geology between Lakes Managua and Nicaragua and the Caribbean, which is a major fault zone, or they were not willing to let this information come to light. Moreover, erupting volcanos, rather than earthquakes, were dramatically publicized by anti-Nicaragua forces in the "postage stamp incident," when Panama came into contention as the preferred route at the turn of the century. Yet the U.S. State Department, at least, had knowledge of the occurrence of earthquakes, near the San Juan and in Greytown. Its consulate had reported "a trembling of the earth" several times during the night and early morning of December 29/30, 1888, which was strong enough to shake beds, awaken their occupants, and to tumble objects from tables, shelves, and walls onto the floor.[21] There was, as well, knowledge of an earthquake in the early 1860s, which many considered had changed the San Juan channel and the bar at its entrance, making navigation more difficult.

In the surveys and propaganda pamphlets for the Nicaragua canal during the nineties, there was again great emphasis on the volcanic geology. They concluded that the canal route would not be endangered by volcanic eruptions, and this was probably correct; however, earthquakes were another matter. Many assumed, falsely, that because there was no volcanic activity in the canal zone, there was no earthquake danger. Adherents, in support of their argument, repeatedly cited the fact that the old fort at Castillo had remained intact. One report concluded that the whole matter was partisan and born of bias: "The risk of injury to Nicaragua Canal constructions by earthquakes only exists in the theories of those who are interested in the making of a canal at some other locality, or in the mind of the man who is naturally a pessimist and opposed to all bold undertakings."[22]

Through the years, the old part of Greytown, since the closing of the transit route, had handled much of Nicaragua's foreign trade. For many years, the Pellas fleet of river steamers had transported rubber, coffee, hides, dyewood, and other products from the interior on a regular schedule, taking back imported goods that had been transferred (with great difficulty) across the bar. But until the coming of the construction company, the town had a sleepy, decaying ambience. Now, although changes came more slowly than in the company town of America, the old port began to be revitalized: "This hitherto dull little town, destined to become the Atlantic port of the Nicaragua Canal, is rapidly awakening into a new life, and is already blossoming out as the scene of considerable activity."[23]

Its second boom began in 1889, when the population had reached 2,000.[24] After three years' impact by the Maritime Company, the town, with its white houses, green shutters, and brown roofs, presented an attractive appearance. Its tropical vegetation was particularly appealing: palms, breadfruit, citrus, and mango trees in the yards, which often had colorful flower gardens as well. The grass-covered central square was shaded by numerous coconut palms. Because of Greytown's free-port status, its stores were well stocked. Prices on food and all imported goods had risen, but so had property values, in the town and along the canal route. There were semimonthly calls by ships from New York and a weekly coastwise service to Bluefields, with connections to New Orleans. In addition, a British mail steamer called once a month. There were two main hotels, one noted for its better rooms, the other for its food. A traveler gave this description of the hotel in which he stayed, which had been recommended by the American consul:

> This one consisted of a very large barroom opening on a broad veranda that ran the length of the building, a smaller diningroom, and back of that a number of small closets called bedrooms, separated by partitions about six feet high. In each of these apartments was a canvas cot with a grass mat, a sheet of muslin, and a small, very hard hair pillow. A washstand, with a grass mat before it, completed the furnishing.[25]

A well-appointed clubhouse was frequented by the foreign population, and a horse-drawn tram went up and down the main street. Like most boom towns on isolated frontiers, with many outsiders and transients, it was bawdy. For example, gambling flourished in the saloons (Sundays were no exception) and cockfights were a popular amusement. As a moral counterweight, the company offered a stipend for a Protestant minister; the first one, a Jamaican black, advertised the opening of his church on the main plaza.

But none of this would last. Eventually the Nicaraguan canal company failed, due to lack of funds and inability to get government assistance during the Panic of 1893. Observers reported that work had practically ceased by 1892. However, the promoters presented an optimistic front. While admitting that no extensive work was being done, pending the outcome of Menocal's trip to London on a capital-raising venture, they emphasized that scores of men were still on the payroll and that work was progressing, though slowly. They drew attention to the fulfillment of the terms of the company's concession from Nicaragua: the company had put more money into the project the first year than required in its contract. Moreover, the Nicaraguan government had been sufficiently satisfied to extend the concession for ten years beyond the originally projected completion date.

Indeed, the accomplishments around Greytown were impressive, particularly the harbor improvement, and much money had been spent; but there had been little progress on the canal. Its 1-mile length proved to be the full extent of accomplishment.

Even though both the Panama and the Nicaragua canal projects had collapsed by the early 1890s, their proponents were not idle on either side of the Atlantic. The Nicaragua route remained the favorite, because it was an American concept and work had been started by an American company. Little thought was given to the possibility of the United States' taking over in Panama, where the French had failed. There was simple glee that this project had not succeeded. To Americans, Nicaragua was the only site, and Gulf Coast interests, such as those represented by Senator J. T. Morgan, busied themselves to see that this remained Washington's view. They hoped that the government would help the Maritime Canal Company get on its feet again and resume work, and eventually this gave way to outright pressure upon the government to buy out the company and finish the job.

Conventions were held in the United States—first in St. Louis, then a much larger one in New Orleans—in support of the foundering project. Represented at these conventions were business interests from all over the country and leading chambers of commerce. They were gala affairs, with flags and bunting decorating the main streets and buildings, and parades.

Their objective, and that of smaller regional conventions as well, was government control and completion of the canal, with government financing. State legislatures passed supporting resolutions.

For the remainder of the decade, Nicaragua's proponents carried on a massive propaganda campaign through speeches and pamphlets and articles, all expounding the physical advantages of the route and its commercial imperatives.[26] They urged unilateral abrogation of the long-unpopular Clayton-Bulwer Treaty to enable the U.S. government to take over the project.

Up to the turn of the century, a great part of America's experience in Central America had been with Nicaragua: Vanderbilt's San Juan transit route for the California gold rush, William Walker's filibustering in the 1850s, the aborted Maritime Canal Company operations at and near Greytown, and the banana interests in the Mosquito Reserve in the 1880s and 1890s. It is no wonder that most Americans and their government were disposed to consider "the canal" and Nicaragua as synonymous.

An American Colony
in the Mosquito
Reservation and
Affairs at Bluefields,
1880–1905

The large district known as the Mos-
quito Reserve stretched from the Rama River in the south to the Hueso
River in the north and westward from the Caribbean to beyond the 85th
meridian. Thus it contained the Escondido Valley, Monkey Point, and the
towns of Bluefields (which became the capital of the Reserve), Rama, and
Pearl Lagoon. By the terms of the Treaty of Managua in 1860, this territory
had autonomous status under Nicaraguan sovereignty. The British, because
of their long-standing commitment to the Mosquito people, had insisted
upon self-government for them as part of the agreement to end its protectorate. The Nicaraguans, for their part, expected this self-government to be
free from further foreign influences and completely in the hands of the
native people. As noted, this did not prove to be the case during the following two decades.

British influence (at least indirectly, through pro-British Jamaican factions) upon the Mosquito "autonomous" government prevailed. While the
Nicaraguan–British controversy continued during the 1870s over what each
country perceived as treaty violations by the other, the Reserve did not
appear to offer sufficient stability and protection to entice American investors. The threat of the area's coming under increased Nicaraguan control,
possibly endangering foreign business interests, was a disincentive. In
1879, however, when arbitration by the emperor of Austria upheld Britain's
right to intervene on behalf of the Mosquito government, this gave the
assurance that American banana interests (planters, shippers, merchants)
felt they needed.

As mentioned, conditions were propitious for the beginning of American
settlement in the reservation early in the decade of the 1880s. A major
economic inducement was the suitability of the alluvial flats of the Escondido River between Bluefields and Rama for banana plantations at a time

when this fruit was becoming popular in the United States. Like the British before them, Americans were free to acquire concessions at low cost and to operate without economic restraints. A willing Mosquito government offered these advantages. Because of its incompetence and strongly anti-Nicaragua feeling, this government aided Americans in their business conquest. Colonists arrived from New Orleans in increasing number, bought tracts along the river, and planted banana plantations. With them came merchants who settled in Bluefields, following in the footsteps of the Keith commissary. In addition to banana cultivation, the large American wood products company, the John D. Emery Company of Boston, established itself in the reservation in 1884 to cut mahogany.

Bluefields received a new lease on life with the banana business. It became for a time, in the words of Parsons, "one of the major outposts of Yankee 'Manifest Destiny' in the Caribbean."[1] With the tracts obtained (at very low prices) along both sides of the Escondido River, each with a 3-mile river frontage, the Mosquito Fruit Company was formed. The natives also were urged to cultivate bananas and were told there would be a market for all they could produce. There is little evidence, however, that many natives participated in the business, except as laborers. The first shipment, in 1883, consisted of a few hundred bunches. A steamer made monthly trips between New Orleans and the upriver plantations, and later, as the production and number of plantations increased, almost bimonthly. By the end of the first year, several thousand bunches had been shipped. (There were, of course, peak periods: the banana business was seasonal, due to the fact that fewer were in demand during the summer months, when domestically grown fruits were available in the United States.)

By 1885, Bluefields bananas had so established themselves in U.S. markets that competitive companies in New Orleans and Baltimore entered the picture, making more of a sellers' market for the planters and bringing them better prices. Eventually, ships were calling from Baltimore, Philadelphia, and New York, as well as New Orleans, to pick up freshly cut bananas at the river landings, from large dealers and small growers alike. The latter would send canoes, containing a few bunches, to meet the steamers as soon as they received information that the ships were in the river. Some U.S. companies were so sure of the market possibilities that they were willing—in fact, preferred—to commit much larger ships to the trade if they could be assured of a capacity cargo each trip. It would be more economical. There was difficulty with the shallow bar off Bluefields, but, once across it, ships had wide and deep access to the plantations along the river. For this reason the river plantations had an advantage in banana export over those on Pearl

Lagoon, which had no deep-water approaches. In these cases, lighters had to be used to get the fruit to the steamers, and this extra handling meant greater possibility of damage and greater cost.

When Americans entered the reservation during the 1880s, they found numerous Moravian missionaries at work among the natives. On the Mosquito Shore since the late 1840s, the Moravians almost a half-century later included some American missionaries, and their little churches and schools were scattered all over. The center of the mission was Bluefields, which had—according to a probably careful Moravian census—800 or 900 inhabitants in 1882.[2] Like other nineteenth-century missionaries, the Moravians considered the native people almost savages—ignorant, degraded, and possessed of undesirable culture traits. They were dedicated to bringing education, uplifted morals, and relief from squalid living conditions to these people—along with the word of God. Polygamy and alcoholism were of particular concern, but getting the natives to wear clothing and to abandon dancing were also considered important. The Moravians were often discouraged by the response of the natives to their evangelical endeavors: in a typical service, held in an Indian dwelling, several persons might lie listlessly in their hammocks, and another, stationed at the door with a stick, would keep out dogs and cattle, noisily drowning out the voice of the preacher. The missionaries, nevertheless, had added their imprint to the changing culture of the reservation, parallel to the secular transition in the 1880s and thereafter. As in similar instances elsewhere, the missionary and secular foreign influences were not altogether reconcilable. The Moravians attributed much of the natives' degradation to British and American contacts, and perhaps were not enthusiastic about the impending Americanization. Their schools, on the other hand, became highly regarded assets for the American population, and for this reason (if no other) the Moravian presence was appreciated by most of the newcomers.

In the early 1890s the reservation, under its native leaders and still influenced by the British, was thriving. During this early phase of the banana trade, Bluefields (with Limón, Costa Rica) was a world leader in exports of the fruit. Among the shipping companies was that of Jacob Weinberger, whose Bluefields Steamship Company was established in 1890 and soon became dominant in both transport and production. Over 90 percent of wealth, enterprise, and commerce in the Reserve was estimated to be under American control, and Bluefields was described as "American to the core."[3] The area thus presented a picture quite different from other parts of Nicaragua, and of Central America as a whole.

Bluefields by 1893 had a population of about 1,500.[4] Its one main street,

King Street, led up from the wharf and contained most of the town's shops. The remainder of the widely scattered settlement did not have a street plan and its houses were haphazardly situated. Resident Americans built their homes of lumber brought from the States and in a style reminiscent of small towns back home. However, all buildings were elevated on posts, well above the ground, following Mosquito practice, to avoid the wetness and mud.

Under a permissive, pliable, and not energetic Mosquito government (which still had British backing), Americans had utmost privilege and freedom. The chief, Robert Henry Clarence (a descendant of the "kings") was a handsome, full-blooded Mosquito Indian only 20 years of age. The vice president and guardian of the chief during his minority, Charles Patterson—and the other four members of the executive council, who had most of the power—were of Jamaican extraction. A leisurely governing body, it spent much of its time at Pearl Lagoon, where the chief kept three horses

Mosquito Chief Robert Henry Clarence (seated, center) with his executive council, 1893 (*Popular Science Monthly*, vol. 45, no. 6, June 1894)

Bluefields in 1893 (*Popular Science Monthly*, vol. 45, no. 6, June 1894)

and frequently went riding. Here, also, the secretary of the executive council, J. W. Cuthbert, led a fourteen-piece brass band which often played familiar American arrangements for visitors.

Life in Bluefields became more and more like that to which Americans were accustomed in the United States. They had their own newspaper and Protestant churches. Sundays were not unlike those in most small American towns at the time, with churchgoing the central activity throughout the day. Their schools, run by the Moravians, were not only good but in keeping with American educational systems and values.

The English-language *Bluefields Messenger* reflected the "cosmopolitan" character of the town in 1894. It carried daily advertisements of the Bluefields Banana Company, with its biweekly passenger service to New Orleans; of wholesale grocers, with fancy lines; of U.S. and British trading and insurance companies which maintained agencies in Bluefields. The town supported a bottling company, producing "ginger ale, ginger beer, potass water, champane, lemonade, sarsparilla, seltzer," which boasted two newly imported bottling and corking machines.[5] Patrons of the numerous restaurants and hotel dining salons must have been accustomed to the "better things" of life, if one is to judge by a typical advertisement:

Finest and complete as-
sortment of Wines, Li-
quors and Cigars.

Cold and Warm Lunches
Imported Fancy Eatables
Regular Meals from 9 to 10 a.m.
    and from 3 to 4 p.m.
    Lunch at any hours.
Also a variety of all the
most popular Fancy and
Mixed Iced Drinks:
    Cocktails, Punches,
Souris, Fizz, etc.[6]

A mark of the relatively gracious life that Bluefields' "colonials" had developed was their German Club, which lent a "civilizing" influence to the town for many years. With its spacious lounging and reading-correspondence rooms, smoking rooms, its gymnasium and shower baths, and its sleeping rooms and card rooms (on the upper floor), it was an enclave of European life for its members. In exotic contrast, across the street, was the native-style "governor's palace," which was occupied by the Nicaraguan chief officer.

Bluefields' activity and Americanization reflected developments upriver. Many Americans lived on their plantations, which began about 20 miles upstream and thereafter covered both banks of the Escondido, almost with-

Banana plantation on the Escondido River, 1893 (*Popular Science Monthly*, vol. 45, no. 6, June 1894)

out interruption, to Rama and beyond.[7] By now, several ocean steamers, of competing companies, were ascending the river each month to collect the fruit. In addition, an old Mississippi River steamboat made a regular run between Bluefields and Rama, serving the plantations (each of which had a wharf at the bank) and carrying passengers.

Planters' homes, in clearings in the tropical forest, were constructed of bamboo and thatch, and while the steamers loaded or unloaded supplies it was possible for passengers to disembark and walk about. One of the sights they often observed was a tract of land in the process of being cleared, with machetes as the only tool, by Mosquito Indians or blacks. Each worker cleared at least 20 square yards a day, requiring only two to three hours, then quit before the day was finished.[8] The extra money they might make by clearing additional land meant little to them. Even the established plantations were disorderly, with banana plants growing amid the remnants of unburned logs and debris, but they were productive and profitable. Side by side, the plants were in various states of maturity, and harvesting and planting were conducted almost simultaneously throughout the year. Green bunches, covered with banana leaves to inhibit ripening, awaited the steam-

Loading bananas on Escondido River steamer, 1893 (*Popular Science Monthly*, vol. 45, no. 6, June 1894)

ers and barges along the banks at each plantation. During those days there was little interruption in the calls of boats, as fruit was shipped out and profits flowed in. Life was easy, and even occasional floods were a blessing in disguise:

> In 1897 the famed banana fields of the Rio Escondido (on the "Mosquito Coast" of Nicaragua) were so deeply flooded that the steamship "Saga" voyaged through the main streets of Rama, fully sixty miles from the mouth of the river, to pick off from their roofs the dwellers in that town. The bananas barely showed their tops above the yellow flood. Along the coast flew reports that the plantations were ruined; subscriptions were asked to help the planters—and three months later they were harvesting better crops than in years before. Their plantations had been so enriched that they bore most bountifully.[9]

Many workers for the plantations arrived from the United States when the native labor proved inadequate. Earlier, it had been possible to "get by," for only small numbers of men were necessary; they could be hired for short terms, and quantity, quality, and regularity in the labor force were not considerations. However, as time went on this changed, and nearly every steamer from New Orleans brought a few laborers. Recruited by the larger American companies, which operated on a substantial scale in the Escondido (such as the Bluefields Steamship Company, which, besides its shipping business, had several plantations), many of these laborers were former dock workers in New Orleans. Despite the isolation, some of them adapted and proved efficient. Their pay was good, and they had both the experience of working regular hours and the self-motivation that was often lacking in the natives. Some became supervisors. However, there were also drifters and misfits—as there had been among those who had worked on the canal project at Greytown—who perhaps signed on only for "adventure," and they proved to be problems. Some of them drank excessively, such as the unfortunate described in the documented report of Bluefields Steamship Company to its home office in New Orleans:

> Enclosed we beg to hand you report of the drowning of J. M. McGee and trust that his father will be convinced that we did all in our power to give him a decent burial.
>
> It is a sad mission to perform but his parents should have expected some misfortune to befall him and this on account of his fondness of liquor. We had him down on Providence for quite a while, but could not keep him out of Rama and every time he would get a chance he would get on a drunk, so we removed him to Guadalupe thinking in that way he would be away from liquor but such an arrangement was useless and the writer was upon the eve of discharging him when the climax of all his drinking occurred.[10]

The report went on to describe how McGee, after steadily drinking beer, rum, and wine from before noon to after midnight, jumped out of a boat (while crossing the Rama River), started to swim ashore, and "before any one could save him . . . passed out of sight." In one way or another— though not always due to alcohol nor ending in tragedy—the American labor force was beset by turnovers, and maintaining it at an appropriate level was difficult.

In 1893, a change in government in Nicaragua signaled a less comfortable life for Americans in the Mosquito reservation. The harmonious coalition of Granada Conservatives, which had ruled for thirty years, had begun to dissolve in 1889, when President Evaristo Carazo died in office and was succeeded by his vice president, Roberto Sacasa, who was from León. Sacasa completed Carazo's term and was elected in his own right in 1891. He made the mistake of selecting his friends from León for major posts in his government, thus alienating his party associates of Granada, who felt shut out—a status to which they were not accustomed. The old intercity rivalry came back into play, but this time to disrupt the long unity within the Conservative ranks. The Liberals took advantage of this disunity and in 1893 overthrew the government, placing one of their own in power, a young Managua politician named José Santos Zelaya. This assertive leader dominated events in his country for the next sixteen years and exerted a powerful influence in Central America as a whole.

Before the enormous increment in productivity in the Reserve, the Nicaraguan government had been mainly concerned about its national prestige, insofar as the Mosquito question was concerned. It had always been so: the Mosquito Shore was part of Nicaraguan territory, to which no foreign power had the right to extend a protectorate, open or disguised. But by the time Zelaya came to power there was a new element: the Reserve was perceived as an economic asset. There was now a substantial difference between the prosperous banana-growing, mahogany-cutting economy, with its associated shipping and mercantile interests, and the remainder of the country. Nicaraguans were becoming jealous of the profitable development, mostly under foreign auspices, in this eastern enclave, from which, because of Mosquito autonomy, they received no benefits. There had already been disputes on the margins of the Reserve between Nicaraguans and Americans, and increasingly, the validity of Mosquito concessions to Americans was contested. Zelaya, who came into power when these feelings were strongest, turned out to be an advocate, and the first important action of his government was directed to the Mosquito reservation. Determined to incorporate the Reserve into the republic in order to control it (already Nicaragua had titular sovereignty), Zelaya sent troops to Bluefields in February of 1894 and declared martial law. For some months previously, Nicaragua had been engaged in a border war with Honduras, and it was upon the basis of providing protection from a rumored invasion of Bluefields by Honduran forces that the government justified its military occupation of the town.[11]

The resident Americans were alarmed, fearing not only for their lives at the hands of "barbaric" Nicaraguan soldiers (who did, apparently, commit atrocities) but also for their homes, businesses, and plantations, which represented considerable investments. The rumor was abroad that it was official Nicaraguan policy to rid the Reserve of foreign interlopers, and the following year, this incident brought into conflict the governments of Nicaragua, the United States, and Great Britain, along with the foreign colony of the Reserve (mainly Americans). Each looked upon Nicaragua's avowed intent to incorporate Mosquitia in its own way. The viewpoint of the Mosquito government was not considered important.

Nicaragua, though she had her economic reasons, expounded her legal right to the Mosquito Reserve, on the basis of noncompliance with the terms of the Treaty of Managua, which had granted autonomy to the Mosquito Indians. Nicaragua now claimed that the natives were not in control of their government, that it had been subverted and had lost its identity as a local government, by and for the Indians, and had passed into the hands of long-resident Jamaican blacks and Creoles and other foreigners. (This indeed had been the trend for several years.) For Nicaragua, the arrangement harked back to the days of the "Mosquito kingdom" and the British protectorate, a sham and facade for foreign domination; and in this view she had the concurrence of the U.S. government. Secretary of State Walter Gresham expressed the official Washington position:

> An alien administration, in other interests than those of the Indians, notoriously exists, especially at Bluefields. Nobody is deceived by calling this authority a Mosquito Indian government. No matter how conspicuous the American or other alien interests which have grown up under the fiction of Indian self-government, neither the United States nor Great Britain can fairly sanction or uphold this abuse of the sovereignty of Nicaragua.[12]

The Americans in the Mosquito Reserve had a different view. The Mosquito government had functioned so inefficiently, and with such corruption, that American business interests had suffered; yet it represented safety and they had learned to live with it. Now, suddenly, they were faced with Nicaraguan intervention. Under martial law, the Nicaraguan authorities did not recognize the leases, concessions, contracts, and grants which foreigners had obtained from the Mosquito government. Nor was there protection from fire losses, because the existence of martial law voided insurance coverage of U.S. businesses.[13] Along with bureaucratic restrictions, such as the requirement of consular invoices (entailing additional expense), there was the imposition of export taxes on bananas. The Nicaraguans clearly intended to collect these and other duties, and this was particularly disconcerting to the Americans (the Mosquito government had been lax in collecting duties). Finally, under martial law, foreign businesses were required to use the Spanish language in all official transactions.

All of this brought fear and uncertainty to the American colony in the Reserve (estimated to consist of about 500, a fifth of whom lived in Bluefields).[14] They were ready to recognize Nicaragua's rights of sovereignty, but this did not eliminate the fact that their own rights seemed seriously threatened. They claimed that their investments of capital and labor in the reservation had been made on the assumption that the Treaty of Managua, and particularly its interpretation in the Austrian arbitration, protected them—that they would be secure in an autonomous zone. Besides curtailment of trade, they were concerned about the use of Spanish, the fate of the Moravian and Anglican churches, and the education of their children. Moreover, atrocities by a few Nicaraguan soldiers made the future less than promising. Several residents in outlying parts fled into the bush, or flocked into Bluefields to be under the protection of American marines from the *Marblehead*. By late spring of 1894, business had come to a standstill, due to the uncertain conditions. Fruit on plantations was rotting; labor was unobtainable on the upper river and its tributaries because of fear of violence; banana ships and barges were detained and fruit was not collected from the docks. The Reserve was no longer the comfortable safe haven, under mild and permissive (if incompetent) rule, that foreigners had previously enjoyed.

The long-resident Jamaicans, who had risen to positions of advantage, were vocally anti-Nicaraguan. They valued the reservation in terms of its similar culture and institutions, which now seemed threatened. A Jamaican leader of Bluefields, a Mr. Thomas, wrote to the American consul:

The Nicaraguans have no sympathy for the inhabitants of the Mosquito Reserve. They are jealous of the prosperity of the reserve. We do not speak the same language, we do not profess the same religion and our institutions and laws and manners and customs are not agreeable to them, and their manner of life and mode of government are obnoxious to us; and both Indians and foreigners within the Mosquito Reservation are unwilling that these men shall have the rule over us.[15]

In his communications with the U.S. government, President Zelaya's spokesman, Foreign Minister José Madriz, denied that the Nicaraguan government was hostile to the interests of Americans in the Reserve. However, he made it clear that the Zelaya government was determined to apply what it considered its rightful control over Mosquitia:

I fully appreciate the fact that the foreigners and particularly the Jamaicans are more in sympathy with the old regime. It would be absurd to suppose otherwise. The reservation has been unconditionally under their control, and therefore the intervention of an authority which watches and corrects irregularities is not at all pleasing to them.[16]

At the height of the controversy, President Zelaya sent Madriz to the Shore as his special representative in an attempt to reconcile the parties and bring confidence in and acceptance of Nicaraguan authority. It was a difficult mission. Madriz managed to obtain the good will of the Indians, discriminated against and exploited by the Jamaican oligarchy, and this was a major accomplishment; but he was not successful in his appeals for cooperation to the American and British consuls or the foreign residents generally, whom he attempted to reassure about their properties and business interests. He investigated the conduct of the military government under General Rigoberto Cabezas, a source of many grievances by foreigners, but found it in accord with the rights, defense, and interests of the nation. He gave it his vote of confidence and proceeded to collaborate in the execution of its policies, which further discouraged reconciliation with the foreign element.[17]

Thereafter, both Madriz and the Nicaraguan ambassador in Washington, while disavowing antipathy toward the American residents, continued to emphasize that Americans would henceforth be subject to Nicaraguan laws. They would not be permitted to ignore commercial regulations, including the payment of duties, and they must not participate in insurrections against the military government. While there was no retreat from these strictures, the government-to-government relations between Zelaya's Nicaragua and the United States remained amicable throughout the turmoil in Bluefields.

Meanwhile, discontented Americans from Rama to Bluefields had appealed to the United States for protection of their interests, and, not obtaining it to their satisfaction, inclined to British intervention. This ran counter
to the U.S. policy of supporting Nicaragua in her claim, which was related
to revived interest in an American-controlled Nicaragua canal and in conformity with the Monroe Doctrine and the Clayton-Bulwer Treaty. Although the United States did not countenance the harassment of American
business interests in the area, she shared Nicaragua's fear of revived British
control through the Mosquito government, which had turned to Britain for
help.

There was conflict, as well, between Washington's position and that of
consular representatives in Bluefields, and even the minister in Managua,
Lewis Baker. Baker, dedicated to protecting the interests of the Americans,
had called the Nicaraguan provisional government in the Reserve a "bold
usurpation."[18] The State Department thereupon admonished him: "Take
care to say nothing tending to disparage Nicaragua's rightful claim to paramount sovereignty or to encourage pretensions to autonomous rights incon-
sistent therewith."[19]

It appeared, as the year progressed, that Britain was disinclined to have
further dealings with Mosquitia, other than protection of its resident citizens during the upheaval. British ships, sent to Bluefields, had instructions
to withdraw as soon as they were no longer needed for this purpose, and the
American ambassador to London, Thomas Bayard, confirmed to the secretary of state his belief that Britain's intervention was solely for protection of
its residents and not for upholding the Mosquito government.[20] The British
minister in Managua, Audley Gosling, told the vice president of Nicaragua
that any idea of Britain's desire to resume her protectorate was "farcical" and
that his country welcomed the Reserve's incorporation into Nicaragua, if
that proved to be the wish of its people.[21] However, American residents and
Mosquito government leaders did not recognize or accept the restricted
British objectives. There were reports that the British were going to restore
the deposed Mosquito chief, Clarence. These reports met with enthusiasm
by American residents, though not by their government: "This news created the wildest excitement here and much rejoicing. The Americans were
particularly happy, though they regretted that what they had been pleading
for so strenuously should be done by the British instead of by the American
Government."[22]

The Mosquito government, under its Jamaican leaders, expected Britain
to come to its aid. After all, the British presence had been manifest, from the

outset of hostilities, in its ship *Cleopatra*, anchored off Bluefields. But in the end, this presence proved no more significant than that of the U.S. man-of-war *Marblehead*; they were there to assure stability in a volatile situation that involved nationals of both countries—not to assist or oppose the Mosquito government. Nevertheless, in the summer of 1894 the Mosquito government was so confident of British backing that it was successful (for a short while) in reinstalling itself, along with Chief Clarence. The Nicaraguan troops were forced to withdraw upriver; however, they were back in Bluefields a month and half later. Their reentry, in August, created a wild exodus of some 600 Jamaicans and natives from Bluefields, who took advantage of a British offer to transport them to Puerto Limón. Hearing reports that the Nicaraguans intended to kill them all, "some left all that they had and rushed to the wharves, willing to go in any sort of a craft, their only desire being to get away from Bluefields at once."[23] Meanwhile, the American residents· felt that their interests had not been protected by the marines when the crisis came.

During the year, incidents involving American citizens caused friction between Washington and Managua. The military governor of Rama shot and killed William Wilson, an American employee of the Brown and Harris Company, as he intervened in an arrest on the company's property. The governor afterward fled from Rama, allegedly with the assistance of the local police, and it appeared that the Nicaraguan government made little effort to apprehend him. Accused of anti-Nicaragua activities and collaboration with the pro-British faction, two leading American citizens of Bluefields, John S. Lampton and George B. Wiltbank (both longtime settlers and members of the Mosquito Council), were virtually kidnaped and forcibly taken to Managua by Nicaraguan authorities. (Arrested in the same incident were several British citizens, including the vice consul in Bluefields.) After imprisoning them in Managua, the Nicaraguan government prepared to expel the Americans from the country, without a trial and no charges having been proved. With U.S. intervention, however, these matters were settled amicably.

The proposed Nicaragua canal was always in the background of negotiations, and both countries diligently attempted to be conciliatory. Washington's position on Nicaragua's rights in Mosquitia was clear from the beginning, and the State Department soon dispelled any doubt or ambiguity on the part of its diplomatic and consular representatives who were inclined to favor the *status quo* vis-à-vis American-Mosquito arrangements in the Bluefields-Rama area. Apparently—come what might for the business and culture of American residents on the Shore—they could look to their government for intervention only to assure their individual safety and just treatment, as normally accorded U.S. citizens in foreign countries. Good relations with Nicaragua were desirable because of the proposed canal, and inseparable from this was a long-prevailing policy of thwarting any form of British control or influence in Mosquitia. This would take precedence over any disruption in the lives of American planters and merchants, who lately had established themselves on the Escondido.

That there was still ambivalence, as late as August 1894, in British policy—caused by lingering concern for the Mosquitos—is indicated in this letter from Thomas Bayard, U.S. ambassador in London, to the secretary of state:

> . . . The trace of responsibility for the personal safety of a feeble remnant of an inferior and deteriorating race who were once under her protection in some degree survives, and creates hesitation on the part of Great Britain formally and finally to abandon her obligation to interfere when her former proteges are threatened with gross injustice and oppression.[24]

But this was mainly perfunctory. When the year ended, many notes had been exchanged between Washington and London with regard to "affairs at Bluefields," and it had become apparent that withdrawal, rather than enhancement, of British influence in this area of the world was in the offing. A misreading of British intentions might be excused, after their long involvement with Mosquitia and resulting conflict with both Nicaragua and the United States, but now Britain appeared truly uninterested, and even her post–Treaty of Managua concern for the welfare of the Mosquito Indians, allegedly her reason for continued surveillance, was not voiced very strongly.

Upon regaining control of the reservation in August of 1894, the Nicaraguans, who by then had some experience in dealing with the Mosquito population and were employing more tact, were able to win the confidence of the majority. It was not concerned with the deposed Jamaican government leaders and the foreigners, who were recalcitrant to the last. According to the Treaty of Managua, incorporation could occur whenever the inhabitants of the Reserve freely chose it, and there was little doubt that the Indians, with whom the Nicaraguan government dealt, were ready to choose it. They had long been dissatisfied with the corrupt, self-serving Mosquito government, from which they had been virtually excluded. Accordingly, delegates from all of the native tribes in the Reserve attended a convention and, by unanimous consent, declared for incorporation. Thus, technically at least, the treaty provisions were adhered to.

The declaration reserved for the Mosquito people defined privileges, such as exemption from military service and from personal taxes. Of considerable significance—if it had been carried out—was a provision that revenues produced by the Shore be used for the benefit of its inhabitants. The government of Nicaragua gladly accepted the "free will" act of incorporation, which acknowledged that the area would henceforth be subject to the laws of the republic, that revenues would be collected and administered by the national government, and that no persons, other than Mosquito Indians, would hold elected office in the communities and municipalities. However, because the Mosquito representatives were unable to write, their consent had to be certified by the U.S. consul and three American officials of the Bluefields city government, who signed the document with General Cabezas, the "Intendent-General of the Atlantic Coast of Nicaragua." Consequently, it is questionable if all of the native representatives understood what they were consenting to. In any event, the Nicaraguan government was satisfied that its objectives had been achieved.

Nicaragua assumed control of the Reserve officially in November of 1894 and incorporated it as the Department of Zelaya. At the time, according to estimates (there was no official census), the territory contained over 6,000 Mosquito Indians, mostly scattered in coastal and riverine villages. In addition, Bluefields had a population of about 1,500. Of the 500 Americans in the Reserve, 100 lived in Bluefields, and the remainder of the town's population was mainly Jamaicans and Creoles. The Moravian Church reported that it had thirteen congregations in the Reserve, comprising "5,500 souls— 75 per cent Indians, 25 per cent colored people."[25]

The incorporation ceremony was an inaugural victory for President Zelaya. The prestige he gained by this development, nationally and throughout Central America, was considerable, and his fortunes and those of the Mosquito Coast became closely linked in the following fifteen years.

The United States government was pleased with the outcome. So were the British. The U.S. ambassador to Great Britain, Thomas Bayard, reported to Secretary of State Gresham that the British Foreign Office was satisfied and relieved, as if having ridded itself of something burdensome.[26] When the *Cleopatra* steamed from the roads off Bluefields, it marked the close of the half-century Mosquito controversy between Britain and the United States, and between Britain and Nicaragua.

American commercial interests had lost. Britain, the "ally" they and the Mosquito government had counted upon, had quietly withdrawn and the U.S. policy of support for Nicaragua had prevailed. As Morrow states, "thus passed into history one of the few conflicts between United States governmental policy and United States business men."[27] But despite the abolition of the reservation and their reluctance to submit to Nicaraguan control, Americans and American business interests remained the mainstay of the Mosquito Coast society and economy. As they had anticipated, however, they never again had the freedom to pursue their gains as in previous years.

Zelaya, like his contemporary, Porfirio Díaz of Mexico, recognized the value of foreign investment in the economic progress of his country. However, he was unwilling to let Nicaragua be exploited freely, without restrictions—what many foreign businessmen wanted. The hitherto profitable business interests of the Mosquito Shore now faced strict controls in the form of discriminatory tariffs; grants of monopolies for imports, exports, and the marketing of products; and awards of concessions (subject to arbitrary cancellation if better terms could be anticipated elsewhere) for land exploitation or projects. The practices had the effect of favoritism for a few—at a price—but denial for most. There was no longer the extreme *laissez-faire* arrangement, previously enjoyed by all foreigners in the Mosquito Reserve, and this was resented by both the British and Americans. There is no doubt that Zelaya and his close associates personally profited from the controls. That was part of the objective. But now, for the first time, the Caribbean enclave, especially its economic center of Bluefields, was under the direct supervision of the Nicaraguan government—another objective. Meanwhile, Americans on the Shore became embittered and complained to their government.

According to a census compiled in 1899 by the U.S. consul in Bluefields, there were in that city fifteen American firms or individuals engaged in wholesale and retail trade, with a total capitalization of over $1 million. The largest mercantile companies were Brown and Harris and Samuel Weil and Company, each with a capitalization of $250,000. On the Escondido and its tributaries were fifteen large banana plantations, owned by American individuals. Much larger were the four owned by corporations, and especially those of Brown and Harris and Weinberger's shipping company, Bluefields Steamship Company. Many service activities were also in the hands of Americans, for example, ship repairs, tanneries, ice factories, and hotels. There were eleven American-run transport services, with the Bluefields Steamship Company by far the dominant one.[28] They conducted the steamboat service on the Escondido and other rivers of the former reserve (San Juan services apart), and operated coastal schooner and sloop services connecting Bluefields with Greytown, on the one hand, and with coastal and lagoon points northward as far as Cape Gracias a Dios.

Within the Department of Zelaya, or the former Reserve (often distant from Bluefields but still served by it), were many other American interests. There were a number of isolated gold-mining camps at interior locations, and one of the large operations was that of the long-enduring La Luz and Los Angeles Company at Siuna. However, the most imposing single-company enterprise in the backlands was mahogany cutting and milling, by the John D. Emery Company of Boston. In the years preceding incorporation, its operations had been expanded without much regard to the demarcation line, in some cases into areas Nicaragua claimed were outside the Reserve; so conflict with the government came early. Indeed, one of the first harassing actions by Nicaraguans after the Austrian arbitration was against Emery. Though it was to have more troubles with the Zelaya government, in 1898 it had just renegotiated its contract and was thriving, averaging shipments of 12,500 logs annually. At its main La Cruz camp, it had 20 miles of tramway, and as many miles of standard-gauge railway, and three engines and thirty-two cars. Six hundred workers were employed locating and cutting trees, getting the logs out, and preparing them for shipment. (The company at times exported 2,000 mahogany logs per month from this camp alone.) The concession averaged about one tree to the acre (rosewood and cedar, as well as mahogany, were cut) and each tree produced about 2½ logs.[29] Trails were opened on each side of a stream for a distance of 2 miles, which were paralleled at one-quarter-mile intervals by other trails; then men were dispatched along the trails to locate and count the trees in each tract. Hauling the logs to a river or railway required many mules and oxen. The company constructed camps as the logging advanced, and provided housing, pasturage, and sawmills.

On an experimental basis, a number of Americans established rubber plantations during the late 1890s (most of these were in the Pearl Lagoon area). They were an outgrowth, so to speak, of wild rubber collection, which extended back three decades. Wild rubber production had been on the decline, due to reckless and improvident methods of exploitation, and the Americans hoped that their plantations of *Castilloa elastica* would profit from the greatly increased world demand at the turn of the century. The oldest trees, planted on the Tennessee Plantation in 1897, were tapped in 1904—6,000 of them, all grown from nursery stock to a height of 40 to 45 feet, with circumferences of 17 to 30 inches. Though care was taken to tap the trees (especially the small ones) only slightly this first time, the yield, only 534 pounds of rubber, was disappointing.[30] In the face of the Brazilian boom, rubber was not to have a substantial economic impact for either the Shore or for Nicaragua, and production from the experimental plantations did little to compensate for the decline in wild rubber exports of prior years. This was one of the least promising of American endeavors.

By 1904 there was hardly a major business or import-export activity on the Mosquito Shore which was unaffected by the monopolistic policies of the Zelaya government. Monopolies were granted for the sale of native spirits, native-grown tobacco, gunpowder and dynamite, foreign-manufactured tobacco and cigars, and foreign alcoholic beverages. Monopolies were granted for offshore fishing rights, rights to gather coconuts, to cut mahogany and cedar, and to collect india rubber. A monopoly was granted for the sale of gasoline for the tugs that operated between the Bluff and Bluefields, which had the effect of a monopoly on lighterage, since it was impossible for competition to develop due to the high price on gasoline. A monopoly was granted for butchering, and thus for control of the meat supply and its prices.[31] Americans received many of the monopolistic concessions (for example, the Emery Company held the monopoly on mahogany cutting), but some went also to Nicaraguans and Europeans friendly to the Zelaya regime.

After mergers, Weinberger's Bluefields Steamship Company was the giant in the Nicaraguan banana business in 1897. Soon after its founding in 1899 (by the merger of the Keith interests with the Boston Fruit Company), United Fruit Company began a policy of acquiring controlling interest in competitive companies, and Bluefields Steamship Company was one of these. When it became a subsidiary, it continued to operate under its old name. In 1904 it received the sole concession for navigation on the Escondido River and thus for the shipment of the area's bananas. Individual planters, who did not work the land that belonged to the steamship company, found themselves at its mercy. The company charged whatever it wished for transportation, while paying the lowest price for first-quality fruit. There was no third party to appraise the fruit. Planters had to accept the price or allow the fruit to rot, as there was no alternative way of selling it. In this notice, the company and the Nicaraguan government made it clear that the planters had no choice:

NOTICE

There being rumors in circulation among the public, of the arrival of a steamer in opposition to the Bluefields Steam Ship Co. Ltd., who enjoys the right of navigation on the Escondido River and its tributaries, by reason of a concession granted to them by the Supreme Government of the Republic of Nicaragua; and as I have been informed that planters are deliberately with-holding their fruit in consequence of such rumor, I herewith give due and public notice:

"That no steamer other than those of the Bluefields Steam Ship Co. Ltd. will be permitted to ascend the Escondido River and its tributaries in search of fruit and I do this to protect the planter for the purpose that he may cut and ship his fruit and carry out the obligations entered into by the Government of the Republic."

Bluefields, October 24, 1904

The Bluefields Steam Ship Co. Ltd.

R. C. Bemiss, Manager

The undersigned Governor and Intendente of the Department herewith notifies the public and particularly the Banana Planters that, in conformity with the contract celebrated between the Government and Mr. Charles Wein-berger regarding the exclusive navigation on the Escondido river and its tribu-taries, no steamer will be allowed to navigate said river and its tributaries, other than those of the Bluefields Steam Ship Co. Ltd., which is the successor to the above said contract.

Bluefields, October 25, 1904

The Governor and Intendente

JUAN J. ESTRADA[32]

Output of bananas began to decline, since the prices growers received under the noncompetitive buying and shipping arrangement were not re-munerative. For many planters, this seemed to be the end, and more and more of them felt that they should sell out, for whatever they could get, and leave.

What many Bluefields merchants looked upon as a critical measure also came in 1904, when the government, solely in its own interest, gave a concession for construction of a central, covered wharf. Up to that time, all goods went through the customs house at the Bluff, then were lightered to each merchant's wharf, in front of his place of business on the waterfront. This alone was tedious and time consuming. But under the new arrange-ment, goods had to be lightered to the new wharf for a *second* customs check, before release to the merchants. This superfluous check meant additional wharf charges and the extra expense of lightering goods to their establish-ments. It seemed but another method of extracting more revenue for the government and of making business less profitable for American merchants.

Besides the concessions, high and discriminatory tariffs were imposed by the Nicaraguan government upon the former Mosquito Reserve. This was contrary to terms of the Treaty of Managua, signed by Britain and Nicaragua in 1860, which provided for special treatment in the matter of tariffs for the Mosquito Coast, if and when incorporation took place. Soon after the turn of the century, the Mosquito Shore, with only about 10 percent of the population of the country, was contributing 40 percent of the duties collected by the government.[33] Duties on some imported goods were outrageously high—some amounting to as much as the value of the articles. Added to this were municipal taxes on each package, a tax for the hospitals at Bluefields *and* distant León, a tax for the park in Managua. There were valid grounds for complaints of discrimination against Bluefields, in favor of the interior and the Pacific coast, for it was clear that little tax money was returned to Bluefields in the form of local improvements.

For American families of the Shore, even personal affairs were not exempt from government interference. The old fear, expressed by many in 1894—of losing control of their children's education in the English language and according to familiar cultural underpinnings—became a reality a few years later. The Nicaraguan government demanded that all instruction in the Moravian schools be in Spanish. Apart from the Indians, their pupils were almost exclusively foreigners and Anglo-Indian mixed bloods. Very few in these groups knew or understood the Spanish language. So, rather than attempt what they considered impossible and unacceptable, the Moravians closed their schools—particularly to the detriment of the 400 children of Bluefields, including many Americans.

To those affected, this seemed just another attempt to demoralize and diminish all foreign influences along the Shore. The government was not interested, for example, in a Moravian compromise, which would have devoted two-fifths of the class day to Spanish instruction—a fair proportion, considering the makeup of the student body. Moreover, the application of the decree seemed to point to anti-foreign harassment: Bluefields, where most of the foreigners lived, was made a special case for compliance, was singled out, while other areas were treated with more leniency.

Also, there was obvious antipathy toward the Moravians, who, Nicaraguans thought, were conspiring to reestablish the Mosquito regime under Chief Clarence. This seemed logical to them, since the Mosquito regime had been the benefactor of the Moravians from the start. The Moravians also incurred displeasure because of their influence over the Mosquito Shore populace. This could not be denied, but, in the eyes of the Moravians and their American supporters, their influence had been gained over the years, legitimately and justifiably. The Moravian mission was alleged by Nicaraguan authorities in Bluefields to have "always been unfriendly and even openly hostile towards the Nicaraguan Government," and to have "taught in its schools and churches the natives to disregard and disrespect the laws and customs of the country."[34] This allegation, no matter how valid, constituted a good basis for the discriminatory actions. The fairly extensive property holdings of the Moravians also came under criticism. The Moravians considered their rights to be legally unassailable, but as the lands had now become valuable, the Nicaraguan government coveted them.

In 1904, as the first decade of Zelaya's rule over the Shore ended, many American and some British interests, merchants and planters alike, remained apprehensive.

8   An Unbuilt Canal
and Greytown's Decline,
1893–1906

While controversy over control of the reservation had raged in Bluefields during 1894, Greytown languished. The climactic events surrounding incorporation were confined to the Mosquito capital, and the economic effects of Nicaraguan control were felt mainly there, in the Escondido Valley, and in more heavily Mosquito-populated areas to the north. Greytown, meanwhile, had gone into rapid decline after the American canal company abandoned its work in 1893, and many foreigners had left. The few remaining American and British residents and businesses, however, became subject to some of the same restrictions as their counterparts farther up the Shore. The Nicaraguan governor forced foreign merchants and plantation owners to pay a "Greytown tax," which was, in effect, a duty on their imports, despite the free-port status granted

Greytown in the 1890s, after the canal construction boom (James W. G. Walker, *Ocean to Ocean*, Chicago: A. C. McClurg & Co., 1902)

by the Treaty of Managua. Here, too, foreign nationals were discontented and complained to their respective governments.

Other events had coincided with the failure of the canal project and were striking at Greytown's very existence—its ability to survive over the years, the commercial role which it had managed to retain. These were the deterioration of transport on the lower river and the diversion of traffic to Corinto, the Pacific port (and thence, via the Panama Railway, across the isthmus), occasioned by the completion of railway connections between it and Managua. Archibald Colquhoun, a traveler and author of a book on the Nicaragua route, observed:

> An air of deep depression hangs over Greytown; business seems to be almost non-existent, and people are waiting for the canal, to which they look to make the fortune of the place. I am not inclined to believe that Greytown will ever become a place of great importance; some city on the lake will have a far better chance; and the prospects of a "boom" on any considerable scale are, I should think, somewhat remote.[1]

Despite the canal company's work, the harbor had become as bad as ever. The prospect of keeping Greytown open as a harbor, to serve the canal after it was built, was slight because the port was situated on an unstable shore of shifting sandbars and the lower San Juan tributaries contributed an abundance of volcanic material. This problem had been considered by some observers to be the weakest aspect of the canal scheme. It would have been a difficult and costly undertaking. Much dredging had been accomplished in the harbor by the Maritime Company, sufficient to allow ocean steamers to enter while work was going on, but by 1895 the sand had again taken over and the abandoned dredges were no longer floating but standing high and dry, like islands embanked by sand. The S.S. *Jamaica* arrived on June 15, 1895, with about 5,000 boxes of miscellaneous cargo consigned to the port, but, due to little water on the bar, plus very rough seas, for two days it was impossible to reach the ship and begin unloading. Then, after the harbor tug and lighters were able to go out, they were beached on the return trip. Crews managed to save much of the freight, but the tug, with damage to its propellers and hull, was almost a total loss. Since it was the only tug serving the port, this seriously affected the business of the town. As for the *Jamaica*, it had to go to Bluefields to discharge the remainder of its cargo, which small coastal schooners transported back to Greytown.[2] Thereafter, ships had to be diverted—some to Limón in Costa Rica, others to the Colorado bar (which had enough water to permit a small steamship to cross it and carry goods from ocean steamers to shore). Meanwhile, river boats came up the river from Greytown, to the junction of the Colorado, then down the Colorado to its mouth, to receive the goods for return to Greytown. Inconvenience, delay, and increased cost were the rule of the day.

Indeed, commercial activity in Greytown often suffered as much from conditions in the lower river as from those of the harbor. The upper San Juan and its tributaries were clear and unusually free of sediment, but below Machuca, the river became subject to silting, beginning at the entrance of the San Carlos River. With its tremendous volume of volcanic sand, this largest tributary built a delta at its mouth, and from that point to the sea, the San Juan, greatly overladen, was obstructed by shifting sandbars. The Sarapiqui River, 25 miles downstream, which also originated in Costa Rica's volcanic highland, contributed its addition of sediment, and the delta of the San Juan began 8 miles below this point. Here the river divided into a number of meandering distributaries, the major one being the Colorado. Because of the shoals in the lower river, and especially in periods of low water, Greytown was often isolated for weeks at a time. May 28, 1897—the arrival of the *Hollenbeck*, a river steamer in regular service between the lake and Greytown—marked only the second time in four months that a river boat had reached the port from the interior.

During the dry season of 1897 (as prevailing in the interior of Costa Rica, where the San Carlos and Sarapiqui Rivers have their sources), a sandbar grew to 3 inches above water level, just below the Colorado distributary, and gradually extended across the San Juan to within 3 feet of the opposite bank.[3] Each year during the dry season, which lasted about three months in the interior, such conditions were common. After incorporation of the Reserve by Nicaragua, more passengers traveled between the western part of the country and Bluefields. Many of these were government administrators, traders and men with newly established business and agricultural interests in the former Reserve. The San Juan, as always, was the only way of entry and exit (except via Panama). If the lower river was closed, there was no alternative but to go by sea, to and from the mouth of the Colorado, for rendezvous with the river boats. Likewise, freight destined for the interior (mainly imported agricultural products and manufactured goods) and exports from the interior (mainly coffee and india rubber) had to be routed via the Colorado, at additional expense.

At Castillo, the only rapids of the San Juan that steamers did not attempt to navigate (except in high water), a railway was now available to take passengers and freight around the rapids. Passage of the rapids below Castillo, including Machuca, the last one, was not a great problem, except when the river was extremely low—as it frequently was. There was little fluctuation in river volume and depth in the upper part of the San Juan, due to the equalizing effect of the lake, but from the San Carlos down, channel conditions were unpredictable. The San Carlos could be torrential, discharging vast quantities of water into the main river and causing it to overflow its banks for many miles (the so-called *Agua Muerte*). At other times, it contributed little water, causing the San Juan to become extremely shallow in its lower reaches.

During this time there were schemes (which never materialized) to improve Monkey Point, a natural harbor about halfway between Greytown and Bluefields, known to be a safe haven for ships of deep draft when the wind was from either the north or east. Government authorities thought that, at modest cost, the harbor could be made secure for shipping, regardless of wind direction, and permit freight to be discharged without lighters. One scheme involved building a railway to the Rama River a short distance to the south, selling lands along the river for the production of bananas, and putting a steamer on the river to carry produce to the railway, which would then convey it to ships in the improved harbor of Monkey Point.

The population of Greytown in 1897 was down to little more than 1,000—half of what it was during the canal construction days. The foreign population constituted about one quarter of the total: 11 percent Jamaican, 2.5 percent American, just under 1 percent British, 0.5 percent German,

El Castillo at the end of the nineteenth century (James W. G. Walker, *Ocean to Ocean*, Chicago: A. C. McClurg & Co., 1902)

and 10 percent other nationalities. The remainder were Spanish Nic-araguans, Creoles, and a few Mosquito Indians. Of the 833 persons over 18 years of age, only about 30 percent were married or had been married (widows and widowers), suggesting that the frontier character of the town had altered but little. About a third of the population were Protestants, a group which consisted mainly of foreigners, Mosquitos, and Creoles.[4]

For a population so small, there was a striking occupational variety in 1897. Among the men, the leading occupations were carpenter (50), clerk (12), farm laborer (36), fisherman (19), laborer (55), merchant (18), sailor (23), servant (56), shopkeeper (13), and tailor (17). The primary and/or service nature of these occupations is apparent; however, this hardly indicates the full variety of occupations in the small town, then declining and more isolated than before. There were among the men, for example, 5 bakers, 4 barbers, 6 blacksmiths, 4 bookkeepers, 6 butchers, 7 copyists, 7 engineers, 5 lawyers, 3 machinists, 4 masons, 6 musicians, 4 painters, 2 photogra-phers, 3 pilots, 7 rubber cutters, 6 shoemakers, and 4 teamsters. Again, among the men, there was one each of the following: druggist, caulker, cigar maker, cook, engraver, hotel keeper, mattress maker, printer, tinsmith, and watchmaker. Two men considered themselves hunters, one was an appren-tice, and six were students. Finally, there were 2 male teachers, 2 physi-cians, 2 clergymen, 1 dentist, and 1 fireman. Most of the women were housewives (258), but some were bakers (8), cooks (3), laundresses (18), seamstresses (28), servants (92), shopkeepers (10), hotel keepers (2), mer-chants (2), cigar maker (1), milliner (1), and teacher (1).[5]

Since there was little opportunity to be employed as a farm laborer in and around Greytown, which was almost totally nonagricultural, this category must refer to former occupation (in most instances) or to temporary employ-ment elsewhere. The term "rubber cutter," used in the census, is assumed to refer to the preparation of india rubber for shipment, as it was a major commodity in Greytown exports.

Increased living costs, and failure to adjust wages to meet them, was doubtlessly a major dissatisfaction within the port town as the century ended, and a reason why many drifted away. Some of this cost was due to the rising shipping charges on imported goods; also, the purchasing power of the Nicaraguan peso had fallen significantly by 1897. In 1895, one had been able to buy 20 pounds of flour with a day's earnings or, with two days' remuneration, a pair of shoes. Two years later, a day's pay would purchase only 15 pounds of flour, and a person had to work two and one-half days to buy a pair of shoes.[6]

    In 1897 the former Pellas steamboat concession on the river and lake, with
all its properties, was sold to the Atlas Company, a British enterprise.
Inland navigation had been conducted by the Maritime Canal Company
from 1889 to 1891, and after it ceased canal construction, steamer service
again became highly irregular as commerce along the route declined and the
Pacific port of Corinto, utilizing the Panama Railway, obtained four-fifths of
the import-export trade of western Nicaragua.[7] The British company, nevertheless, sensed renewed commercial opportunity by 1897. With improved equipment, better management, and the removal of certain
obstructions in the river, it hoped to improve the San Juan's competitive
position and restore some of Greytown's importance as a port. On favorable
terms, it acquired the navigation rights on the San Juan and Lake Nicaragua. To meet the problem of low water and silting of the lower San Juan
(for at least half the year), and to eliminate the necessity that passengers and
freight use the Colorado entry and exit (and thus transshipment), it proposed to construct a railway to Silico Lagoon, at the Colorado confluence
with the San Juan, which had deep water throughout the year. Moreover, in
case a canal should *not* be constructed, it intended to make substantial
improvements of the Greytown harbor and river channel.

    This was the first time, since the days of the American transit companies,
that foreign interests had viewed the San Juan—without a canal—as a
possible commercial asset. Indeed, the Atlas investments (the railway bypass of the lower river was eventually constructed), as well as the river
shipping business, could be lost if the United States constructed a canal.
The company contended that such a project should not be undertaken
without a satisfactory disposition of its concession rights. The U.S. government, however, did not agree that the two matters were related, and refused
to accept responsibility for any damage to enterprises that a canal might
bring.

    Even after the failure of the Maritime Canal Company, the U.S. govern-
ment and public had continued to be concerned with the prospects of a
canal across the Central American isthmus. When a Republican administration returned to power under President William McKinley in 1896, the
movement for a U.S. government–constructed and –controlled canal gained
momentum, which was intensified by the demonstrated need during the
Spanish-American War in 1898. There was consensus that, when an isthmian canal *was* built, it would be through Nicaragua, utilizing the route
projected earlier. Early in his administration, accordingly, McKinley appointed a new commission to survey the Nicaragua route and to make
recommendations. Headed by Admiral John G. Walker, the commission,

with 100 technicians, arrived in Greytown in December of 1897, conducted field surveys throughout 1898, and early in 1899 submitted its report to the president, recommending several modifications of the Maritime Canal Company designs. Apparently, it found that none of the work done by the canal company at such great cost, almost ten years previously, was of any use; and its proposal—assuming the Nicaragua route were chosen—was to begin anew and to relocate the entrance. It emphasized the harbor problem and its urgency in terms almost identical to those which preceded the works of the early 1890s. (The Maritime Canal Company buildings at La Fe ["America"], however, were utilized to house the commission's engineers. These structures, after some ten years of abandonment, were in fairly good condition.)

With the arrival of the commission in Greytown, hopes for the town's revival had been aroused once again. Little though it had to offer, Greytown still seemed disproportionately attractive—in comparison with what surrounded it. In the report of one of the commission engineers are the following comments, referring to the encampment at the old headquarters at La Fe: "This location is healthier and freer from distractions than Greytown,"[8] and later: "I started for Camp Sarapiqui, after experiencing much difficulty in getting the men away from the allurements of Greytown."[9]

There were certainly no "allurements" for the consuls who were stationed there, most of whom considered it a hardship post, and remained only briefly. Increasingly, after the 1860s, there had been dissatisfaction; the pay was too low, according to them, to warrant putting up with the conditions. A consul who wrote to Washington in 1898, requesting a raise, gave ample support for his request:

> . . . San Juan del Norte (Greytown) Nicaragua, is an undesirable and expensive place of residence; and yet it is commercially and politically an important port.
>
> The climate is hot and unhealthy, the society is poor, there are no places of amusement or recreation; there are but few conveniences of life, and communication with the outside world is difficult, infrequent and irregular. It rains almost perpetually—the average annual rainfall being more than 265 inches. Desirable and even comfortable business and dwelling houses are scarce, and living expenses generally are high—nearly everything consumed by foreigners is imported in tins from New York.[10]

Commission engineers found the labor situation very unsatisfactory. Typically, appraisals of the labor force attributed its low quality to lack of initiative and incitement to incentives, as normally felt by "people of better races."[11] This attitude toward work was very frustrating to the American engineers, who sometimes minimized the enervating climate and the natives' physical capacity as factors.

The commission was impressed that there seemed to be no attempt to cultivate crops in the San Juan Valley. (Actually, this was more the rule than the exception, and the situation was not to change in the twentieth century.) The relative abundance of fruits, vegetables, coffee, and sugar cane, grown in riverside clearings during the 1880s, was no more, and the cattle were few and extremely inferior. Banana production was minimal, due to shipping problems. Bananas and plantains, nevertheless, were generally well suited to conditions of the valley and constituted the staple food of the few natives along the river. The delta soils, of volcanic origin, were not lacking in fertility; but there was the problem of excessive rainfall, with no dry season, which made the delta unsuitable for most food crops. Where the soils were good, the cost of clearing the forest and providing adequate drainage was prohibitive, and away from the delta and the river, the soils became poor sands and leached clays. That the commission soon recognized the area's low potential is obvious in its report:

> Considering the location, present condition of river and seaport, the climate and rainfall, I deem this valley about as valuable as our western deserts, and that it will take as much energy and industry to develop it as it has to transform these western wastes with which we are familiar.[12]

This is an interesting and unusually candid commentary, compared with the almost unanimous praises of the country's productivity and promise for agriculture, by observers earlier in the century. (Most of them, proponents of colonization schemes or a Nicaragua canal, were limited in objectivity and anxious to impress, even at the cost of accuracy.)

However, the geologic report, submitted to the Nicaragua Canal Commission of 1897–99, had only this to say about fault-related earthquakes:

> Earthquakes of the latter class, due to dislocations of the strata, are perhaps no more liable to occur in the vicinity of the Nicaraguan Canal route than elsewhere, and hence they do not constitute a danger which is peculiar to this region any more than to almost any other in which a ship canal might be constructed.[13]

According to this report, the only danger from earthquakes to the eastern division of a canal was the Costa Rican volcanos, which the report discounted because of the distance. Although volcanic activity and faults are geographically related in Nicaragua, some of the most destructive earth-quakes have resulted from displacement along fault lines, and not from volcanic explosions.

In June of 1898, after receiving an offer from the Maritime Canal Company to sell its concession and holdings to the U.S. government for $5.5 million, Senator John T. Morgan of Alabama, the foremost Nicaragua proponent, introduced a bill providing for government construction, operation, and fortification. However, the Senate postponed action on the bill until the next session. The following December, when the session convened, President McKinley's message to Congress urged construction of an isthmian canal under U.S. control, though not specifying that the site be Nicaragua. McKinley's secretary of state, John Hay, who did not support unilateral abrogation of the Clayton-Bulwer Treaty (favored by some of his predecessors), immediately opened negotiations with the British, aimed at mutual abrogation.

In the spring of 1899, congressional proponents of the Panama site were successful in delaying further Nicaragua considerations by the creation of yet another presidential commission to reinvestigate the matter of isthmian canal locations, this time to include Panama and other sites. The Second Walker Commission, as it was called, engaged a force of engineers and laborers, totaling 850 men, and dispatched the majority (more than 600) to Nicaragua. Separate parties conducted surveys at all sites during the next two years.[14] Early in 1900, the commission members themselves inspected the entire San Juan route before proceeding to Panama. As chairman, Admiral Walker made inquiries of the French company as to the sale of its Panama assets, but in November of 1900 the commission recommended Nicaragua as the preferred route. The decision seemed not to be based upon technical advantages that the route might have over that of Panama; in fact, most of the commission members were inclined toward the latter in this regard, and the report admitted that the Panama project would cost less, provide a shorter canal, and require less transit time. The recommendation for Nicaragua resulted from failure to come to terms with the French company over the purchase of its concession and anticipated difficulties in obtaining an agreement with Colombia on territorial rights in Panama.

In the frenzy caused by the possibility of the United States' constructing a canal after the Walker Commission's survey and report, land speculation was rampant along the sleepy tropical banks and in the rainforest fastnesses of the San Juan. The Nicaraguan government granted huge land concessions to its high officials, not only within the vicinity of the proposed canal but wherever rock and other construction materials were available, as at Monkey Point. The idea was to "corner" the lands that might be affected by the canal, even those beyond its immediate vicinity, and to realize enormous profits from the U.S. government and sales to individuals.

Anticipation at Greytown was so great that it was almost impossible to buy real estate at *any* cost—in this decrepit and decaying port, whose harbor and river had long been incapable of sustaining even its earlier levels of activity. Nor was it at all certain, furthermore, that Greytown would be the terminus of the proposed canal, as several other sites were under consideration. The U.S. consul reported to his superiors in mid-1901: "There is no consulate subject to harder conditions and less conveniences of life, that has more adverse climatic conditions to contend with."[15] There was still no agricultural production. Besides the expense of imported food, the boredom of eating canned foods—without ever anything fresh—made for discontent. Yet there were redeeming features, it was said, such as freedom from yellow fever, the scourge of other tropical places in Central America. And officials did not hesitate to emphasize Greytown's importance as the seat of a consular district, containing American investments exceeding $4 million, with more American residents than any other consular district in Central or South America at the turn of the century, in their requests for pay raises.[16] Although this was true, the town (as opposed to the district it administered) had obviously become a struggling backwater outpost, abandoned by most Americans (except the consuls).

San Carlos, the Lake Nicaragua approach to the projected canal (at the other end of the San Juan), was also the site of many land grants to favored persons within or close to the government. No matter that San Carlos had deteriorated to little more than a crumbling village surrounding a military fort. It appeared that its new day would come, as one of the canal-route cities.

From December 1900 to June 1902, a battle raged in the United States between the Nicaragua and Panama forces. Commercial interests, which had previously thought only in terms of a Nicaragua canal, began to consider any route across the isthmus that would serve their economic interests as of equal value. A distinction was no longer made. And in the accounts, propaganda, and quotations of the period, amid all the drawn out congressional debates, one can trace the transition of sentiment: Nicaragua canal to isthmian canal, and finally to Panama canal. As soon as the Walker Commission recommended Nicaragua as the proposed route, powerful Republican opponents in the Congress had swung into action. They had the assistance of Philippe Bunau-Varilla, indefatigable propagandist for a Panama canal, who, as a major stockholder in the French company (and a former engineer in its Panama venture), had become vitally interested in selling its concession and properties to the U.S. government. His greatest hope was that French interests could be persuaded to "rescue" the canal and he continued to work toward this end, but to no avail.

The Panama-oriented coalition of Frenchman, business magnates, and Republican leaders in the Senate and House of Representatives became formidable. Its great advantage was the Republican victory in the presidential campaign of 1900. Besides, Senator Mark Hanna, won over to the Panama cause, was the most powerful political leader of his time and very close to both Presidents McKinley and Roosevelt. After a year of Bunau-Varilla's lecturing and pamphleteering in the United States on the merits of the Panama route and speeches by its proponents in the Congress, another break occurred when the French company offered, in January of 1902, at Bunau-Varilla's urging, to sell its Panama concession and properties for $40 million (approximately the value estimated by the Isthmian Canal Commission). Only two months previously, the company had asked for more than 2½ times as much—which had been considered unreasonable and unacceptable by the United States. Although this latest offer did not come in time to keep the bill for a Nicaraguan canal from passing in the House of Representatives, there was still the Senate hurdle. Only two weeks after receiving the French company's offer, Admiral Walker's Isthmian Canal Commission reversed its recommendation and, with President Roosevelt's backing, recommended Panama as the most feasible and practicable route, considering the changed circumstances.

When the House-passed Nicaragua bill came up in the Senate in late January 1902, Panama partisans introduced an amendment which authorized the president to purchase the French company's rights in Panama at the offered price and to secure a canal zone from Colombia. In effect, the amendment made Nicaragua the second-choice site, to be used only if a satisfactory title could not be obtained from the French company and negotiations for territorial rights with Colombia should fail. During the next five months, despite Senator Morgan's efforts, the Panama forces gained momentum. Meanwhile, Secretary Hay's long negotiations with Great Britain reached fruition. It was a period of uncommonly good Anglo-American relations, and the British government, supported by public opinion, gradually became willing (by 1902) to concede to a completely U.S.-controlled isthmian canal in Central America. Britain's control of the Suez Canal, her engagement in the Boer War, the growing animosity of the Germans, and the desire for a firm alliance with the United States were factors. Ratification of the Hay-Pauncefote Treaty and its proclamation in late February 1902 removed the diplomatic obstacle long imposed by the Clayton-Bulwer Treaty.

During the spring of that year, there were Senate hearings in preparation for the forthcoming floor debate which would decide the site of the canal. The hearings drew an admission from most commission members that they really had favored Panama over Nicaragua, but had recommended the latter in their two earlier reports only because of the excessive price originally demanded by the French company. Bunau-Varilla was propagandizing again, this time emphasizing the danger of volcanos and earthquakes in Nicaragua, as opposed to Panama, and converted some highly influential newspapers to the cause. The disastrous and highly publicized eruption of Mt. Pelee (in Martinique) in May 1902, only a month before the Senate debates were to start, alarmed the U.S. public and placed the "volcano issue" in the forefront at the right time. Immediately after that, Mt. Momotombo, on the shores of Lake Managua in Nicaragua, erupted, causing an earthquake which destroyed railway docks. All of this was extremely beneficial to the Panama advocates. Bunau-Varilla bought blocks of Nicaraguan postage stamps, bearing a view of the Momotombo volcano, and sent one to each senator and congressman as a reminder of Nicaraguans' identification of their country with volcanos—and the menace.

The Nicaragua forces in Congress made many attempts, in the debates of June, to refute the volcano-earthquake danger, emphasizing the infrequency of eruptions and the distance of active Nicaraguan volcanos from the proposed route. To counter the citation of centuries-old Panama City edifices, which were still intact, they cited El Castillo, which, though built in 1675, retained its central tower and high parapets. They referred to the findings of earlier surveys, even those of the Walker Commission, which had not been unfavorable with regard to volcanic activity and seismic disturbances.

However, the threat remained convincing, and Senator Hanna's skillful arguments for Panama were persuasive in the end. Both houses passed the amendment calling for Panama to be the site of a U.S.-constructed canal, and the bill was signed into law on June 28, 1902. Bunau-Varilla afterward expressed his belief that the Nicaragua route would have been chosen had it not been for Mt. Pelee and Senator Hanna.[17] Also, it was known throughout the debates that Panama was the choice of President Roosevelt.

The pro-Nicaragua forces, led by Senator Morgan, did not give up. It was thought that complications over the title and acquisition of rights from Colombia would arise (which Senator Morgan had unsuccessfully attempted to assure by proposing amendments to the Panama bill) and that the choice would ultimately revert to Nicaragua, as the alternative provided for in the legislation. (This is why Senator Morgan finally was willing to vote for the Panama amendment and why he persuaded pro-Nicaragua House Democrats to do the same.) Although complications with Colombia *did* arise, these were resolved by the revolution and the declaration of independence by Panama in the fall of the following year, and there was never a need to consider the second choice.[18]

Throughout this controversy in the United States and afterward, when problems with Colombia stalled definitive action on Panama, the Caribbean and Pacific Transit Company, offspring of the Atlas Company, had trouble with the Nicaraguan government. After the company had completed the short-line railway between Silico Lagoon and the San Juan, according to the terms of the concession, the government claimed that the railway was inferior (its bridges being temporary and of wood) and annulled the contract. The company viewed this as an evasion of the government's commitment to grant it an exclusive monopoly of traffic on river and shore for thirty years. Nevertheless, operations continued without a formal concession; the company carried mail without charge and the government received reduced freight rates, but there were daily harassments, and fear of sudden interruption of services was ever present. In developing its stranglehold on the company now engaged in San Juan shipping, the government was attempting to seize the old Maritime Canal buildings and workshops, which Atlas had bought at auction. Apparently, it was waiting for the opportune moment to seize the steamer fleet as well.

The government planned to open Monkey Point, with its natural deepwater harbor, as a new port; and back of this, in the view of some, was the desire to put Greytown out of business once and for all. Greytown's status as a free port, under the terms of the Treaty of Managua, had always been distasteful to the government, which perceived the advantages of a completely new port and a customs house under its control. Improvement of Greytown's harbor and the lower river was not necessarily in its best interests.

The possibility of a U.S. canal also figured in the Monkey Point plans. President Zelaya and his confidantes owned the surrounding lands in the

Rama Valley. Because the heavy machinery and other materiel that would be necessary in constructing the canal could not be unloaded at Greytown, due to its bar, wharfage at Monkey Point or Punta Gorda might profitably be sold to the United States, as well as the coastwise steamship concession between those two harbors. The plans also envisioned an extension of the old Maritime Canal Company railway (12 miles of which had been completed) from its seaward terminus at America up the beach to Monkey Point. Some bridges would be necessary and, at the 1-mile segment of canal at the seaward end (the only part ever constructed), possibly a causeway. Otherwise, the government seemed to view the project as relatively easy and inexpensive.

Another plan was to extend the railway from its interior terminus to the San Juan above the section that became impassable during the dry season. Thus if both the lower stretch of the San Juan and Greytown harbor could be bypassed by rail, traffic could once again move between the Pacific and Caribbean, and connect with overseas shipping, without major hindrance. Although none of these plans materialized, they were part of a deliberate (and finally successful) effort to destroy the Caribbean and Pacific Transit Company's operations, which had worked to the advantage of Greytown.

After it became certain that a U.S. canal would not be built in Nicaragua, but in Panama, there was such an exodus of Americans from Greytown that the U.S. consul recommended a British-subject appointment as his vice consul. There were no eligible persons of American birth from whom to select one.[19]

Consular fees for the fiscal years 1902 through 1905 declined from $1,184 to barely over $150.[20] In July of 1904, the Caribbean and Pacific Transit Company finally made the decision to suspend all river service, with notice to the Hamburg American Steamship Company that no more import or export freight could be handled. The mother company, the Atlas Line, also ceased calling at Greytown, after its scheduled steamer arrival that July. The American consul, John Hill, wrote to Washington as follows concerning this calamity for the river route and its port, which Atlas had attempted to save:

> The C. & P. Transit Co. have been forced to take this step and give up what has been and still might be a lucrative business by a succession of obstacles caused by the necessity of crossing an ever changing and dangerous bar and by the navigation of a river filled with perilous rapids, but more than all by the systematic persecution of the Nicaraguan Government.[21]

The company had just lost a tug to the bar, and this influenced its decision to withdraw. In these circumstances of extreme uncertainty, the company was not willing to build a replacement. Shortly thereafter, the Nicaraguan government let it be known that the New Orleans–based Bluefields Steamship Company—the same company that had been given the Escondido and banana-shipping monopolies—would replace the British company on the San Juan and Lake Nicaragua, with exclusive privileges.

Discussion of channelization of the San Juan became more common in Greytown after the canal fantasies evaporated. The cost of channelization would have been a small fraction of the cost of a canal, and it would have allowed all-season shipping from the lake directly to the sea, eliminating the seven dry-season transfers. However, there was little likelihood that even minor improvements in navigation would be made by the new, monopolistic enterprise, operating hand in glove with the Zelaya regime. In the atmosphere recently created by the Nicaraguan government, investment by other interests (feasible though it might be) was not likely. In fact, improvement of the San Juan route would have been counter to the government's plans for Monkey Point and the railway to it. The latter was the project into which the government put whatever funds it had—reportedly enough to construct about 20 miles of railroad to open up lands owned by the president and his friends for banana production. Even so, few in Greytown believed that the railroad would be extended farther. Talk of pushing the line through to Managua, most believed, was meant to hasten the demise of San Juan del Norte as a free port by frightening the remaining merchants away. In any case, the river improvement and the Monkey Point projects were rivals for the same trade potential and investment dollar, and both could not be supported simultaneously. As it turned out, *neither* would be.

After the loss of the Caribbean and Pacific Company's tug in 1904, the only means of reaching an ocean vessel beyond the bar at Greytown was by dory or canoe. The vessel in question was a Bluefields Steamship Company vessel out of New Orleans, which, by terms of the contract with the Nicaraguan government, was obligated to call at Greytown every three weeks. It was the town's sole contact with the outside world. The ship would anchor outside the bar, blow its whistle to announce its arrival, and, unless someone in a small boat took the risk and ventured over the bar, weigh anchor and proceed to Bluefields, where it would discharge any passengers or freight destined for Greytown.

Downriver transport bypassed Greytown completely. Flat barges went down the Colorado branch to the ocean, where a Nicaraguan government-subsidized schooner met them and transferred their passengers and freight directly to Bluefields. There was no longer any booking of passengers to and from Greytown; tickets were sold only to or from the Colorado's bar or its junction (with the San Juan). Inbound or outbound Greytown passengers had to make their connections by canoe. Regardless of the delay, inconvenience, and extra expense, they were required to pay the full fare which had previously been in effect. Freight destined for the interior also had to be delivered to either of these two points, and freight destined for Greytown was brought only to these places. The river journey to the interior had become very primitive, even by comparison with earlier times, and was to remain so. It was described as follows:

> The transportation facilities on the San Juan River, for the interior, are inadequate, three trips being made each month, with flat lighters poled by boatmen to Colorado Junction, a distance of twenty miles, where a transfer is made to small river steamer to Machuca rapids, then to barge to head of rapids, then to small steamer to foot of Castillo rapids, then to tram-car around the rapids, then to river steamer to Fort San Carlos, the whole comprising a distance of less than 90 miles and consuming three and one-half days in the trip, to say nothing of the hardships endured by the passengers who have scarcely standing room on these disgusting flat boats, not even a bench for a seat, must take their own blanket for a covering at night and a mosquito-bar as protection from insects at night, or day, where they must stand or lie on the cargo, which invariably receives more attention than the passengers.[22]

A great blow to Greytown was official annulment, by the Nicaraguan government, of its free-port privileges. This status, established by the Treaty of Managua in 1860, had been tolerated after incorporation of the Mosquito reserve as part of the republic in 1894, but only to a degree. As noted, merchants and plantation owners had been compelled to pay taxes to Nicaragua, purportedly for port maintenance (promises to maintain and improve its facilities were not kept) and municipal services. This was equivalent to paying import duties on their goods. After the decree abolishing free-port status, the government agreed to credit these payments against future duties.

During its free-port heyday, Greytown had been a center for smuggling by blacks and Mosquito natives, who, to make things look legitimate, lived ostensibly as fishermen. These men were expert boatmen—a talent handed down from the early Mosquito Indians, with the propensity to engage in contraband traffic. They built their canoes for speed, and with the concealment afforded by the bars and lagoons of the area and the maneuverability of their craft in such waters, they operated profitably, with little danger of detection. The smugglers obtained goods that came into Greytown free of duty and hid them in caches up and down the Coast, in both Nicaragua and Costa Rica. They sold these goods periodically, as the opportunity afforded, at much lower prices than the merchants outside of Greytown, subject to the stiff Nicaraguan duties on imports, could afford to. Even so, the smugglers made substantial profits. A large part of the goods that entered Greytown free of duty, particularly liquor, tobacco, boots, and shoes, were not consumed there.

Greytown lost this thriving segment of its economy when the port became no longer "free" and Nicaraguan customs officials arrived. The smuggler population, in their shacks along the beach, no longer had any reason to remain, and had to seek sustenance elsewhere. There was no demand for labor in the port any more, and even if there had been it would not have attracted any of the smugglers, who were disdainful of any kind of laborer classification, and really too lazy, and too accustomed to the "free" life.

In full control at Greytown, the Nicaraguan government now confiscated the remaining property of the Maritime Canal Company, under the forfeiture provisions of the concession. But it found little of value. In a state of virtual abandonment were a few locomotives, some tow boats, boilers, and an abundance of rails and pipe. The dredges that had been left were in bad condition. The many tons of steel rails, used and unused, could be utilized for the government railways in the interior. The locomotives, however, though in fair condition but needing repairs, were of much broader gauge than those on Nicaragua's railways. The buildings (at La Fe) could be disassembled and the serviceable lumber used for public buildings in Greytown or transported to the interior. Whatever lumber was not rotted was worth the effort, in view of the fact that it had been imported from the United States and was unavailable locally.

The condition to which Greytown had been reduced by 1905 is summed up in the following excerpt from a dispatch of the U.S. consul, Frederick M. Ryder:

> In the present decadent state of San Juan del Norte, with its former business interests crippled almost beyond resuscitation; its warehouses falling into decay—and into the river in many instances; with positively no future, from a business standpoint, to relieve it from the present conditions; with practically no transportation facilities; with direct steamer communication with the United States, via Bluefields, once in three weeks; with only two American subjects in the town, and these having no business interests worth mention-

ing; with so little employment for the inhabitants that the small coasting
schooners are carrying away more passengers than they should with safety, as
the residents, who have lived here for many years, are so anxious to get away,
to Bluefields or elsewhere, where they can secure work—and this has been
carried on for some time, and to such an extent that, I firmly believe, the
population will not at present exceed 350 to 400 people. Under these conditions, which exist to-day, what necessity is there for a resident Consul at this
port?[23]

The consul also pointed out the lack of logic in Greytown's remaining the
chief consulate post with authority over Bluefields, which had simply a
consular agency. He rebuked his predecessor for misleading the State Department in a report of 1900, in which the latter stated that American
interests in the consular district had increased so greatly that his office
should be elevated and that he should receive a higher salary. He should have
admitted, Ryder wrote, that all of the increase had occurred within the
jurisdiction of the Bluefields agency, and for this reason should have recommended that the consulate be transferred to Bluefields and the consular
agency established at Greytown.

It was Bluefields which needed stronger, official U.S. representation.
Instead, a resident had been chosen as agent to represent U.S. interests
there, who often had conflicting interests and was involved (and therefore
biased) in local undertakings and activities, political and otherwise. Moreover, communications between Bluefields and Greytown were so poor, time
consuming, and unreliable that when matters of vital importance, involving
American citizens, had arisen, the Bluefields agent, needing advice from his
superior at Greytown, was unable to take the proper action at the proper
time.

For his part, regardless of whether the consulate remained in Greytown
or was transferred to Bluefields, Ryder had apparently had enough, and—
like many of his predecessors—requested a transfer. "I much prefer wearing
out in a temperate climate [he wrote] to rusting out in a tropical one."[24]
Nevertheless, almost a year later, he was still in his unappealing and inactive
post and still writing his pessimistic reports. Greytown's American population at that time was exactly six, and none was engaged in a commercial
enterprise. "Many Americans," he said, had "removed" themselves, and
"the remainder [were] in the cemeteries."[25]

9   American Business
along the Shore
in Unstable Times,
1906–1920

                        If American business interests in Nicaragua were unhappy with President José Santos Zelaya, so, increasingly, was the U.S. government. The deteriorating relations were linked to many complaints in Washington about Zelaya's inimical practices toward Americans doing business in Nicaragua, mainly on the Mosquito Shore. But there were also other reasons for the growing ill will. In 1901, Zelaya's nationalism had obstructed any compromise over extraterritorial rights for the United States if a Nicaraguan canal should be built, and this was a factor in turning the United States toward negotiations with Colombia for Panama rights. With the abrupt ending of U.S.–Nicaragua negotiations over a canal, the United States incurred Zelaya's enmity. Bad relations with the U.S. government also developed after 1903, as a result of his belligerency toward neighboring Central American states, which he had previously attempted to rally to unionism. While not wishing to intervene actively, the United States attempted, during the years following the Panama decision, to keep Central America peaceful and thus stable. But Zelaya's policies, seemingly designed to dominate the other countries, led to greater and greater turmoil. With Manuel Estrada Cabrera, a rival dictator in Guatemala, Zelaya flouted peace treaties and fought over control of Honduras and El Salvador. The United States restrained from physical intervention on behalf of Nicaragua's beleaguered neighbors, but its mere presence as a moral force, diplomatically engaged, was an obstacle that intensified Zelaya's anti-American feelings.

Things appeared encouraging when the Central American states agreed to meet in Washington in 1907 to resolve their difficulties. In an unusually conciliatory atmosphere, all five countries signed a compact which, had it been respected, would probably have brought peace and stability to the isthmus. It provided for a Central American court to settle disputes, refusal to allow their territories to be used for revolutionary movements against other countries, restriction of the activities of political refugees from other states, nonrecognition of governments that gained power by revolutionary means, and the permanent neutrality of Honduras, whose weakness and central position had been critical in the recent isthmian conflicts.

There were violations of the Washington accords during the following two years, however, and peace was jeopardized. The William Howard Taft administration blamed Zelaya, but Guatemala's Estrada Cabrera was equally responsible. Of the two, Zelaya was more openly defiant of the United States, and his many offensive actions (beyond the flouting of treaties) could not escape notice. There were disputes over cancelled American concessions, including the sizable Emery one, whose holders pressed for compensation. The Nicaraguan government rebuffed the U.S. representatives who were sent to Managua to discuss the matter, and this further soured relations. Zelaya negotiated a British loan for construction of the long-proposed railway to the Atlantic coast, and made overtures to Japanese interests about building a canal. This met with U.S. disapproval, as any foreign connections or indebtedness on the part of Central American states were abhorrent.

It was within this antagonistic atmosphere that incidents on the Mosquito Shore proved climactic. In May of 1909 the independent native and foreign banana planters went on strike against the Bluefields Steamship Company, and there was much destruction of property. This unrest was followed, six months later, by a full-scale revolution against the Zelaya government, starting in Bluefields. The east coast city had become a stronghold of dissatisfaction with the regime, and Conservatives could rely upon much support there, including financial assistance from the foreign colony. As a springboard for revolutionary activity, it also provided a measure of protection because of its location, distant and separated by wilderness from the rest of the republic. Also, Juan B. Estrada, the Liberal governor of Zelaya Department and an appointee of the president, defected to the Conservatives and became the revolutionary leader. His assistance was critical to the initial success of the revolution, for the Conservatives were thereby able to secure control of most of the east coast, as the garrison at Bluefields was turned over to them. The Conservative rebels raised a sizable army and established a *de facto* government, with Estrada as provisional president, before the Managua authorities were able to take the offensive.

Although local representatives of the U.S. government appeared to encourage the revolutionary activity, the official policy of Washington was

initially neutrality. In the beginning, the rebels, and their American supporters on the scene, hoped for help, but had no assurances. War vessels,
sent at the outbreak of hostilities, had instructions from the Navy Department to protect American interests only. Despite this formal neutrality,
there was little doubt that Zelaya's overthrow would be welcomed in Washington.

The occasion to abandon neutrality came when Zelaya's forces, proceeding down the San Juan River to attack the rebels on the coast, captured two
American soldiers of fortune (officers in the revolutionary army) while they
allegedly were attempting to blow up a government ship with mines. The
men were executed, which Zelaya claimed was justifiable under the circumstances of capture and Nicaraguan law, which provided the death penalty
for rebellion. The U.S. position was that the men should have been treated
with the humanity accorded to prisoners of war. Moreover, the incident
appeared to be pointedly anti-American in view of the fact that Frenchmen,
captured with the Americans, were not executed.

Since the Americans were part of the revolutionary army, engaged in
sabotage, and it was a time of war, the unfortunate fate of the American
mercenaries was hardly extraordinary. For the United States, nevertheless,
it was the final offense in a long series of grievances against Zelaya, and
sufficient to cause a break in diplomatic relations and abandonment of
neutrality. The secretary of state, Philander C. Knox, in a bitter note,
emphasized Zelaya's aggressive and obstructionist acts of destabilization in
Central America over the years and his refusal to abide by the Washington
agreements of 1907. He did not disguise the U.S. government's moral
support of the revolution and implied that a heavy indemnity would be
demanded for the execution of the Americans, if the Liberal government
remained in power. With the prospect of physical intervention by the
United States in support of the rebel cause, Zelaya's hopes to continue his
long dictatorship dimmed. His friend, Porfirio Díaz of Mexico, concerned
about the strong reaction of the United States and fearful that a Conservative
victory in Nicaragua might bring Guatemala's Estrada Cabrera to power
over all of Central America, attempted to defuse the controversy by urging
Zelaya to resign in favor of José Madriz, another Liberal, who was thought
to be more acceptable to the United States. Zelaya resigned in December of
1909 and went into exile.

It was at this point that a lengthy period of U.S. intervention in Nicaraguan affairs began. The revolution continued, with the U.S. State Department refusing to recognize the Liberal successor government, which it

considered too closely linked with Zelaya's policies. With the security of the Panama Canal (under construction) at stake, American businesses clamoring for protection, and the ever-present fear of excessive foreign influences, a stable, friendly government and a viable economy in Nicaragua became major objectives of U.S. policy as formulated by Secretary of State Knox. In his view, accomplishment of these objectives rested upon Nicaragua's financial rehabilitation. With the concurrence of President Taft, he initiated arrangements to have American banks extend loans to the country, to be secured by customs collections under the direction of State Department appointees. Under such a system, Taft and Knox expected that Nicaragua's reliance upon foreign loans could be reduced; claims (many by American concession holders) against the Zelaya regime, resulting from the revolution, could be settled; and economic development could ensue. Not forgotten in these considerations was the fact that Nicaragua still possessed the alternative canal site, whose exclusive rights the United States was later to secure.

These plans for Nicaragua appeared to rest upon a rebel victory and a government thoroughly purged of Zelaya influences. The United States played a decisive role in bringing this about. When the forces of Zelaya's successor Liberal government attempted a blockade of Bluefields, the only important place held by the Conservative rebel army (which had been surrounded), a U.S. warship stood by and refused to permit military actions which might endanger American lives and property. Furthermore, it prevented any disruption in shipping. Because of this, the Liberal forces were compelled to withdraw and the rebels followed them to the interior. New outbreaks of rebellion, in various parts of the country, further weakened the government, and its army was defeated at Granada in August of 1910, whereupon the revolutionists entered Managua.

After two decades, the Conservatives were again in control of the presidency. Estrada, the first of the rebels to assume the office, and his vice president, Adolfo Díaz (a former employee of an American gold-mining company in the Atlantic region), were willing to cooperate with the U.S. State Department by making the desired financial reforms. The new government committed itself to negotiation of loans with U.S. banks, customs collections under the control of American representatives, and the establishment of a Nicaraguan-American commission to review the many claims. Meanwhile, however, the two other revolutionary leaders, who also were members of the Conservative coalition, Generals Emiliano Chamorro and Luis Mena, were rival contenders for power and did not give their full support to the Estrada regime. Opposition to the close alliance between the new government and American interests mounted, and interfactional strife, manifested in the new cabinet and in the national assembly (which eventually convened), together with continuing provocations by pro-Zelaya elements, kept the government unstable and delayed progress in carrying out the promised reforms. Mena, the minister of war, with the army behind him, assumed more and more control. Estrada, finally, resigned in May of 1911 and Díaz took over as president. However, this did not improve matters.

Mena, with his eye on the presidency, refused to cooperate with either Díaz or the United States in their arrangements for the financial "protectorate" in Nicaragua. Díaz, convinced that a new revolution was coming, informed the U.S. State Department of his wish that the "protectorate" be expanded to include the right of American intervention in behalf of his "lawful government," if needed. By this time even Chamorro, leader of a third Conservative faction (he, too, wished to be president), was wary of Mena's ambitions and began to oppose him.

Mena, the dissident general, mounted his revolution in July 1912, with the assistance of pro-Zelaya Liberals and elements of the army that were loyal to him. This attempt to bring down the U.S.-supported Díaz government, using Zelaya forces, was interpreted in Washington as a clear defiance of the Taft-Knox "dollar diplomacy" in Nicaragua; and at this point another form of U.S. intervention was introduced: military engagement—but no longer simply a show of force, as at Bluefields.

After an appeal from Washington for protection of American lives and property during the revolution, President Díaz invited the United States to send its own forces to provide this protection, not only for U.S. citizens but for the Nicaraguan populace. The response was immediate. Within one month, a force of U.S. marines and navy men, numbering in the thousands, was in the country. Not only did they assist in protecting the capital, they held the vital railway line to Corinto and kept it open for the government. Later, they joined in attacks upon rebel-held positions. All of this alarmed the neighboring Central American states, which entered futile protests. After two months, discouraged by American intervention and a series of defeats, the rebel forces surrendered.

The Conservative government of Adolfo Díaz remained in power, although still beset by interfactional strife. The president was not the most popular leader of his party, but he continued to have the backing of the United States. When, after withdrawal of most U.S. troops, a legation guard of 100 marines remained in the country, it was a symbol of the support that the incumbent government could rely upon against future revolutionary (Liberal) uprisings. In the eyes of the State Department, this was for the benefit of the people of Nicaragua, in that it discouraged restoration of any regime resembling the Zelaya dictatorship.

The marines would remain in the country thirteen years and the objective would be accomplished, but at the price of much Latin American ill will. Despite the internal political "stability," the financial reforms that finally were instituted were not initially effective in eliminating the country's economic ills—the government was constantly faced with insolvency and, unable to meet its expenses, had to resort to new loans. Customs receipts, intended to reduce indebtedness on prior loans, had to be released in order to meet the immediate expenses of the government: unpaid government employees, unpaid awards of the claims commission, and scores of other demands.

Under the circumstances, it is not surprising that civil disorder was widespread in Nicaragua during the decade. The army had been reduced in size, and the salaries of already-underpaid provincial government employees were often in arrears. The Mosquito Shore, remote from the capital, was especially affected by the decline in law and order. For example, the Bluefields business district was subject to numerous fires, whose circumstances suggested arson, and in the confusion following these fires, looting was widespread. Store proprietors and townspeople complained of inadequate protection. During a fire of July 18, 1911, which destroyed about forty houses and stores, the police force itself came under suspicion; policemen were accused of being intoxicated when the fire broke out (in the early morning hours) and of participating in looting a Chinese store.[1] For their negligence, the governor threatened to discharge the entire police force—but this would have meant bringing another indifferent police contingent from the interior, which would not have improved the situation, and there was little hope of drawing replacements from the local population.

With the damages of the revolution itself, much of it fought in eastern Nicaragua, added to the turmoil and economic disarray that followed, Mosquito Shore services deteriorated and businesses suffered. It was soon apparent that the new government was both unwilling and unable to assist with recovery financing, insofar as public works were concerned, to repay its debts to Bluefields merchants who had helped to fund the revolution, or to honor concessions granted by the Zelaya government to "favored" American interests.

In the early part of the decade, following the revolution, an unfortunate situation developed regarding Rio Grande Valley investments by Americans, and the U.S. government was powerless to help. This valley, north of Bluefields, was the second one along the Mosquito Shore (after the Escondido) to be developed for banana plantations. Occupied only by Mosquito Indians until late in the Zelaya years (after the turn of the century), it later became Nicaragua's principal producing zone, reaching an apex in the 1920s under the Cuyamel Fruit Company. It was in this valley that scores of unsuspecting but gullible Americans had purchased land, sight unseen, as shares in bogus stockholding corporations engaged in fraudulent colonization schemes. Once the revolution was over and a new administration in Managua had taken over, uncertainty and worry among the American investors mounted. It appeared that their claims would not be honored by the new government, which they considered to be arbitrary and unjust. It took them a long while to realize that they had been duped by fellow Americans. They wrote frantic letters to the new president of Nicaragua and to the U.S. State Department, to no avail.

By 1912 *The American*, the English-language newspaper of Bluefields, was exposing the banana-land promotion schemes in the United States for the frauds they were. According to the newspaper, even the Pan American Fruit and Fiber Company of Minneapolis, the first company to commence planting in the Rio Grande Valley and the only one to ship out substantial amounts of fruit, had engaged in the most deceitful and exaggerated propaganda to sell its stock to gullible Americans. *The American* contended that Pan American's claims about the possibilities of spectacular production and profits for stockholders, with tiny investments, were not only out of proportion to all prior accomplishments but unattainable. In an article that appeared August 6, 1913, headlined "Come All Ye Banana Suckers," the newspaper made this comment:

> The latest literature to come under our observation is a half-sheet in two colors and much resembling a circus poster, issued from 1102 Plymouth Building, Minneapolis, Minn. It says: "$1.00 down and $1.00 per acre per month pays for your plantation and brings it to bearing. No work — No labor — No worry – No loss." It is a safe bet if the promoters of this scheme can secure enough "banana suckers" they will neither worry, nor labor nor lose.
>
> A banana plantation will come into full bearing in from 12 to 18 months and it can be brought to that condition at an approximate cost of $30.00 per acre. How these promoters can guarantee to buy the land, plant it and care for it up to the complete bearing stage for from $13 to $19 is a financial problem that only a promoter or an expert who has solved the ramifications of the Nicaraguan monetary system would have any business to tackle.[2]

And this was the company which had *done* something. Others, which had sold stock to thousands of small U.S. investors, apparently never made any pretense of cultivating or shipping bananas. At last, some investors discovered that "plantation companies" which had sold them shares of stock in the United States did not even exist.

Not all companies of the valley were merely "fronts" for bogus stock sales in the United States, but few were what they purported to be in their literature. Inspection disclosed that many "plantations" were very poorly cared for and produced very little: there was no thinning, they were overgrown with weeds and bush, and poorly drained, or simply unplanted in many places. In addition, shipping facilities at the river's mouth were inadequate and not in accordance with conditions reported to stockholders. Transport from field to river was frequently unavailable, there being no mules, and the fruit often had to be packed out on men's backs, if it was to be gotten out at all.

Despite the outright fraud, deception, and false propaganda, some U.S. land development companies were responsible in carrying out their commitments in the Rio Grande Valley—an area not lacking in potential. By 1914, several recently initiated plantation enterprises seemed to be getting off to a good start. Some stockholders of Iowa and South Dakota sent an investigator, William H. Miner, down to see, firsthand, one of the plantations owned and operated by a Sioux Falls company, and he appeared to be pleased with what he observed at this and other American plantations along the river. As he proceeded up the hundred-mile length of river, his launch stopped at several plantations to give information as to when to cut and carry bananas to the bank. Sometimes the river boat dropped off empty barges, to be filled for the return trip. Arriving at the Sioux Plantation, Miner found a large-scale establishment, responsibly managed by an American superintendent and foreman, and consisting of a good, comfortable residence house, commissary, storehouse, and outbuildings, including chicken houses.

Of the 5,000 acres owned by the company, 230 had been planted in less than a year, and the banana plants were 2 to 8 feet tall by the time of his visit. Fourteen laborers lived on the plantation, in quarters provided by the company. With the exception of the French, German, and Hungarian plantations along the river, which had almost ceased operations, plantations he visited on his return down the river appeared to be sound enterprises. The most important and best managed of these was the three-year-old Kansas City Plantation, which was shipping over 1,000 bunches of bananas per week from its 400 planted acres (of 10,000 owned). Farther along were seven adjacent plantations, with a 20-mile river frontage, under control of a Chicago corporation, directing operations from a central riverfront office. Finally, the investigator spent a few days at the comfortable, airy, screened and verandahed home of the American manager of another plantation. His wife, with assistance from the laborers, had converted the place into a veritable garden, having planted seed brought from the United States, as well as native transplants, all over the cleared grounds surrounding the house. In the rear was an orchard, with oranges, limes, grapefruit, guava, and other tropical fruits. In sum, Miner was favorably impressed by his trip, and he wrote and published an account of it upon his return to the United States.[3]

But in general, economic conditions were far from healthy along the Shore. Bluefields merchandising firms, which formerly had acted as the bankers for the region, were no longer able to make loans. The long-established private banana plantations, now deteriorating, had depended upon these. Disease was a factor in the decline of these plantations, but the lack of "cleanings" (thinning and weeding) and proper care, because of the shortage of funds, encouraged inroads by disease. Also, the banana plantations had suffered enormous losses during the campaigns of the Zelaya revolution along the Escondido, from Bluefields to Rama and beyond, and no governmental reimbursement or assistance was forthcoming. Trade with the interior, upon which Bluefields depended for its food necessities (such as sugar, coffee, and corn), also relied upon the banking and exchange function of Bluefields' merchandising houses. This trade, consequently, dried up.

Five years after the revolution ended, Mosquito Shore residents had many grievances against the central government. Its officials were corrupt and demanded bribes from businesses to compensate for not being paid by the government. The judiciary was ineffective in the redress of injustices. Geographic separation was as bad as ever. Communication with the interior and with the capital remained, as always, difficult. There was little knowledge in the rest of the country of the Atlantic coast, which, with a small proportion of the total population, contributed the bulk of the national revenue.

Undoubtedly, administrative expenses in the region were inordinately high because of inefficiency and poor management. However, according to residents, the government transferred the substantial amounts collected by the three custom houses on the Coast—enough to make that region self-sustaining—to Managua for application on national debts or expenses that did not benefit the Shore in any tangible form. It failed to settle debts of the revolution, incurred for funds, supplies, and services furnished in its behalf by Atlantic coast inhabitants and businesses. This was particularly embittering because many parties had themselves become indebted to foreign interests, with evidences of the government's indebtedness to them as collateral.

Bureaucratic hamstringing was another grievance, coupled with unethical practices. Americans, interested in mahogany cutting, complained about their treatment. After searching the forests for months, looking for tracts containing merchantable timber, they would file the information with the local governor, as required by law. Shortly thereafter they might receive notification that prior application had been made for the land in question. The information they had turned in to the local government had been used for the benefit of (perhaps) an associate of the governor, who, claiming first discovery, then attempted to realize some personal gain at the expense of the interested Americans.

Likewise, there were many complaints regarding matters in Bluefields. Police and fire protection were almost nonexistent; streets were in a deplorable condition, with bad lighting. A promised waterworks system was not installed (its pipes were removed to Managua). Fire engines, contributed by a foreigner for protection of the city, were badly deteriorated after only six months. "Criminals" served on the police force, having been "exiled" from the interior to the Coast. With government sanction, local officials were free to levy taxes and to use whatever means they wished to secure remuneration for their services. Educational services were poor, no real public school system having been established. To secure even a basic education, it was necessary to go elsewhere, often to a foreign country.

There were no lighthouses at dangerous points along the Coast or at entrances to rivers and harbors. No dredging had been done to improve navigability of the rivers. This had a detrimental effect upon commercial activities, and development attempts seemed continually thwarted. Foreigners who obtained concessions were so burdened with restrictions that profitable operations were often impossible. Eastern Nicaragua had to bear by far the greater burden of existing and rising import duties, compared with the agriculturally productive west, with its much smaller dependence upon imports, especially of necessities, and among the major sufferers were the American merchants. The list of dutiable items grew greater and greater. New tariffs were proposed on corn, rice, beans, salt, canned and fresh vegetables, soap, lard, hams, salt beef, milk, cheese, butter, gasoline, and machinery and implements of all types, used in both industry and agriculture. The tariff on other imports, such as leather, was increased exorbitantly. Having been drawn into the country by liberal concessions, only to have their benefits nullified by exorbitant taxes, some companies had to withdraw from the Shore altogether.

But Bluefields, though suffering in its trade, never experienced the fate of Greytown. By 1914 only small sailing vessels could reach Greytown, and they came at very irregular intervals (the channel over the bar was only 4 to 6 feet deep). There was little to remind one that this had formerly been the largest port on the Atlantic coast of Central America: the wharves were rotting, the wooden houses had collapsed, the main street was a swamp, and there was no longer telegraph service to the outside. Some light steamer traffic still traveled the river, transferring cargo at both Castillo (around the rapids by tramway) and San Carlos, but freight amounted to only a few hundred pounds per month. Shipping charges were higher than ever for such products as cacao, coffee, rice, and corn. The Pacific Railroad was operating the steamers—at a loss—and its main business these days was conveying goods to and from the Pacific port of Corinto.

Discontent became so great that the idea of independence for the Atlantic coast came to have considerable appeal—certainly among the nonindigenous groups: white foreigners, the Spanish-speaking Nicaraguans, and blacks. A source of unquiet in Bluefields since 1894 had been the antipathy between the blacks and mixed-bloods (Creoles) and the Nicaraguans of Spanish descent (called Spaniards), most of whom had entered the region after the incorporation of the Reserve. This often manifested itself in election confrontations, wherein the Nicaraguans felt that they were discriminated against. The uniting force, however, was the independence movement, which was born of frustration and the disappearance of any expectation of betterment from the Managua government.

Secessionist tendencies were not new for Nicaragua's Atlantic coast. Even during the revolution against Zelaya, there were those who urged Nicaragua to relinquish the territory and allow it to become an independent state. Now there seemed to be even more justification for independence, in the failure of the new government to observe the article of the Mosquito convention providing that all revenues derived from the former Reserve be applied to its benefit: hence financial autonomy. This had not been done. With regard to the debts owed Mosquito Coast residents by the government, there could be little expectation of settlement as long as the Shore had no control of its revenues and thus no leverage. One American adventurer, Clifford Sands (who had been unable to collect money he claimed was due him from the government in Managua for his services during the revolution), became so vexed that he teamed up with a disgruntled American railway engineer in an abortive revolution and attacked the government headquarters at Bluefields, with a small party of natives, in July 1914. He issued a "declaration of independence" for a republic which he called Caribbea, absolving it from all allegiance to the republic of Nicaragua because of a long list of grievances, which he published. It turned out to be futile, however, for he was apprehended and forced to leave the country, by order of the U.S. government.

The representation of the national government in Bluefields consisted of a governor and 24 barefoot soldiers, who obviously could not deter a secessionist revolution. As the Sands incident indicated, there was steady opposition by influential residents to revolutionary methods in finding relief for their grievances. The sufferings of the populace during the Zelaya revolution were still fresh in their minds. Also, a vital element in the separatist movement was the reaction of the United States—and there was little indication that it would support secession. Legation officials in Managua passed on to the Bluefields consul a telegram from Washington which made it unequivocally clear that, this time, participation by Americans in revolutionary activity would not be countenanced. Some Americans, consequently, felt that their own government, as in 1894, was deserting them. Less responsible elements, both Creoles and "Spaniards," still clung to the belief that if disorder and revolutionary outbreaks continued, the United States would eventually see to it that their grievances were adjusted. Thus many remained dedicated to a policy of constant agitation.

When President Woodrow Wilson's secretary of state, William Jennings Bryan, assumed office in 1913, he immediately turned his attention to Nicaragua's financial plight. He was not committed to continuation of the methods employed by the previous administration, but pursued a policy of dollar diplomacy of a different sort. Instead of relying upon loans from private banks, which he felt in some cases had been motivated by greed and imposed conditions too burdensome upon Nicaragua, thus impeding its economic rehabilitation, Bryan proposed a direct loan from the U.S. government. When the president refused to approve an outright loan, the secretary sought to achieve his objective by paying Nicaragua a sum of money in return for canal option rights and a lease of Atlantic and Pacific naval bases. This was simply a revival of an unratified agreement made during the final days of the Taft administration (the Weitzel-Chamorro convention). Since a second canal seemed unnecessary and the probability of construction by foreign interests slight, this proposal was clearly designed as relief for Nicaragua at a time when it was in critical need of short-range assistance.

The Díaz government was receptive, and the strategy linkage helped gain President Wilson's support. Negotiations were begun between the two governments and early drafts of a treaty were completed during the summer of 1913. These, however, contained added provisions for a U.S. protectorate in Nicaragua, similar to that in Cuba (which Díaz desired). It was clear that the U.S. Senate would not accept these provisions, and they were removed from the final treaty, which was signed by Bryan and Nicaraguan ambassador Emiliano Chamorro in August 1914. By its terms, the Bryan-Chamorro Treaty granted the United States, in return for $3 million, an option on the Nicaragua canal site in perpetuity, a 99-year renewable lease on the Corn Islands (in the Caribbean), and a 99-year option to construct a naval base on the Pacific's Gulf of Fonseca. That the treaty still did not have wholehearted support in the United States is indicated by the fact that its ratification by the Senate did not come until a year and a half later, after prolonged debates and hearings. In 1916, after ratification of the treaty he had signed, Chamorro returned to Nicaragua to run for president. He won the election, with the full backing of the U.S. government, which, still fearful of Zelaya influences, helped to discourage participation by the Liberal-party candidate.

Although there was controversy as to how the $3 million received by Nicaragua was to be disbursed, with American banker-creditors clamoring for a share as repayment on their loans, a compromise evolved, with about three-quarters of the canal fund going to pay important foreign loans, claims (including the long-standing Emery one), and back salaries.[4] This had a salutary effect upon the country's financial position, and in 1917 a new financial plan was in place, supervised by a U.S.-Nicaraguan high commission rather than exclusively by the banks. By good management, austerity, and fiscal reforms, this body was successful in scaling down the massive indebtedness. By 1919 revenues had increased significantly and loan balances had been greatly reduced. Little of this general improvement was felt on the Mosquito Shore, however.

Meanwhile, the Bryan-Chamorro Treaty, whose options the United States was never to exercise, had stirred a storm of protest, not only in Nicaragua but also in the nearby countries. It was a disappointment that such a treaty should have emerged from a Democratic administration in Washington, which many had expected would abruptly reverse the distasteful interventionist policies of the Taft administration. At home, the treaty appeared to Liberals as confirmation that the Díaz government was a puppet of the United States, willing to "sell out" the country. There were still conflicting claims of Costa Rica, with respect to the San Juan, and of Colombia with respect to the Corn Islands; and their governments were not happy. Likewise, El Salvador and Honduras, both with frontage on the Gulf of Fonseca, felt that Nicaragua had no right to bargain with the United States unilaterally concerning that body of water. The Central American neighbors, not satisfied with an amendment to the treaty "protecting" their existing rights, appealed to the Central American Court of Justice, but its decision in their favor was meaningless. The court had no jurisdiction over the United States, and the Nicaraguan government not only refused to accept its ruling but withdrew from the 1907 accords (which set up the court) in 1917.

While the $3 million paid to Nicaragua might have been the catalyst for general economic improvement there, the Bryan-Chamorro Treaty did not otherwise serve longer-range U.S. interests. It became a symbol of high-handed American domination in the Caribbean and created ill will that lasted for decades.[5]

Nicaragua's economy suffered acutely from the effects of World War I. The major source of foreign exchange in the Pacific coreland was coffee, much of it customarily sold in Europe, and the growers found themselves cut off from their markets. As for the Mosquito Shore, the war's effects upon the British and German markets for pine and mahogany caused almost all trade in these two woods to cease. The banana business suffered too. Shipping schedules were curtailed due to the lack of other types of freight. Production in the plantations of the Bluefields and Rio Grande areas diminished due to lack of capital and labor. French and German interests controlled some of the plantations, and these were, of course, in an especially precarious situation. The United Fruit Company held almost 200,000 acres of banana land, but was not developing it due to the uncertain conditions.[6] Besides the problems connected with the war, banana growers in the Bluefields area were already suffering damages due to soil depletion and the spread of disease in their old plantations. For the first time, some began to recognize the danger of excessive dependence upon banana production and to consider conversion of their plantations to cattle raising by planting pasture grasses and importing breeding stock.

The foreign complexion of Bluefields, insofar as control of businesses and institutions was concerned, still prevailed in 1919. There were still the large mercantile companies, Samuel Weil & Company and Belanger's Incorporated, each with its resident American manager. There was also the Bluefields Fruit and Steamship Company, handling the banana business, also with a resident American manager. Besides these were nine smaller mercantile houses: four American, two British, two Nicaraguan, and one Belgian.[7]

The commercial and services structure of the town consisted of the following: a British-owned restaurant and hotel, three lumber businesses (two American and one British), an ice and bottling works (American), a bank (American), a transportation company (British), a printing company (American), and an insurance agency (American). The population included two doctors (one American and one Italian), a British dentist, five British clerks, one British bookkeeper, one American bank employee, one British carpenter, one British domestic, one British clergyman, and five landowners or agents of plantation companies resident in Bluefields (three American and two British).[8]

Among the other foreign interests, the Chinese had, since the turn of the century, made great commercial inroads. On the Mosquito Coast they were like the so-called "Turks" (Syrians and Lebanese), who often controlled the retail trade in outlying parts of Latin America, including the north coast of Honduras. It was estimated that by 1920 they controlled 90 percent of the retail businesses in Bluefields (nine establishments), other coast towns, and up the rivers. Their population had doubled in two decades, finally numbering about 300.[9] In many cases they married native Nicaraguan or Mosquito women. The large American import houses, from which the Chinese merchants bought most of their merchandise, considered them valued and reliable clients, who paid their bills promptly and caused no trouble. In fact, they were the major victims of burglars and arsonists. Descendants of the original Chinese merchants remained and continued to operate most of the retail establishments of Bluefields, becoming, with the departure of the Americans, even more exclusively dominant.

A good picture of the types of stores in Bluefields and the tastes of the populace during this period may be had by examining the inventory of Chee Lee, a Chinese, whose store was looted in 1919.[10] With its great variety of items, this could have been any general store in the United States. His inventory listed patent medicines, notions, toothpaste, soaps, canned and dried foods, beverages, clothing, household needs (such as brooms, lamps, candles, kerosene, ax handles, and washboards), and even guitar strings. The Americanization of the customers, as well as their almost complete dependence upon imports, was evident: the only clearly native products among the more than 200 items carried by the store were home-made brooms, lard, *aguardiente*, sugar, coffee, and beans. The rest were products of an industrial and consumer-oriented economy, many identified by their American brand names. To a considerable degree, products reflected a bit of America transferred to the tropics and the tastes of expatriate Americans. There was preoccupation with keeping clean, or at least smelling clean, in the great number of brands and scents of soap. Men's white shoes, presumably fashionable in the tropics, were available, along with white shoe polish. But only occasionally was there a sizable inventory of *one* item—more then five or six boxes, bottles, jars, or tins.

By 1919 the Atlantic coast had achieved a reputation for lawlessness unparalleled in its history—or in other parts of Nicaragua. Crimes were committed with impunity. Facilities for imprisonment were poor and escape was easy. There were no funds for the prolonged containment of prisoners. The poorly paid law enforcement officials were ineffectual, subject to bribes, and often collaborated with criminals. In March of 1919, a tremendous fire destroyed the Bluefields Tanning Company. This large installation burned down, with its adjoining salesroom and warehouse (with a complete supply of shoes and other leather articles), before the fire spread, uncontrolled, to consume eight or ten other buildings (including the major hotel, the Victoria). The town had no usable fire-fighting equipment. According to newspaper reports, armed police not only continually hindered the volunteers from fighting the blaze, but aided, abetted, and even participated in the simultaneous looting. At the height of this fire, a gang, allegedly police-led and armed with axes, broke into the large store owned by Chee Lee, the Chinese merchant, and emptied it of its contents, while fire fighters battled to save it and other police stood by and watched, with drawn rifles.[11]

All of this was reflective of economic and social breakdown in this part of Nicaragua. More and more discontented with the state of things, most businesses and businessmen of Bluefields, including several Nicaraguans, sent a petition to the American consul, appealing to the U.S. government to come to their aid. The dissatisfaction which it expressed cut across all nationality and ethnic lines. The petitioners called particular attention to the conditions of lawlessness under which they had to live: almost daily murders and robberies; frequent fires, obviously arson, and the consequent refusal of insurance companies to carry policies at affordable rates; ineffective law enforcement and the inability or unwillingness of the Nicaraguan government to provide adequate police protection and jails.

Although the petition to the consul was vague as to methods, it asked that the United States take steps "to obtain for us, in whatever way may seem most proper and effective, protection for ourselves and property to the end that we may continue to reside here and follow in peace the pursuit of our legitimate occupations."[12] The petition had been signed by practically all the American and other foreign interests in the Bluefields area. There seemed little doubt that they wished for armed intervention by the marines. This, in any case, was the way President Chamorro interpreted the petition.

This Conservative president was unlike his predecessor; he had proved much less pliable in dealing with the U.S. State Department throughout his administration. Confident and secure in his military and political situation, he had balked on several occasions at American pressure regarding financial arrangements. He reacted immediately to the Bluefields petition by throwing a wholly unexpected "bombshell" (as it was called in the local press): he ordered the expulsion of all foreign signatories of the petition as "dangerous aliens," giving them three months to get their affairs in order and leave.[13] This appeared to be the end for the American colony's interests, which had hung on in Bluefields through many trials for over a quarter century. Unlike the Americans who had lately come to Managua to manage the customs, these Americans considered Bluefields their home.

Although John Sanders, the consul at Bluefields, was reluctant to interfere in the administration of the Nicaraguan government, he pressed the American minister in Managua on behalf of the petitioners. Disclaiming the dark political motivations apparently perceived by the Nicaraguan government, he wanted to get the expulsion order rescinded. Time passed, and the only satisfaction for these foreigners in Bluefields was that the president did not seem persistent in carrying out the order. This was not altogether reassuring, for there had not been an official revocation. According to the governor of Bluefields, the petitioners were *persona non grata* and still subject to expulsion. His orders from the president specified that the only exemptions must be signatories who declared "they had no intention of causing embarrassment or injury to the government."[14] The declaration demanded in Bluefields, however, was the equivalent of an apology or retraction, in the eyes of the petitioners, and most of them refused to agree to it.

After lengthy uncertainty, during which the American minister in Managua gave little support to the consul's pleas (the consul later complained to the U.S. State Department about this), the matter was resolved a mere two weeks before the deadline through the efforts of the consul. Sensing that he could not depend upon the minister in Managua, the consul busied himself, soon after the expulsion order, in obtaining information (through private contacts) about the deliberations of the Nicaraguan government. He learned that the minister of foreign affairs had withheld his approval of the expulsion, but was swaying. Fortuitously, the minister's brother-in-law passed through Bluefields (instead of the usual route, through Panama) en route to the United States on personal family business and paid a visit to the consul, who, recognizing him as an emissary of the minister of foreign affairs and one who was willing to help resolve the problem, explained the matter to him from the viewpoint of the victims. Apparently convinced, the Nicaraguan wrote letters and sent a telegram to Managua immediately, and shortly thereafter the president suspended his order. The governor was so informed less than a week before the deadline.[15] Thus was the most serious threat to American influence in the Atlantic Coast since the Zelaya revolution finally averted by a conscientious consul who was loyal to his local charges and who had the good fortune of finding a personal conduit to those in power.

10   National Upheaval
and Its Impact
in the East,
1920–1940

In the early 1920s the Conservatives still ruled in Nicaragua. Emiliano Chamorro's term as president was ending, but a hand-picked relative, Diego Manuel Chamorro, succeeded him. Meanwhile, the financial situation of the country had greatly improved and U.S. policy, under President Harding, included plans to liquidate the intervention in Nicaragua, as elsewhere in Central America and the Caribbean, as soon as political stability could be assured. Unfortunately, the prospects for that appeared discouraging, as there was unrest throughout the isthmus. Governments were still forcibly overthrown, despite the Washington peace treaties of 1907. Nicaragua and Honduras seemed on the verge of war, the Liberals having returned to power in the latter country by a *coup d'etat* in 1919. Each distrusted the intentions of the other, and exchanged accusations of encouraging revolutionary activities along the border. The Central American Court, designed for the arbitration of disputes, no longer existed, due to Nicaragua's withdrawal following the adverse decision pertaining to the Bryan-Chamorro Treaty. Attempting to rebuild the peace structure, the United States called another conference of Central American states in Washington early in 1923, from which treaties, signed by all five republics, resulted. The agreements established a restructured court, more acceptable to all, and the countries confirmed their pledges to settle disputes by peaceful means and not give aid to revolutionists. They made a firmer, more explicit commitment not to recognize governments that assumed power by revolution or *coup d'etat*. The United States also proclaimed this to be its policy henceforth.

The United States then turned its attention to promoting conditions in Nicaraguan politics sufficiently stable to permit its disengagement. It pressed President Diego Chamorro (and after he died in office, his vice-presidential successor, Bartolomé Martínez) to allow free elections in 1924,

199

and made clear its intention to withdraw the marines after the installation of a strong, freely elected government. The ensuing election was relatively free and fair, but did not prove to be the long-range solution that the United States desired.

All the while the Mosquito Shore was approaching its peak in banana production, and the early 1920s seemed promising for the large American companies. The general economic situation had notably improved, due in no small measure to increased revenues from banana exports. While the older plantations of the Escondido Valley were in decline, those of the Rio Grande, farther north, were still producing well. By the 1920s, the Cuyamel Fruit Company had the largest operation in this valley, having obtained thousands of acres for planting, and was also a buyer of bananas from small plantations along the river. Shipping from the Rio Grande region was a continuing problem, however. The closest deep-water anchorage was near small keys 8 miles offshore, some 30 miles northeast of Bluefields and about the same distance south of the Rio Grande bar. These islets offered no protection from the northeasterlies, and frequently the waters were so rough that barges could not be towed out to the ships. When the risk was taken, costly losses of fruit and damage to the barges and other craft were common. Ultimately, the company selected a more protected anchorage for its ships, at Man of War Cays, in an effort to reduce the risk and shipping time, but the lack of wharfage facilities at the river's mouth was a weakness in the competitive position of Cuyamel's Rio Grande enterprise.

The greatest stimulus to banana production came with the entry of Standard Fruit Company of New Orleans, which eventually became the largest American business ever to become established in eastern Nicaragua, accounting for almost half of the nation's output of bananas.[1] This company began its Nicaragua operations in 1921 by acquiring pine-timber interests in the Puerto Cabezas region through a New Orleans–based partnership arrangement. Founding Bragman's Bluff Lumber Company, it obtained 50,000 acres of land, extending to the interior from Puerto Cabezas, by concession from the Nicaraguan government. At first, the emphasis was upon timber cutting and lumber production, with construction of a railroad, installation of several saw mills, and improvement of wharf facilities. However, the plan had always included production of bananas, using the same railroad and docks. During the first year, the company planted approximately 10,000 banana suckers in the expectation that the plants would be ready for cutting by the time the railroad was completed.[2] Puerto

Cabezas was rapidly converted into an American-style company town, with hotels, office buildings, a commissary, residences for a doctor and assistant manager, laborers' quarters, mess halls, and a large water storage tank. The company recruited unskilled laborers locally, but a number of Americans were attracted by the developments, and many brought their families with them.

Standard Fruit plantations shipped their first bananas in 1925. By this time Puerto Cabezas was thriving, with excellent docking facilities. The railroad was being extended ever farther to the interior, with hundreds of workmen laying ties. The company employed almost 500 men on the banana farms, with timber-cutting and saw mill operations proceeding simultaneously as the rail line advanced.[3] However, most of its food had to be imported, at considerable cost, and there were problems of preserving fresh produce and meat.

Unfortunately, government concessions to the Standard Fruit–Bragman's Bluff Company placed in jeopardy the land rights of native Indians in the Wawa region. By agreement with the government, in conformity with the Mosquito conventions of 1894, these Indians had been awarded sizable allotments of agricultural and grazing land, extending back from their riverfront villages. However, surveys of the land had lagged (the government attributed the inaction to cost and inadequate funds), and only 1,000 hectares were surveyed by 1923.[4] The outcome was that Indians were considered squatters on "company lands," once the Standard Fruit concession was granted. They complained, on the contrary, that the government and the company were depriving them of lands they had been promised, but the government refused to make another definitive survey. This was but one of several instances in which Indian rights had been violated since the incorporation of the Mosquito Reserve.

Lost for several decades in the fastnesses of the tropical rainforest, inland from Puerto Cabezas and beyond the banana plantations and the pine forest savannas, had been the gold mines of the Piz Piz district. Situated in the Sumu Indian country of the headwaters of the Coco and Prinzapolka rivers, the mines were so isolated from the general activities of the Mosquito Shore that it could easily be forgotten that they were a tributary development (albeit with slight economic impact within eastern Nicaragua), dating back to the late nineteenth century. Gold mining had been started in the remote area by Germans, Canadians, and Americans, who prospected on the basis of tales of gold brought back by rubber gatherers. Although there was never a significant gold rush, the first quarter century was marked by the establishment of several mining interests, all quietly and undramatically carrying on; their activities were eclipsed by other developments along the Shore.

In those days, before air transport became common, access—as well as living conditions—was a monumental exercise in endurance. Only gold could have made it worthwhile. As late as the 1920s, the only access was by river, as far as possible, then by mule and oxen, or by foot. Some mines had tramway access for short distances in the immediate vicinity. After one arrived at Bluefields or Puerto Cabezas, then was transported by a small schooner to Prinzapolka, there were four transfers of conveyance before the mines were reached. Passengers traveled up the Prinzapolka-Banbana River by motorboat or canoe to Tunky, head of motorboat navigation, then by smaller canoe up the Tunky River to Miranda, then to the mines by tramway or mule. Ordinarily, the trip from New Orleans required about twenty days; on rare occasions, when conditions were most favorable, this could be reduced by half. Freight shipments, delayed by multiple handlings en route and the slowness of movement occasioned by their bulk and methods of transport, required at least a month and sometimes two.

The Banbana River, a tributary of the Prinzapolka, quickly became a narrow and crooked stream, full of rapids and shallows, after about 30 miles. Barges of 3- and 5-ton capacity, towed by gasoline launches of shallow draft, carried the freight. If the river was high, they were pulled through the rapids with the aid of winches on the river bank, finally to reach Tunky. There the native handlers reloaded the freight on dugout canoes, carrying from 500 to 1,500 pounds, and poled them upstream, if the depth of water permitted, or dragged them by hand through shallows and rapids. Finally, where progress by water became impossible, the cargos were unloaded again and hauled to the mines by tramway, oxen, or whatever overland conveyance was available (even, occasionally, native porters). Frequently, low water in the streams or too-swift currents, because of floods, prevented upstream progress altogether. In any case, the channel was always blocked by tangled masses of logs and other debris. Hawxhurst wrote in 1921: "In no other country in the world would such a stream be utilized for purposes of transportation, and its use here would be impossible but for the exceptional skill and hardihood of the Indian boatmen."[5]

The heavy rains in this mining district turned it into a quagmire for part of the year, especially in July and August. Except where there were aerial tramways, rough trails connected the mining sites, and transport of freight between them was exceedingly difficult, requiring ox teams, and even packs of oxen, to haul mudsleds and drags. Despite the discomforts of rain and mud, the district depended upon heavy precipitation to keep the rivers high, so that the lifeline for food and supplies could be kept open to shipping. Also, the mines depended upon hydroelectric power for their operation. Whenever precipitation was below normal, the results were delays in river traffic and curtailment of mining operations because of reduced flow at power plants.

While Puerto Cabezas was growing, Bluefields—now distant from the major new banana lands—failed to improve. Still a center of Liberal dissidents and foreign malcontents (some of them separatist agitators), the town seethed under the Conservative government, still in power in Managua. The "exploitation" of the Atlantic coast by western Nicaragua had not abated, the residents claimed. They contended—with a great deal of reason—that the Atlantic coast served simply as a "political El Dorado" for the politicians of Managua, who received appointments to all of the better posts, though ignorant of the conditions and traditions of the eastern coast. Considering this to be colonial status and the West Nicaraguans "foreigners," they repeated their demands that governors, magistrates, judges, chiefs of police, and postmasters be appointed from their midst. This, they felt, was their just due, because they contributed a disproportionate share (considering the small population) of public revenues.

"For want of a respectable government," Bluefields by 1924 had become a lawless, morally degraded pesthole, according to bitter American and Jamaican residents who wrote to the secretary of state.[6] The streets were in such bad shape that "after thirty years of 'Nicaraguanism' mule carts can hardly get over the roads," and even 2-ton motor trucks were repeatedly stuck in the ruts. In vivid terms, they described the lack of sanitation:

the never-swept sidewalks covered in all seasons by orange, banana, and mango peel, the stomach-sickening mouthfuls of consumption germ-breeding sputum on sidewalks, the crows and other small animals remaining dead in the streets until they rot, causing people often times to take the next street, the pools of stagnant water forming in the streets and remaining seven to eight months every year forming breeding places for all sorts of disease germs, and the Government having dozens of condemned murderers constantly in jail but too ignorant to set them to work to fill up these ruts.

They also described the immorality and corruption they saw. Drunkenness was widespread among men, women and children, accompanied by all forms of disorderly conduct and obscenities. These offenses went unpunished when the chief of police saw "a chance of getting a few dollars' fine for his drinks that day." Not only did the Nicaraguan government sell licenses for public gambling establishments, but on holidays allowed the gamblers to block street corners and sidewalks with their tables, put out to attract all ages and both sexes of the populace.

As for Greytown in the early 1920s, it was moribund. It had become so silted in that it could be reached only by a maze of waterways. Visits of small craft (now motorized) from upriver were infrequent, and only in the wet season. No oceangoing ships called beyond the bar. The few remaining residents criticized the Nicaraguan government for its neglect over two decades and abandonment of the port to natural forces:

> The harbour that sheltered Nelson's great fleet, today after a few years of occupation by Nicaragua is so overgrown by weeds, and so filled up by the sand from the San Juan river as well as the sand from the ocean, that flat-bottomed barges of thirty or fifty feet length and from four to five feet deep displacement can hardly traffic any more in this once beautiful harbour.[7]

Conditions within Nicaragua, as a whole, worsened after 1925, and the Mosquito Shore was caught up in the maelstrom. The ensuing eight years of political upheaval and civil war proved to be its final undoing. The country indeed had appeared sufficiently stabilized and financially viable by mid-decade for the United States to withdraw its marines, an action much desired because of pressure at home and abroad. However, the plan was for the marines to stay long enough to oversee the election of 1924 and its results. The new, elected government was a coalition of Conservatives (president) and Liberals (vice president). However, Emiliano Chamorro, the strongman of the Conservative party and former president (1916–1920), had returned from his post as Nicaragua's minister to the United States to campaign in the election. Defeated, he contested the results, alleging fraudulent "irregularities." The United States, nevertheless, recognized the new government, and, presuming that all was well, withdrew the marines in August of 1925, six months after the inauguration. This was the signal for Chamorro to mount a *coup d'etat*. In a few months, he was president of Nicaragua, having been appointed by congress, which he had come to control, as well as the army. The United States refused to recognize his regime and a revolution broke out in Bluefields, led by Liberal supporters of the ousted vice president, Juan B. Sacasa, who had fled the country. The United States sent American forces back to protect American lives and property—the beginning of the second U.S. intervention, lasting until 1933.

With an armed vessel obtained in the United States and with assistance from Mexico, a group of Liberals, close to Sacasa, stormed and captured Puerto Cabezas in August of 1926. By now there was civil war throughout the country, but the Liberals were most successful in the east. The revolution was taking a heavy toll economically: on the Mosquito Shore alone, the important banana plantations were suffering from a shortage of workers (forcibly recruited as soldiers by both sides) and from fighting in the river valleys and ports. The following October, after a fruitless attempt by the United States to mediate, Chamorro resigned, and Adolfo Díaz, appointed by congress, again assumed the presidency. Díaz had not obtained control of the government by *coup d'etat*, as had Chamorro (contrary to the provisions of the Central American conventions of 1923, which he himself had signed for Nicaragua). Therefore, the United States was willing to recognize his government. For Sacasa and the Liberals, however, Chamorro's exit was not enough. (Sacasa had been vice president in the elected constitutional coalition government of 1924, overthrown by the *coup*, and thus the only legitimate successor to the presidency.) They resolved to carry on the war against Díaz and his Conservatives. In December, Sacasa returned to his homeland, installed by his supporters as "Constitutional President of Nicaragua," and set up his government in Puerto Cabezas.

Meanwhile, additional marines had arrived in Managua and were deployed on both coasts and in the interior. Ostensibly, their purpose was protection of Americans, but in effect the American military forces aided in preserving the incumbent Conservative government. Their policy of establishing neutral zones in various parts of eastern Nicaragua, including Puerto Cabezas, in which fighting between the opposing armies was prohibited, was more a deterrent to the Liberal forces than an advantage. It had been instituted very early as a result of appeals from mahogany companies, which were prevented from getting their logs out; from banana companies, whose boats and barges were taken over; from gold mining companies, whose installations were raided; and from other American businesses along the Shore that were endangered in the conflict.[8] Sacasa protested this obstacle to his army's movements and contended that the real purpose of the neutral zones was not so much protection of American lives and property as keeping the Díaz government in power. As more and more marines poured into the country and established additional neutral zones in western Nicaragua, this limited the Liberal army's new offensive in that part of the country. Criticism of the policy of the Calvin Coolidge administration mounted in Washington: the need for so many marines, simply to protect American interests, appeared hardly credible.

Numerous offensive actions of the Liberals in and around Managua threatened the Conservative forces, despite the advantages of the marines' presence. The neutralizing function of the marines did not appear to be enough. Díaz was losing heart and offered to resign, if it would bring peace; however, the United States was determined that he remain in office until the elections of 1928. This precluded reconciliation with Sacasa's Liberals, whose prime demand was that Díaz step down. Finally, having rejected a Díaz proposal that the United States take a more active military and political role in the country, the Coolidge administration determined to impose a peace. Sacasa was invited to send delegates to Managua to discuss with President Coolidge's personal representative, Henry L. Stimson, a peace settlement.

Besides its disarmament, amnesty, and property-settlement provisions, the terms of the agreement proposed by the Díaz government and the United States assured U.S. supervision of the elections of 1928, participation of Liberals in the interim government, the maintenance of marines "temporarily" within the country to enforce the peace, formation of a Nicaraguan National Guard (initially trained and commanded by Americans), and the continuance of President Díaz in office until the elections. There was no objection from the Liberal delegates to any of the terms, even those permitting continued U.S. influence and presence, except that of Díaz remaining in the presidency. Stimson was just as adamant on this point, believing that Díaz had to remain in order to prevent chaotic instability and infighting prior to the elections. Finally, the Liberal delegation put the matter to their commanding general, General José Moncada, to decide.

The influence of Moncada, who had led the fighting forces throughout the war and to the very threshold of the capital, had grown while that of Sacasa, in Puerto Cabezas, had waned. Although receptive to the other provisions in the initial stages of his conference with Stimson in early May 1927, the general, too, was unwilling to agree to Díaz' retention. After Stimson insisted that this provision was requisite to U.S. supervision of the elections of 1928 (a vital issue for the Liberals), and after concluding that the United States would put forces into the field against him if the war continued, Moncada acquiesced. In the following days, all but one of his generals agreed to lay down their arms. Sacasa's delegates and Sacasa himself also still refused to accept the settlement, but their refusal, due to Díaz' remaining, was of little consequence, and Sacasa left the country. The refusal of the general, Augusto Sandino, was linked to the Americans' remaining, and it meant that the war was far from over.

Thus began for the U.S. Marines (after initial withdrawals, the force was rapidly expanded again) a tough guerrilla war against Sandino and his "bandit fringe"' of hold-out revolutionaries. This time it was Americans fighting Nicaraguans (plus some Honduran guerrillas). No longer were the marines simply policing "neutral zones" in the interest of protecting American lives and property. Eventually, the government employed the newly created and marine-trained National Guard, and there was also air support, with bombing and strafing. Within a year following the Stimson-Moncada agreement, three major battles had been fought, starting in the northern mountains (Sandino's stronghold) and extending to the coffee district around Matagalpa and to the gold mines of the east. None had been decisive. The hit-and-run tactics of guerrilla warfare in difficult terrain served the Sandinistas well. Operating in small bands, their total number was never large at any time during the long campaign, and did not match that of government forces and U.S. Marines. The undeclared war was unpopular in the United States, not only within the Congress but also in the press and on the streets, where demonstrators decried the continued American intervention in Nicaragua and many appeared to be sympathetic to Sandino.

Tardily, after a raid on the American-owned gold mines between Matagalpa and Puerto Cabezas in April 1928, the government bolstered its forces on the Mosquito Shore. Ambushes and battles continued between this augmented eastern contingent and the Sandinistas all through the following summer. Although pursued, Sandino was illusive in his temporary jungle camps. With repeated reinforcements, the marine force in the country during the first year reached well over 5,000, and $3.5 million had been spent in support of it.[9]

The 1928 elections were now at hand. This time the U.S. policy was clearly neutral; it was concerned only that candidates of all parties be eligible to hold the office of president (under the 1923 conventions) and that the elections be fair. Chamorro again wished to run for president, but the United States declared him ineligible because of his assumption of the office by *coup d'etat* earlier in the decade; and the State Department informed him, if he were elected, he would not receive recognition. Chamorro, however, had his supporters, and they tried for many weeks to gain control of the Conservative party and to void the plan for strict U.S. control of the elections. In the end, they tried to split the vote and throw the election into the Conservative-controlled congress by encouraging minor parties. None of these tactics was successful, and General Moncada, the Liberal candidate, was elected over the Conservative party's nominee, a Chamorro surrogate, in November of 1928.

Although Sandino attempted to disrupt the elections (he considered

Moncada a traitor) by terrorism and anti-election propaganda in the countryside, his efforts were largely unproductive. The election had been scrupulously supervised by the Americans, utilizing marines at polling places throughout the republic, and was considered notably fair. The Liberals were back in power after eighteen years of Conservative regimes, mostly American supported. In Moncada, however, the United States again had a friend, though he was a Liberal.

After the election, an overture of conciliation was made to Sandino; but it soon became clear that the Liberals' return to power, with his former chief now president, and the impartiality of the U.S. government in the recent elections, were not enough for the guerrilla leader. He would neither deal with the Americans, who, in his eyes, had no business in Nicaragua's internal affairs, nor would he lay down his arms until all American troops had departed from the country. Despite increasing pressure in Washington, after the Coolidge administration ended, to terminate all American military presence in Nicaragua, the marines remained and the war continued. Now their main function was to train and command a National Guard, which the U.S. government hoped would eventually be able to cope with the situation.

Meanwhile, a movement in the U.S. Senate, favoring construction in Nicaragua of a second canal, was beginning to bear fruit and it looked as if the option in the Bryan-Chamorro Treaty might be implemented. Proponents contended that the Panama Canal would in a few years be insufficient to accommodate the traffic. There was much opposition to an appropriations bill to conduct a new survey, but Congress finally passed the measure, which newly inaugurated President Herbert Hoover signed early in 1929. Hopes were again aroused in Nicaragua and there was another resurgence along the San Juan when a battalion of U.S. engineers arrived the following August, to spend two years in the field.

The operations were as difficult as if the area had never been penetrated. The lower channel of the river leading to Greytown was weed choked and hardly wide enough for the exploration boat and its two barges to pass, and Greytown could be reached only by a 4-mile walk along the old railway embankment of the Maritime Canal Company. Overland transport for materials and supplies was impossible, and it was many months, using axes and dynamite, before workers opened the narrow, shallow, and tortuous water passage sufficiently for *bongos* to be poled, paddled, and portaged through. Eventually, they made the channel usable by motorized dugouts, which speeded operations, but at a high cost. "Pins were sheared off by the score, propellers bent, shafts twisted and whole motors knocked off and lost overboard . . . spare parts were rushed down from the States by the box and every motor rebuilt from the tank down time and time again."[10] One of the engineers, Lewis R. Freeman, gave this appraisal of conditions:

> If you have not penetrated the jungle of the San Juan River you do not know what real jungle is like. Can you imagine a rainfall of about 300 inches a year? Perhaps not, unless you have been to Greytown, at the mouth of the San Juan, for that is the wettest place in the Americas. In such a country tents merely filter the water; thatched native shacks are the only solution to the temporary housing problem.
>
> Have you ever tried to make a map in a continuous downpour, in a jungle so thick that you cannot see ten feet in any direction, where foliage is so dense overhead that little light penetrates and a permanent gloom pervades? Have you ever tried to run a traverse across many miles of swamps where at no place is the footing sufficiently secure to keep you from sinking to your waist, to your neck, and often over your head? Imagine unnumbered mosquitoes, insects by the million, so varied as to size, shape, bite and method of locomotion that classification is impossible. Throw in some alligators, snakes, scorpions, vipers and poisonous reptiles, not to mention the ticks, and you have a picture of the conditions under which the Engineers have been working on the San Juan.[11]

The survey was completed—but all for naught. There is no assurance that its findings would have led to serious consideration of construction, but two events conspired to nip the possibility in the bud. To proponents, it must have seemed a cruel turn of fate when the earthquake-volcano alarm sounded again, as it had thirty years before, to prejudice Nicaragua as a canal site. In 1931, in the final stages of the survey, a particularly disastrous earthquake struck Managua and received wide publicity. Also, a world depression had set in. Not only was the commercial reason for a second canal no longer valid, for international business was plunging headlong, but the cost to the U.S. government during these times of other pressing priorities would have been prohibitive. Moreover, construction in Nicaragua would have had little impact on U.S. unemployment, for most of the labor would have been done by Central Americans. The survey was put on the shelf, after due perusal of the voluminous data. The conclusion was that this was not the time to give the project serious consideration.

Unlike earlier periods when American engineers had come to town, stirring canal hopes, even Greytown seemed little affected by the latest visits. It slumbered on. Passing through the town in the early 1930s, Beals wrote:

210 National Upheaval and Its Impact in the East

Every one of the wooden houses was rotting, warped out of proportion, the gingerbread work broken and fallen, upstairs piazzas sagging dangerously. Half the houses were abandoned, their windows broken, the roofs fallen in, here and there . . . heaps of charred ruins. In one pile of black beams I saw a big safe. These houses, I was told, had been burned down to get the insurance. Many had once been covered with galvanized tin, but these roofs were rapidly disappearing, carried off to the more prosperous community of Bluefields. The unprotected walls were tottering. Not a house, save the customs office in charge of a courteous, alert negro, had a fresh coat of paint. The streets, once paved with cobblestones, were cushions of green grass, and the jungle, which circles the town, seemed to be pushing in, preparing to strangle it.[12]

In early 1931, with the Hoover administration half over and both the United States and Nicaragua suffering from the depression, the U.S. government decided to withdraw most of the marines. It realized that its military presence in Nicaragua was counterproductive in bringing peace to the country, and it appeared that the National Guard was strong enough to handle the Sandino threat. The U.S. government, moreover, was increasingly preoccupied with its domestic economy and could ill afford such foreign adventures, long opposed by many. Under the plan for a staged withdrawal, however, a few hundred marines would remain until after the 1932 elections. This was not satisfactory to Sandino, who began making plans for a large-scale assault on American interests along the Mosquito Shore, particularly Standard Fruit Company in and around Puerto Cabezas.

The onset of the world depression coincided with Nicaragua's peak banana production. According to approximate dollar figures, compiled by the *New York Times* in 1931, over 85 percent of American investments in Nicaragua were on the east coast. Of those investments, almost 90 percent were in bananas and lumber.[13] While composing but 10 percent of Central America's production, bananas alone were close to 50 percent of the nation's exports in terms of value (up sevenfold in a decade).[14] The giant in banana production was Standard Fruit Company—and in lumber production as well through its subsidiary, Bragman's Bluff Lumber Company. But low prices and high unemployment began to cause considerable unrest in the banana districts by early 1931, and the lumber and gold mining interests were hard hit as well. It seemed a propitious time for Sandino to strike against the greatest representation of American corporate enterprise in his country. Winning the allegiance of some Mosquito Indians and taking advantage of the devastation caused in Managua by the earthquake in late

March 1931, Sandino's forces attacked the Bragman's installations at Logtown, 70 miles inland, along the rail line from Puerto Cabezas. After looting
and burning most of the buildings, the hundred-man band, with some local
recruits (dissatisfied fruit and lumber workers), set out for Puerto Cabezas,
raiding banana plantation settlements along the way.

Two small detachments of Guardsmen, led by marine officers, were sent
to the scene as soon as word of the raids was received in Puerto Cabezas.
Along the entire east coast, the National Guard numbered only about 150
men, and not even a third of them were stationed in that port.[15] (Most of the
Guard was engaged in earthquake relief work in Managua.) Sandino's guerrillas ambushed both detachments, and one of them was unable to return to
Puerto Cabezas. Its train had been halted and disabled at a bridge, where
the rails were torn up. By this time, aid was forthcoming in the form of
planes sent from Managua, but their bombing and strafing was not effective
in routing the guerrillas, concealed in the hills. When word was received
that a force of Guardsmen was cut off from Puerto Cabezas, leaving the
town practically defenseless, panic broke out. The population of the town
and vicinity, including some 300 American employees of Standard Fruit
Company, with wives and children, left their homes and gathered at the
wharf, awaiting a U.S. naval vessel en route from Panama.[16]

By the time that other Guardsmen reached Logtown, the guerrillas had
massacred eight American field employees of Standard Fruit (with machetes). After evacuation and their arrival in the United States aboard a fruit
company vessel, survivors told grim tales of their ordeal. Under attack by
Sandino's men, as they awaited rescue along the railway track, they had
escaped by submerging themselves in creeks and drainage ditches and
covering their heads with brush and leaves. Others had hidden among the
banana plants.[17]

A few additional marines and Guardsmen, arriving from Bluefields,
proceeded up the damaged rail line, fording rivers and replacing rails along
the way, to join the main group of beleaguered forces at a banana plantation.
After engaging the guerrillas, while benefiting from air support and killing
one of the leaders, the full Guard force (about 50 men) moved within 15
miles of Puerto Cabezas. Other units of Sandino's army then surrounded
the port. Because access by rail seemed impossible (a trestle ahead of them
had been burned), the Guardsmen descended the Wawa River on a banana
launch and reached the port by sea. Meanwhile, the American gunboat
Asheville had arrived and belatedly received the order to station its men in
the town until such time as National Guard reinforcements arrived from

other parts of Nicaragua. This show of force appeared to be sufficient, for the Sandinistas then withdrew from the area, after four days of terrorizing.

Meanwhile, the Standard Fruit Company evacuated the wives and children of its resident employees in Puerto Cabezas to New Orleans. The majority of field employees who had fled to Puerto Cabezas returned to the interior plantations as reconstruction of four railroad bridges commenced. Besides the loss of lives, the fruit company had suffered tremendous loss of property. It had hoped to be better protected.

In earlier and in recent times, an assault upon major American businesses, and certainly the killing of eight American citizens, have provoked more substantial U.S. military action. But in this instance the pleas of business interests, primarily Standard Fruit Company, met an uncommon lack of receptiveness in Washington. Secretary of State Stimson and the Hoover administration used the Sandino offensive on the east coast to announce that not only would the exit of U.S. Marines proceed as scheduled, but that Americans in the interior of Nicaragua could expect no protection from the U.S. government. If they did not feel secure, they would have to evacuate the country or withdraw to coastal points; otherwise, it would be necessary to rely upon the Nicaraguan National Guard. The policy—so radically different from preceding ones—took American business interests in Nicaragua (and many in the United States) by surprise. Despite criticism, there was no retreat.

The State Department's position was that there was no comparison between this situation and the earlier civil war, when the United States had employed general military intervention. There were at that time neutral zones, more or less respected by the armies of both sides. There had been no organized attempt to murder private citizens of any foreign country, and the problem was only to protect them from the ordinary consequences of being caught in a conflict. The earlier war was not a guerrilla operation, in which marines fought an illusive enemy in unknown and difficult jungle country. Much of the interior battleground now, the State Department contended, called for "native troops," and was not adapted to regular, large-scale offensive military operations.[18]

It is clear, therefore, that the State Department was aware that the presence of marines had thus far been ineffective in bringing down Sandino. Pertinent to the U.S. stand was the fact that no National Guard had existed in 1926, and since then a major objective had been to train just such a force (expanded to its present strength of almost 2,000 men) which would be capable of waging an offensive in interior Nicaragua, as dictated by Sandino's tactics.

The new policy was the culmination of a determination, earlier reached by the Hoover administration, to extricate the United States from further involvement in Nicaragua. The same consideration applied in the extension of the policy to limit protection of Americans as in the original intention to withdraw the marines. Moreover, there was much less sympathy in the United States for American businesses abroad, now that a depression threatened the collapse of the whole domestic economy. The policy had many supporters, as well as critics. None was more pleased than Republican Senator William E. Borah, chairman of the Senate Foreign Relations Committee, who had long been an opponent of U.S. actions in Nicaragua.

> I take it [Borah said] that all these things are steps toward our getting out of Nicaragua. In that view of it, I am in hearty accord with the program. We sent our marines to Nicaragua twenty-one years ago. We have been there practically ever since. We've set up governments and taken down governments and run governments. Conditions in respect to disorder and banditry are as bad as when we first went in. I'm in favor of the Nicaraguans having the kind of a government that they want, changing it as often as they want and in the manner they want. I hope it is true we are not going to let anything change our plans to get out and stay out.[19]

The new policy did not escape the attention of the Sandinistas. Sandino's spokesman in Mexico City sent a message to President Hoover, commending what he considered to be a step in the right direction. However, he pointed out, "not until the last American marine has been withdrawn from Nicaragua will there be peace there."[20]

Although disappointed with the State Department's announcement, in the wake of restored calm at Puerto Cabezas, Americans on the Mosquito Shore took it seriously. Almost as soon as Standard Fruit employees had returned to the interior plantations, many retraced their steps to the port city, some to evacuate the country. They had no confidence in the National Guard. The Moravian Church, because one of its missionaries was killed during the Sandino raids, ordered the remaining ones to east coast seaports. After less than two weeks, the United States withdrew the warships dispatched to Puerto Cabezas and Bluefields, with their landing forces.

Sandinista raids on National Guard posts continued throughout the summer and fall of 1931, and were effective. No department north of Managua was spared, and by November the guerrillas even threatened the capital, when they temporarily occupied the town of Chichigalpa on the Managua–Corinto railway. For the first time since the previous spring, U.S.

marines were authorized to leave the capital—to be stationed on the trains to protect them.

The greatest threat to the Mosquito Shore was past, but raids continued in that area: on the gold mines of the Piz Piz district, once again; on Rama, at the head of the Escondido River, for the first time. Guerrillas also attacked in the lower Coco Valley, long one of their major strongholds. Here they gained support from the Mosquito Indian population through its influential half-English–half-Mosquito "chief," a Liberal congressman, hacienda owner, and dedicated Sandinista. The following October, they again raided some of the Standard Fruit plantations along the rail line to Logtown, which had been attacked with such fury earlier, and looted their commissaries.

The war continued another year, while steady reductions were made in the U.S. marine force and the National Guard made a generally poor showing against the guerrillas. With the approach of the elections of November 1932, both Nicaraguan parties were apprehensive about the withdrawal of all the marines afterward. This drew them together, and they agreed that, whichever party won the election, peaceful and conciliatory methods would be used in dealing with Sandino. True to its promise to the Nicaraguan government, the United States kept marines in the country to supervise the elections, while they continued to train and command the National Guard. After Juan B. Sacasa, candidate of the incumbent Liberal party, was elected president, the Americans prepared to leave, and the last marines departed immediately after the inauguration of January 1, 1933. Former President Moncada's foreign minister, Anastasio Somoza, appointed by the outgoing administration with U.S. concurrence, took over as chief director of the National Guard. Other command positions, replacing the American marine officers, were divided between Liberals and Conservatives in accordance with a pre-election agreement.

Also true to his promise, Sandino ceased his guerrilla offensive immediately after the marines' departure, as he prepared for a peace conference proposed earlier by President-elect Sacasa. In early February 1933 he came to Managua, amid popular acclaim, for his meeting with the president and the subsequent signing of the peace agreement.

In return for laying down their arms and accepting the authority of the elected government, the Sandinistas received amnesty and special concessions in the northern departments, where most of them lived. One of these was a tract of unused government land in the Coco Valley, to be developed as an agricultural colony. During the following months, Sandino was occupied with ambitious plans for this cooperative project, which had a degree of autonomy and permission to maintain a small militia for internal order.

Relations with President Sacasa were supportive on both sides, but by the fall of 1933, clashes occurred between the Guard and the colony's militia. General Somoza had opposed its formation, and when it requested additional arms from the government, his opposition mounted. Sandino, for his part, called the National Guard "unconstitutional" and vowed resistance. President Sacasa, caught in the middle of this conflict, summoned Sandino to Managua for a conference in February 1934. With the American ambassador participating in the discussions, the two sides attempted to settle their differences; however, nothing was accomplished. Somoza was disturbed when it appeared that President Sacasa was on the verge of making concessions to Sandino, at the expense of the National Guard and its control of the northern departments.

Despite efforts by the American ambassador to pacify him, on the night of February 21, 1934, Somoza met secretly with his chief officers of the Guard and they determined that Sandino should be eliminated.[21] That evening, while Somoza attended a recital, his Guardsmen arrested Sandino and two of his top aides as they left a dinner at the home of President Sacasa. Apparently not realizing Somoza's key role, Sandino hoped for his intervention, at one point getting his captors to telephone their chief at the recital— to no avail. With Sandino's brother, who had been arrested elsewhere in Managua, the four were taken to the airfield and executed by machine-gun fire. Soon thereafter the Coco Valley project, now leaderless, was eliminated by National Guard troops. With Sandino gone, Anastasio Somoza, chief of the National Guard, which the United States had instituted, was undisputed master of Nicaragua. In 1936, with Sacasa out, his long dictatorship and that of his sons, lasting until 1979, began.

When the Somoza family rule began, it brought to Nicaragua a period of imposed stability and close relationship with the United States which would last for almost half a century. Had it come earlier, this political change might have been highly favorable for American interests on the Mosquito Shore. Americans there had yearned for long-term security, order, and cooperation, which the Somozas would have provided. But by the mid-1930s the long period of significant American presence in the east was approaching its end. At Bluefields and Greytown, this had been evident for a number of years, and the Standard Fruit Company was about to make its exit from Puerto Cabezas.

Quite aside from property losses occasioned by the Sandino raids and low prices due to the depression, poor soils and the spread of Sigatoka and Panama diseases in Standard's plantations had a long-term damaging effect. The Nicaraguan Mosquito Shore had never compared with the Honduran north coast in suitability for banana cultivation, and the neighboring country's exports were eight times those of Nicaragua in the early thirties.[22] A major factor, besides its better soils, was the possibility of large-scale flood irrigation in Honduras, which had the added advantage of controlling Panama disease and replenishing depleted alluvial soils. Topographic conditions in banana districts of the Mosquito Shore did not permit this. United Fruit Company, which, unlike Standard, did not make heavy investments in Nicaragua, made extensive surveys and concluded that banana lands there were not "first class."[23] Through the 1920s, while planting in the best available virgin soils and before the spread of root-and-leaf diseases, Standard Fruit Company had been successful in its Nicaraguan location. But by 1935 it was beginning to realize an inadequate return on its investments and adopted a policy of retrenchment and curtailment. The banana boom in the Mosquito Shore was ending.

During the late thirties the company abandoned more and more blighted and unproductive plantations, and pulled up much of the railway track that served them. In 1942 the company announced that it had been forced to cease banana operations entirely and to turn to lumber production to recoup some of its investment, which, it stated, totaled $10 million for the port and railway alone.[24]

Abandonment of Nicaragua by the last of the banana companies was a serious blow, and whatever remnants there were of an earlier, distinctively American way of life on the Mosquito Shore mostly disappeared. By and large from this time forward, the area was a self-contained backwater of very limited foreign influence, and more than ever neglected by the country of which it was only territorially a part.

The Mosquito Shore
since 1940

For four decades the Mosquito Shore subsisted without a strong foreign imprint—economic, cultural, or political. The American-controlled extractive industries, lumbering and gold mining, were highly localized (in the northern part of the Shore) and, by their nature, involved few resident Americans. Of the port cities, only Puerto Cabezas had a small American colony.

During World War II, two American-related developments affected the Shore: one was war stimulated and thus ephemeral, and the other had no immediate impact. *Castilloa* rubber collecting made a brief comeback in the area as a result of the U.S. government's interest in and subsidization of alternative sources of natural rubber in the Western Hemisphere. Nicaragua was one of the promising Latin American sources because of its early San Juan River Valley rubber boom in the late nineteenth century. During this latter period of rubber collecting, tapping was centered mainly on the area north of the Rio Grande River. By the end of the war, in the face of labor problems and high costs, over 3,000 tons were being produced. Due to the type of operation, there was little effect upon the towns, but the developments resulted in construction of an extensive network of access trails and numerous scattered commissaries for the 5,000 Indian and Creole tappers recruited.[1] Base camps received their supplies by air. With the war's end, tapping stopped, the trails were grown over, and only a few landing strips (later used by mining companies) remained as reminders of this rubber venture.

All through the thirties, the Nicaraguans had felt keen disappointment over the aborted outcome of the 1931 canal survey, and in 1939 Presidents Somoza and Roosevelt exchanged correspondence concerning barge-canal construction via the San Juan. Because of such purely executive agreements, which later stirred a lively congressional inquiry, the U.S. government made another survey—this time for barge canalization of the San Juan—and, finding the estimates too high, made a commitment for construction of a road connecting the Pacific and Atlantic parts of Nicaragua as an alternative. Such a road, pushing eastward from Lake Nicaragua (via Juigalpa), was to terminate at Rama, at the head of navigation on the Escondido. As indicated in the relevant memoranda, the official justification for this commitment, as well as the authorization for the barge-canal survey, was hemispheric defense, but that justification was highly debatable. World War II was starting, and projections were that the road would take at least four years to complete—an estimate that was to prove exceedingly conservative. In an enlightening account of the "Rama Road Affair," Rippy comments: "A road to be completed in no less than four years and to be reached when finished by no other means than barges on 60 miles of a muddy river in a rainy tropical jungle could not have been planned to serve any pressing military purpose."[2]

Far more probable reasons for the commitment related to international politics: placating the dictator of Nicaragua, helping him to maintain stability (a prime objective, seemingly at any cost, in U.S. Nicaraguan policy from the days of Zelaya) by better control of the Atlantic coast, until then the seedbed of revolutionary activity. Of particular importance was the desire to free the United States of the pressure by Nicaragua to "do something" about a canal or canalization. Ever since the Bryan-Chamorro Treaty, the interpretation of the Nicaraguan government and people appeared to be that the United States was obligated to construct a second canal, rather than having an option to do so. Perhaps they would be satisfied with a road, and good relations could be maintained. Not only was the long-standing American influence in Nicaragua worth being maintained, but also the exclusive option on second canal construction rights. For three more decades, the possibility lingered that the United States might wish to exercise that option, while Nicaragua continued to be considered the second-best site.

Pine lumbering, begun during the 1920s by Bragman's Bluff Lumber Company, in conjunction with the banana operations of its sister company, Standard Fruit, continued under another New Orleans company after World War II. By 1950 this company, the Nicaragua Longleaf Pine Lumber Company (locally known as Nipco), had extended its network of logging roads and exploitation of the pine savannas as far as the Rio Coco. A large, modern mill at Puerto Cabezas turned out 60,000 board feet daily. Later, when this mill burned down, the company moved its mill operations inland, closer to the remaining stands, which were far from the port city. Exports of pine lumber, two-thirds of it shipped from Puerto Cabezas, became five times what they had been in the late thirties, with markets mainly in Europe and the Caribbean.[3]

After the mid-1930s, air transport was a stimulus to greater development of the American and Canadian gold mining interests in Bonanza, Rosita, and Siuna. All equipment, materials, and food supplies arrived by cargo planes, making over 2,000 round trips yearly. Compensation for the high transport costs came in the form of low labor costs. In the 1950s, wages were no more than about $1.50 per day for the 2,500 Nicaraguan, Mosquito, and Creole workers (although there was price subsidization of meat and basic foods in the company stores). The foreign companies found a favorable political climate in which to operate, as gold production from these mines came to play an important role in the national economy. It was the leading export for almost the entire decade of the 1940s, and Nicaragua was one of the three leading Latin American producers.[4]

The company towns, each with a substantial population (about 5,000), had few amenities. Isolated in the rainforest, they were crude and unkempt throughout their lengthy history. This was in striking contrast to the well-built bungalows, provided with electricity and hot water and surrounded by lawns and gardens, where the 100 American and Canadian technical personnel and their families lived. (Without such amenities, it is doubtful that foreigners could have been persuaded to live in such unappealing locations.)

With economic alternatives diminishing along the Shore, the mines took on greater significance and their influence became more widespread, extending to Mosquito villages along the coast, through employment opportunities; to the port towns, with their dock workers; to the airlines, increasingly important as freight carriers; and to farming enterprises, large and small, which supplied food. Puerto Cabezas particularly benefited. It was the port which received most of the freight destined for the mines, from heavy machinery to food, which arrived by sea and was forwarded by air from its new, American-built airfield. It had a population of 3,500 in 1950, was the most active port on the Shore, and was called by all "The Port."[5]

Much food for the mines and lumber camps came from the Rio Coco Valley. It had considerable agricultural potential (Sandino had recognized this) and was navigable for a long distance throughout the year. Thus Waspam, 138 miles up the river free of rapids, became an important center for the production and shipment of lumber, bananas (bought by independent buyers from small growers, as was the case on the Rio Grande, Escondido, and San Juan during the 1950s), rice, and cattle. Here developed the Shore's most outstanding modern agricultural enterprise, Brautigam and Company. With its fleet of river boats, it collected bananas on a regular basis up and down the river. It produced substantial harvests of rice and beans on its bottomlands and bought the harvests of other producers. It milled rice and raised beef cattle. This agricultural development, and Waspam itself, depended largely upon the markets provided by the lumber and mining camps. From Waspam's modern airport, rice, red beans, and meat from the Brautigam warehouse were flown out daily to Bonanza and Siuna and to isolated Nipco camps. River and plane were the best means of transport in this frontier zone; there was a road of sorts to Puerto Cabezas, but several kilometers were so bad that the trip by vehicle was a long ordeal.

Riverside farmhouse (*above*) along the Escondido River and bananas (*below*) from small riverside farm, ready to be taken to Bluefields by rowboat, both 1957 (From the collection of the author)

Banana growing continued on the Mosquito Shore after the plantation era, but it was mainly the small-scale production of scattered farms along the Escondido. Foreigners were rarely involved, and its commercial impact upon the Shore was slight. As for the farms, carved out of the forest, and their thatched houses on stilts (because of flooding), there was little to recall of the era of American-owned plantations which had stretched almost continuously along both banks decades ago. With rice, bananas were still a major cash crop of these farmers. Survival of the Escondido, in even limited banana production, was due to its access to Bluefields and marketing possibilities. Two Bluefields trading companies continued to purchase bananas from these farms, sometimes collecting them by barge. However, due to the irregular shipping schedule, dugouts often carried the fruit to Bluefields for local sale—a trip sometimes requiring fifteen hours. The trading companies resold the bananas to a Tampa, Florida company when the arrival of its ships coincided with the uncertain arrival of barge loads from upriver. With such unreliable marketing arrangements, these small-scale, private "hangers on" could not provide competition for the U.S. companies—whose plantations were now removed to other parts of Central America—in the export business. However, there was a local market in Bluefields, and small loads of fruit could be sent by air to Managua and Pacific coast cities. There was no access by road from the Escondido to western Nicaragua until the late 1960s.

There was no foreign influence and little economic activity on the southern Mosquito Shore by the 1950s. Its only important agricultural enterprise was copra oil. El Cocal, the largest independent coconut plantation in Nicaragua (owned by the Brautigam family), just north of Greytown, stretched 33 miles (with a width never more than a mile) along the sandy coast between the bar and the Maiz River and contained 40,000 producing trees. Since coconuts in this extremely wet area do not sprout if left on the trees, harvesting was a simple matter of gathering fallen coconuts throughout the year, which reduced labor costs. Four gatherers, followed by four huskers, covered a 4-mile strip each day. Later, the operation was almost completely mechanized. Tractors and trailers carried the husked coconuts to the mill, where women, using machetes, chipped off the shells. The copra then passed to dryers, then to "breakers," and finally, by conveyor belts, to the oil press. With a double passage through the press, rendered oil amounted to about 1,000 drums per year. The dryer furnaces used husks as fuel, and a herd of 300 cattle fed on the pressed copra (or bran) and grazed on the "pastures" between the coconut trees. With hogs, these cattle provided meat for the plantation workers. (Due to transportation and refrigeration problems, there was no marketing of meat.) One of the few employers south of Puerto Cabezas, the plantation provided work for about 100 laborers, all from Bluefields, who received above-average pay in addition to free housing and the opportunity to buy coconuts (a staple) and meat at low cost.[6]

During World War II, when Asian supplies of copra and coconut oil were cut off to the United States and Western Europe, this area, and islands of the Caribbean, received a stimulus. Afterward, however, lower-cost Philippine production eliminated export possibilities, and the Mosquito Shore and the Corn Islands had to rely on soap and margarine manufacturing companies in Granada as their sole market. Transportation was of course a major problem. There was the long trip up the San Juan River and across the lake, and in certain months, due to water conditions, river boats and barges could not dock directly at El Cocal because of sandbars and shoals. Therefore, the drums of oil were carried to the bar in small boats, then reloaded for the river journey.

Because of the processing mill at El Cocal, it appears that coconut production by small growers in the Greytown area would have been more promising. The plantation was willing to buy from small producers, if the coconuts were brought there fresh. There were numerous advantages: ease of management, little care, no need for machinery, little overhead for fertilizers and insecticides, minimum labor (mainly for gathering and husking), year-round production (providing a steady source of cash), suitability to sandy soils (other crops were not), and an assured domestic market for vegetable oils. However, while the coconut, as well as wild plantains and fish, was a major item in the subsistence economy in and around Greytown, there were no substantial surpluses for sale to the mill by small producers.

Since the 1890s, Greytown had become a virtual ghost town. It was too far from the banana plantations and lumbering camps to experience an economic impact from these twentieth-century developments along the Shore. Only nearby El Cocal had any semblance of economic life by the late 1950s, and it was a self-contained "island." Nothing had changed in Greytown, except that it deteriorated. A pathetic monument to a hundred years of waxing and waning canal hopes, it received few visitors. The journey downstream from San Carlos, by whatever conveyance one might be fortunate enough to obtain, was long and tiring; besides, there was very little occasion to go to this small village of about 300 persons, who had almost no money to buy things. Since its economy never rested upon agriculture but upon a commercial and strategic function that was doomed to disappear, the town never produced more than a very small portion of its needs from cultivation of the land. Nor was it near the Mosquito villages, possible sources of food, as Bluefields and Puerto Cabezas were. The population thus remained dependent upon shipped-in rice, corn, beans, and other basic foods. Much of its cash came from remittances sent by relatives who had moved to other parts of the country.

Still standing in Greytown were about 40 habitable houses, surrounded by rotting shells. Empty expanses marked the sites where fine houses had decayed and became unlivable. After abandonment, people had pulled them apart, one by one, for material to patch the remaining buildings. One of the inhabitants bought the ruins of the formerly elegant Pellas residence and constructed four houses out of the material. In his own house was a stairway of Carrara marble, imported from Italy, which had been in the Pellas home. There were two dilapidated churches: the Anglican in ruins and boarded up and the Catholic in little better state, without a resident priest. In the deserted spaces, goats, cattle, and horses grazed on the weeds and grasses. More durable were steel reminders of the past: the old tramway (Greytown–America), its rails rusting in the rain and sun; two large dredges, mired in the shallow water; weather-beaten locomotives alongside

Main street, Bluefields, in 1957 (From the collection of the author)

Flatboat and passengers (*above*) on the San Juan
River, and "carrying" barges across the rapids (*below*)
at El Castillo, one at a time, both 1957 (From the
collection of the author)

stacked up rails and abandoned machinery.[7] All of this desolation and
demoralization were summed up in a remark of the Nicaraguan *comman-
dante: "El espíritu está muerto."*[8]

Prospects for lumbering and mining, the Mosquito Shore's economic
mainstays, have not been promising in recent years. Like the mahogany
before it, the pine resources have been much depleted. Lumbering in Mosquitia has always been exploitative, moving ever inland and northward
toward decreasingly accessible stands and leaving vast, cut-over areas behind, subject to fires which destroy the pine seedlings that would otherwise
provide regeneration. Efforts to put the forests on a sustained-yield basis

have been lacking, and the last frontier of lumbering on Nicaragua's Mosquito Shore proved to be the Rio Coco. Honduras claimed the territory north of that river, along with its unexploited pine forests, and in the boundary settlement of 1960 obtained them. Thus, with inadequate conservation, the possibility of expansion is very limited in Nicaragua.

By 1971, one of the large mining companies of long standing, La Luz Mines, Limited (Canadian), was curtailing its operations at Siuna. By then, gold ores (first mined in open pits and later underground) had been considerably depleted and copper was a major product. The company suspended all exploration; reduced maintenance to the minimum required for the curtailed mining, milling, and freighting; and cut the work force by approximately 40 percent. Among its reasons were the decline in the grade of copper ore and the increased waste in making the remaining ore available for treatment. Future mining and processing of the company's reserves at a profit was improbable at foreseeable copper prices.[9]

Even though great quantities of timber and gold were extracted from Mosquitia over several decades and tremendous profits were made, benefits to the region and impact upon the economic life of most Nicaraguans were never significant. The isolation and secrecy in which foreign companies

Isolated dwelling on lower San Juan River, 1957 (From the collection of the author)

Greytown in 1957, with grass growing in the street, and boarded-up houses
(From the collection of the author)

were allowed to operate worked to their advantage and that of the Nicaraguan dictatorship. Aside from them, the ones most directly involved
were the Indian miners (the combined labor force of the various mines was
estimated to be over 2,700 in the mid-1960s),[10] and they continued to work
under appalling conditions.

As time passed, Nicaragua looked upon the Bryan-Chamorro Treaty as
immobilizing her development because of the uncertainty of U.S. action
and the inability of other foreign governments to become involved. In
holding out hope that a second canal might be built, the treaty reduced
whatever initiative Nicaraguans might have exerted with respect to eastern
development. Not until late 1970 was the dream of an isthmian canal across
Nicaragua laid to rest. In response to anti-United States riots in Panama in
1964, Congress authorized another Atlantic-Pacific Canal Study Commission to study all possible sites for a sea-level canal. Nicaragua was fully
investigated but the commission rejected it in favor of another Panama site
because of much greater cost in Nicaragua and seemingly insurmountable
physical and human problems. At approximately the same time that the
commission's recommendations were submitted, the United States and
Nicaragua, by mutual agreement, abrogated the Bryan-Chamorro Treaty,
which apparently was considered no longer of any future use to the United
States.

With these developments, hopes for Greytown's revival vanished completely. A short time previously, moreover, the long-promised U.S.-constructed road from Rama to the Pacific plain had been completed, and this, though of benefit to parts of the Mosquito Shore, would divert even more activity from the San Juan Valley. After a quarter century of discontinuous construction, it had proved to be unusually difficult and costly, particularly as work advanced beyond Muelle de los Bueyes and on to Rama. Work was confined to about three months of the year, due to the heavy rainfall. Torrential rivers and the necessity of building many bridges slowed progress.

With the foreigners mostly gone and the Spanish imprint (from western Nicaragua) slight, the Mosquito Shore became more than ever the land of the Mosquito and Creole people, the two majority groups. The population of the Atlantic zone (departments of Zelaya and Rio San Juan) constitutes only about 10 percent of Nicaragua's total, although the region comprises over 50 percent of the national territory. The Mosquito population is concentrated north of Bluefields, along the coast and up the major river valleys, especially the Rio Coco. A rural people for the most part, they live in small, scattered villages, each with a population rarely exceeding 500. They speak their own language, related to South American Chibchan, and most of the men also speak English.

By tradition, Indian men are primarily subsistence hunters and fishermen, although for generations they worked as wage laborers on plantations, in forest operations, and in the mines. (Some still do when jobs are available.) Mosquito women attend to subsistence agriculture in or near the villages. Unlike the men, they have had little contact with foreigners and usually speak no English.

By contrast, the Creoles are primarily town dwellers, in the two largest urban centers, Bluefields and Puerto Cabezas, but also in some of the small market towns of the Mosquitos at the mouths of rivers, such as the Rio Grande and Prinzapolka, at Waspam on the Rio Coco, and around Pearl Lagoon. They also make up the bulk of the small population of San Juan del Norte (Greytown). English speaking, they engage in commercial activities, as well as a wide range of occasional jobs and services and some subsistence agriculture and fishing. Although many Mosquitos and Creoles have some knowledge of the Spanish language from the schools, it is little used throughout the east.

Also mainly town dwellers are the small minorities of Hispanics and Chinese. The Spanish-speaking Nicaraguans handle political and administrative functions in the towns and are often shopkeepers, as are the Chinese (almost exclusively). Even small Mosquito villages are likely to have a Chinese shop. On the other hand, Hispanics are rarely found in the villages.

Finally, the present-day population of eastern Nicaragua includes two small remnant Indian groups, each with a population of less than 1,000. The Sumu, descendants of a much larger and warlike coastal group, culturally related to the Mosquitos, now inhabit the isolated headwater areas of several tributary streams far to the interior. The Ramas are more localized, in the river valleys of the Rama and Punta Gorda rivers and near their outlets south of Bluefields, where they have long lived. All of these Indians are primarily subsistence hunters and fishermen, although they also practice subsistence agriculture; and they have little contact with outsiders.

Most inhabitants of the eastern plain are closely tied to the water, either the lagoon-broken coast or the rivers. There are no roads linking the major coastal towns, nor do most of the coastal and interior (mostly riverine) villages have road connections with the outside. The only exception is in the northeast, where old logging roads traverse the pine savanna from Puerto Cabezas to Waspam and other points on the Rio Coco. The only railroad line of any significance ever constructed in the east, which served banana plantations inland from Puerto Cabezas, is now abandoned. Most local and regional transport, therefore, is by diesel-powered boats along the coast and major rivers, by dugout canoes, or by foot along beaches and forest trails.

The Mosquito Shore was touched significantly by external forces, all seeking different things at different times, but it has reverted to a self-contained, indigenous way of life. Through all generations, the Mosquito people never completely lost touch with this way of life (fortunately, as it appears today), but, beginning with the English buccaneers and ending with the foreign companies, the foreign presence decidedly affected their lives.

The greatest and most meaningful impact came within the last century, during which the Mosquito Indians and Creoles sold their labor as plantation workers, rubber collectors, lumber workers, miners, construction laborers, and dock workers. In this manner they became accustomed to a wage and dependent upon goods that money would buy—sometimes completely, for months at a time, or at least as a supplement to their subsistence activities. As a result of the demand for their labor—for they were almost the only source in a region of chronic shortage—there was not a great necessity for them to develop surpluses to sell from their limited resource

Decaying Protestant church *(above)* and remains of a
wharf in silted-in "harbor" *(below)*, Greytown, 1957.
(From the collection of the author)

base. Nevertheless, there was a demand for food (whatever was not imported) by the growing towns and foreign-controlled companies, and bananas could be sold to such companies as Standard Fruit—another way of
gaining cash. They began to depend upon the companies not only for
employment and as markets for their products but also for manufactured
items, clothing, medicines, and new types of processed and canned
foodstuffs, which were increasingly introduced to their diets. These they
purchased in the company commissaries. In brief, there was a drift away

from their traditional subsistence economy to one more and more consumer-oriented, as the wants multiplied.

With the passing of the foreign company and their dependency upon it,
readjustment for these people was not easy. An anthropogeographer, who
recently made an intensive study of the Mosquito economy, expressed their
dilemma very well:

> The economic mainstay of outside inputs of jobs, currency, and inexpensive
> goods has been removed. The company commissaries and supply boats are
> gone, money is scarce, and store-bought items are expensive. With few out-
> side work opportunities the Miskito have become increasingly dependent
> once again on their own subsistence efforts and on their own local environ-
> ments for salable resources, but this time under greatly changed social and
> ecological conditions. The golden boom period is past and the Miskito are left
> with only their subsistence system together with an overburden of desires for
> luxury and foreign goods as a result of contact.[11]

The areas available to the Mosquito population for subsistence agriculture have been, from the practical standpoint, restricted. The vastness of
the Mosquito Shore, much of it virtually empty, cannot be considered a
reserve for subsistence production. The Mosquitos, concentrated along the
coast and up the river valleys, have always walked from their villages to their
plots, which consequently had to be nearby. Nothing short of wholesale
resettlement of the population can change this areal limitation upon subsistence agriculture. Moreover, the soils of interfluvial rainforest and pine savanna, far from Mosquito concentrations, are less productive. The most
favored soils have already been used. To the present, considering the small
populations involved, the land available for "shifting" cultivation has proved
sufficient, and food yields have been fairly high from rather low labor
inputs.

However, there were problems when the Mosquitos were forced to fall
back upon their traditional, subsistence environments, rather than employment, as a source of cash. One notable result has been the overemphasis, in
both exploitation and efforts, upon a narrower range of subsistence activities to provide products with the greatest market demand. This could
lead not only to depletion of various subsistence resources, but, if in the
animal category, to neglect of agriculture. The consequent decline in traditional food production and village sharing could then create more dependence upon bought foods.

A case in point has been the green turtle, the major source of meat protein for coastal Mosquitos and, together with manioc, the traditional mainstay of their diet. Due to the shortage of other types of locally produced meat, demand for turtle meat by foreign-controlled companies' personnel was excessive during the first half of the century. This upset the balance between the turtle population and the food requirements of the Mosquito villages, and tended to deplete the resource. But turtle meat was another source of income for the Mosquito people—commercial marketing of a commodity which was always paramount in their villages—and they welcomed it.

In the late 1960s and early 1970s, foreign companies again set up operations in Bluefields and Puerto Cabezas, this time for the large-scale marketing of turtle meat. With a seemingly unlimited demand and few opportunities to gain cash through employment, the coastal Mosquitos turned to exploitation of the already seriously depleted turtle resource with excessive zeal. After two turtle-processing companies established operations in late 1969 and began buying at higher prices than ever before, the numbers of turtles taken by one coastal community increased 228 percent within two years, while the sale of turtles outside the village increased by 1,500 percent.[12] Conservation of the Mosquitos' most valuable resource was not the only principle at stake here. The supply of this most important source of protein in the Mosquito diet was no longer sufficient, in the face of vastly increased commercialization of the market, to satisfy the food requirements of the villages. The trend was therefore toward greater consumption of carbohydrates, purchased from external sources with the money earned from turtle sales. When the Nicaraguan government, in the interest of conservation, halted these operations of the foreign companies in 1977, the Mosquitos resented the action for it deprived them of one of their last sources of cash. It seemed but another push backward, toward an unwelcome alternative: subsistence fishing, agriculture, and gathering, in the way of their ancestors.

The economic dislocations of the Mosquito population received little attention from the Nicaraguan government during the Somoza years. There were almost no efforts to stimulate the economy of the Atlantic region, to fill the vacuum left by the decline of foreign interests there, or to provide alternatives. Also, the government made few attempts to improve education and health among the Mosquitos. As it had been for years, the Moravian Church was largely responsible for advances in these areas. Yet, despite this neglect by the government, a recent study concludes that the dictatorship was more tolerable in the east, among the Mosquitos, than in the Pacific coreland, among the Hispanic Nicaraguans.

Despite the general dislike and suspicion of "Westerners" on the Shore, Somoza seemed to be an exception. Anglicized themselves, the Mosquito people appreciated his American ties and his bilingualism. On his occasional visits to the east coast, he spoke to them in English and appeared to support their non-Hispanic heritage. Moreover, the Mosquito people, as devout Moravians, were inclined to conservative political views. With a deep fear of communism, and its apparent threats to their traditional land systems and to their religion, they regarded Somoza as a bulwark against alien influences.[13] Their support of the regime was expressed by the disproportionate number of Mosquito men in the National Guard. The Guard had not developed the bad image it had elsewhere in Nicaragua: there were never many Guardsmen stationed in the east and the Mosquito people, for the most part, had not suffered at their hands. Finally, the people appreciated the cultural autonomy permitted them under Somoza. There were advantages in what Alan Riding, a *New York Times* correspondent, called "the independence of neglect": they could continue speaking English and their native languages, could adhere to their Protestant Moravian religion, and could practice their indigenous customs with little interference.[14]

Thus the guerrilla movement, which overthrew the Somoza government in the summer of 1979, received little support among the Mosquitos and Creoles of the east. Except in this region (with a population of 193,835, according to the latest census),[15] the response was mainly positive. The long autocracy, with its suppression of opposition; its family control of much of Nicaragua's wealth; its indifference toward reforms aimed at a better distribution of goods, status, or power; its hated private army—the National Guard; and its close ties with the United States, had estranged many elements of the population—from the rural peasantry to the urban middle class. Many were ready for a change, and this widespread support was important in the ultimate victory of the rebel forces, who invoked the memory of the earlier revolutionary leader, Sandino—still a martyred hero to many Nicaraguans—by calling themselves Sandinistas.

Throughout the buildup of revolutionary sentiment in other parts of the country, there was little opportunity for the Mosquito people to develop close ties with the modern-day Sandinistas, even if they had been disposed to. The rebels' zones of operation were geographically distant. As for the ideological appeal of Sandino, this was not effective in the east. For some Mosquito Shore inhabitants, the memory of the earlier Sandinistas was decidedly negative. Moravian missionaries had suffered at the hands of the Sandinistas in the 1930s, and their Mosquito charges did not forget this.

Many remembered that the Sandinistas had been responsible for the destructive raids upon the Standard Fruit–Bragman's Bluff Company, the
Shore's major employer, in the early 1930s. They blamed the company's
withdrawal upon these raids (although several other factors were involved).
While Sandino had gained allies among the Mosquitos, particularly those of
the Coco Valley, many others had not identified with the view of all foreign
companies as exploiters, but (as noted) were closely tied to them as employees, providers of products, and consumers of goods from the company
commissaries. Granted that the excessive dependency which developed was
not beneficial, the fact is that, for them, the companies were not unwelcome. Former employees looked back on that era as the "good days,"
with fair wages and fair treatment under bosses they admired.[16] It cannot
be denied that there was exploitation, coupled with ethnic discrimination.
This was notorious in the mining communities, where the better-paying
surface jobs went to mestizos from the west while the silicosis-afflicted
Indians labored underground at low wages, in extremely unsafe circumstances. Strict segregation was practiced in the company towns. Nevertheless, such conditions did not appear to have resulted in widespread
dissatisfaction. The mines had provided employment, a source of cash, and
such advantages as subsidized food prices in company stores.

Soon after the revolutionary government was in power, it proclaimed its
commitment to develop the Mosquito Shore and improve the lives of its
native population. Certainly a primary motive was to capitalize upon an
agricultural potential in the virtually empty interior of Zelaya Department
and upon the mineral and forest resources in that part of the country, to
which access had now been provided. The Atlantic coast was heralded in
Managua as the country's great new frontier. Although production in the
American and Canadian–controlled gold mines had greatly diminished,
earnings were high, due to the high gold prices of the time, and the new
government immediately saw the mines of Siuna, Bonanza, and Rosita (the
only significant gold producers) as a source of needed foreign exchange.
They were nationalized in November of 1979. Nationalization of fishing
and lumbering in the Atlantic region followed.

There appeared to be no initial animosity toward the Mosquito people;
indeed, special programs were designed for them by the government. A
bilingual education program—Miskito-Spanish and English-Spanish—was
instituted in 1980 and, simultaneously, the Atlantic region received emphasis in the national literacy campaign. The new government initiated an

indigenous organization, MISURASATA, purportedly to protect the interests of the Mosquito, Sumu, and Rama peoples and to represent them in Managua. (It was also politically useful to the government.) Despite its intentions, the government, in its urgency to integrate these inhabitants, proved inadequately sensitive to their ethnic, cultural, and religious traditions. In fact, it tended to subordinate them in the class struggle of oppressed and disadvantaged peoples throughout Nicaragua. It expected that the Mosquito Shore people, considered to be part of this group, would join wholeheartedly in its plans for a new socialist state, irrespective of their cultural distinctiveness and unique background.

It was not to be. Opposition mounted as the revolutionary government, with its soon-established Cuban and Soviet links, changed the permissive policy of former years to intervention and sought to impose its Marxist reforms. The Mosquitos did not constitute an oppressed, landless peasantry, as existed in other parts of the country, and thus had less to gain from changes. Conversely, they saw their land and resource rights, recognized since the British protectorate, as threatened by nationalization, despite efforts by MISURASATA to protect them. The government also encouraged the colonization of Nicaraguan peasants from the Pacific plain, particularly along the Siuna road, thus incurring disputes with Mosquito inhabitants. Nationalization of the mines did not improve the status of the Indians, who still did most of the grueling and dangerous work down the shafts and could not compete for the desirable jobs above. It appeared that the revolution had brought only a change in bosses.[17]

The two major non-Mosquito elements of the Atlantic population introduced further divisiveness. Within both groups—the Africanized Creoles, who lived mainly along the southern coast and particularly in Bluefields, and the pre-revolution Hispanic (mestizo) inhabitants—was the privileged regional "elite." The Creoles, many of them urban and traditionally the most Anglicized and most foreign oriented (toward the United States and Britain) of the Shore's people, refused any organized liaison, such as MISURASATA, with the Sandinista government. They mounted strikes and demonstrations of protest in Bluefields. The pre-revolution Hispanics (always an alien, unwelcome presence, as far as Mosquitos were concerned), were also adamantly opposed to MISURASATA, but as a manifestation of indigenous power—a threat. The response of the third non-Indian group— the small but very important Chinese population (who controlled most retail establishments along the Shore)—was to depart. Locally, this caused serious economic disorders, with shortages of necessities that the government was unable to supply due to the poor distribution system.[18]

The plethora of government agencies set up in Mosquitia to administer the reforms was staffed by either new Hispanics from the west, with no knowledge of the Atlantic region and its culture, or the disliked Hispanic elite from the east. Better-educated Mosquitos were generally excluded, as were many Creoles, who, in places like Bluefields, had occupied adminstrative positions in pre-revolution government agencies.

One of the many difficulties of establishing workable relationships was communication: the "linguistic barrier." The majority of the population in the Atlantic region, and particularly the Indians of the northeast, had little or no knowledge of Spanish, and most of the new administrators from the west were unable to speak or understand Miskito or English.

A social anthropologist, who made a postrevolution study of government–Indian relations in the Atlantic region in 1980, notes that the first Sandinista fighters to enter Mosquitia were "profoundly baffled by what they found: an apathetic, if not openly hostile, population who 'refused' to understand that they were the victims of imperialism or that General Sandino was a heroic figure."[19] Furthermore, after a year of what he characterizes as notable achievements, "serious cultural animosities persist and continue to evolve in the revolutionary context. A general mistrust or, at best, apathy vis-à-vis the revolution prevails."[20]

Unable to gain the allegiance of the Mosquito and Creole population and fearful of their possible involvement in counterrevolutionary movements, the government turned to increasingly repressive measures. While a perceived danger was undoubtedly a factor, it is not unreasonable to expect that some of the repression, at least on the part of military personnel, resulted from simple prejudice toward an unlike people: Indian, black, Anglicized, and Protestant. In this regard, the reaction would hardly be different in some other countries that have ethnic minorities. In any case, the Mosquito people—especially those in the border zone—suffered the consequences: village raids, casualties, property destruction, detainments, and forced relocation. (The measures were called "defensive" by the Sandinistas.) More alienated than ever, thousands of Mosquito Indians fled across the Rio Coco and, as refugees in Honduras, became recruits of counterrevolutionists who operate from that country: Somoza sympathizers, exiled National Guard members, and disaffected Sandinistas.

Very few tropical coasts have experienced so much activity, so many external influences, and so much expectation—finally to end with so little— as has the Atlantic region of Nicaragua. It appears as if none of these things had happened—there is an amnesic quality about the region. True incorporation, as an integral part of Nicaragua, has never occurred; thus the region is still a geographical and cultural outpost, but now without foreign stimuli.

In the past, the Mosquito Shore had been a special case because of its attraction for the foreigner and his molding of the settlement's history and economy. But from now on its main development will likely follow that of other sparsely populated frontiers in Latin America: internal orientation, with roads of penetration into the area, along which agricultural development and settlement will take place in previously unused land. This is already happening along the Rama Road.

Besides penetration into the eastern interior, the road's completion (in the late 1960s) marked the beginning of a regional exchange between the two sides of the country (Managua–Juigalpa–Rama–Bluefields) in terms of goods and people—despite the fact that it still involved a long boat trip on the navigable Escondido to and from the road's terminus at Rama. The road's significance should be enormously enhanced.

With massive dredging and construction, the Sandinista government is converting Bluefields into a deep-water harbor. Despite its problems with the natives, the government has brought the Mosquito Shore the greatest project since the aborted canal—which, incidentally, has had a salutary impact upon local employment. In at least this way has the relationship between the government and Bluefields residents (almost all have benefited economically) improved. The government seems determined to create, for the first time, an Atlantic port for the country that is capable of handling large cargo vessels and thus open western Nicaragua, via the Rama Road, directly to Atlantic commerce (a much shorter route than through the Panama Canal).

Even prior to the revolution, 90 percent of the country's imports and 50 percent of its exports were associated with Atlantic nations, yet Nicaragua was the only Atlantic-facing Central American nation without a major port on that ocean. There is now an additional incentive for the port developments in Bluefields: more direct access with Cuba and with the Soviet Union and Soviet bloc countries, which are some of Nicaragua's major suppliers, directly or indirectly (especially of military matériel). Already, Cuban and East European ships have unloaded cargos in Bluefields harbor, and many more may be expected to use it when improvements are completed and it is capable of receiving larger vessels and handling their freight.

Whatever the reasons for its transformation, Bluefields appears to be on the threshold of becoming a major Nicaraguan commercial center with elimination of its long-standing problem and that of the Atlantic coast generally: poor harbor facilities. However, the port is simply at the eastern end of the Rama-Escondido funnel to western Nicaragua; it is not connected—except by sea—with other parts of the Shore. Its economic advances may be largely self-contained, and regional interchange and interaction, as far as the Mosquito Shore is concerned, would remain minimal. The situation would resemble that of an isolated but active port of some tropical African country, with a single railway through the bush to the heartland.

Penetration of the extremely isolated northeastern part of the country has also been achieved, by the extension of the Managua–Matagalpa highway to the mining area of Siuna and Rosita, and Puerto Cabezas. This project was begun prior to the Sandinista takeover, and President Somoza inaugurated the unfinished 300-mile highway in April of 1977. Improvement has proceeded since the revolution, and by 1981 the segment as far as Siuna was passable. The remaining portion, to Puerto Cabezas, however, was in poor condition and passable only in the dry season.[21] Once the highway becomes all-weather, additional eastern outposts will have regular land connections with Managua.

The Atlantic coast's second most important population center, Puerto Cabezas, previously accessible from the west only by air or by the Rama Road (after a long boat trip down the Escondido and up the coast from Bluefields), should especially benefit by the extension of the road. Besides bringing Nicaragua's principal timber and mineral-producing zone into the national economy, the road opens new lands for colonization: river valleys which, were it not for floods, have agricultural potential. Stranded populations, repeatedly victimized by floods, can be aided. Unfortunately, the high cost of imported oil will limit some of the advantages of these roads, and the complete absence of railways in the east remains a drawback.

The Nicaraguan government has a late start in frontier development by comparison with many Latin American countries. However, considering the special circumstances (historical and political), perhaps this is not surprising. It is now up to Nicaragua to end the isolation of its eastern half and to initiate durable development.

A major and perennial obstacle, which has always set the region apart and caused Nicaragua much difficulty, is the non-Hispanic culture. In the long view, development that emanates and involves settlers from the west will not be facilitated in a land where other languages are spoken, another religion

and entirely different customs are practiced, and where anti-Spanish sentiments and Anglo-American leanings are long established. For the Mosquito
Indians, blacks, and mixed bloods, English is the *lingua franca*, and Hispanic customs and institutions are alien. Very few are aware of themselves as
Nicaraguans. They still refer to immigrants and visitors from the Pacific
side as "Spaniards," emphasizing their own separateness, linguistically and
culturally.

Despite the improvements in Bluefields, the preoccupation of the Nicaraguan government with the Honduran threat—considered as directed
toward its overthrow—will likely postpone economic advances throughout
the east. For that region, the consuming concern will be military defense, as
long as the threat continues. Besides the unreliability of its non-Hispanic
inhabitants, its remoteness, poor communications, and exposed Atlantic
location appear to make it vulnerable as a haven and springboard for counterrevolutionary forces. (It has been so in the past.) This, no doubt, has also
been part of the incentive for the government's conversion of Bluefields—
the major military base in the region, with scores of soldiers—into a deep-
water port, capable of receiving military supplies by sea for defensive and
offensive purposes, if need be.

Whatever the outcome of the counterrevolutionary threat, the government of Nicaragua is in a poor position to bring about a reconciliation with
much of the Mosquito population, which would be essential to any economic development plans it may have for Mosquitia. Some of its early
problems with the people of the Shore might have found a solution or
compromise, but the repressive tactics it ultimately resorted to have gener-
ated antagonism. The gulf between the two culturally dichotomous parts of
the country appears to be wider than ever.

Beyond all this, it would be difficult for any government to develop the
mostly empty lands agriculturally—if this is the objective of an "eastward
march." The Rama and Siuna roads are a beginning, but only that. The
tropical, high-rainfall environment and the poor soils—often leached,
poorly drained, gravelly, or sandy (except in river valleys and around coastal
lagoons)—will always be major problems for staple crop production. There
is little likelihood that banana planters will make a reentry into abandoned
lands, in light of unprofitable experiences. However, some companies have
used these lands to plant mahogany, cedar, and teak, and there are possibilities for "tree plantations"—a use of land that some consider (along with
cattle raising) the most promising for the Mosquito Shore.

Nevertheless, the eastern plain is not a great bonanza in the geographical sense. Except for its canal potential, the advantages of the Mosquito Shore have been greatly overplayed throughout its history. Facts and events did not bear out the favorable perceptions, and the region's Nicaraguan future is uncertain. True incorporation, whenever seriously attempted, will be slow. It requires an entirely new approach which, one hopes, will be more realistic, more adaptive to real conditions, and less exploitative. Moreover, the human resource of the Atlantic region was grossly neglected during the Somoza years, and, as the Sandinistas have seemed to recognize, massive health and literacy campaigns will be necessary before the inhabitants can begin to contribute to their economic betterment in any significant measure.

The Mosquito Shore's interesting and eventful past offers little to build upon and little encouragement. Largely extraneous and of no lasting accomplishments, it was a response to unique geographical conditions met with peculiar times and perceptions.

Notes

Chapter 1

1. Hubert Howe Bancroft, *The Works of Hubert Howe Bancroft*, vols. VI–VIII: History of Central America (San Francisco: History Company, 1886–1887), VI: 489.

2. Lyle N. McAlister, "The Discovery and Exploration of the Nicaraguan Trans-isthmian Route, 1519–1545," *The Americas*, 10, no.3 (January 1954): 259–76; ref. on p. 273.

3. "La Ruta de Nicaragua a través de la Historia," *Revista Conservadora del Pensa-miento Centroamericano*, 22, no. 108 (September 1969): 3–13; ref. on p. 4.

4. Ibid., p. 5.

5. J. Eric S. Thompson, ed., *Thomas Gage's Travels in the New World* (Norman: University of Oklahoma Press, 1958), pp. 308–9.

6. Troy S. Floyd, *The Anglo-Spanish Struggle for Mosquitia* (Albuquerque: University of New Mexico Press, 1967), p. 56.

7. Thomas Young, *Narrative of a Residence on the Mosquito Shore During the Years 1839, 1840, and 1841* (London: Smith, Elder & Co., 1842), p. 25.

8. See Enrique Sanchez Pedrote, "El Coronel Hodgson y la Expedición a la Costa de los Mosquitos," *Anuario de Estudios Americanos*, Escuela de Estudios Hispano-Americanos (Seville, Spain), 24 (1967): 1205–35; p. 1216.

9. George Hodgson, "Some Account of That Portion of the Continent of America called the Mosquito Shore, as at present actually possessed and used by the Subjects of Great Britain," October 12,1766 (in Walker's report to Foreign Office, February 15, 1847), Public Record Office, London, Foreign Office 53 (Mosquitia) (cited hereafter as P.R.O., F.O. 53), v. 7.

10. Floyd, *Anglo-Spanish Struggle*, p. 139.

11. Stephen Kemble, *The Kemble Papers*, 2 vols. (New York: New York Historical Society, 1884), vol. XVII of Collections of the New York Historical Society, "Documents and Correspondence, Expedition to the Spanish Main and Nicaragua, 1779–1781," pp. 164–431; Polson to Kemble, May 14, 1780, p. 229.

12. Ibid., Kemble to Dallings, May 25, 1781, p. 406.

13. Orlando W. Roberts, *Narrative of Voyages and Excursions on the East Coast and in the Interior of Central America* (Edinburgh: Constable and Company, 1827), p. 265.

14. *Kemble Papers*, vol. XVII, "Journal of Lt. Col. Stephen Kemble, Brigadier-General in Command of the Expedition to Nicaragua, 1780–1781," pp. 1–64; entry of June 9, 1780, p. 14.

15. Ibid., entry of July 7, 1780, p. 22.

16. *Kemble Papers*, vol. XVII, "Documents and Correspondence, Expedition to the Spanish Main and Nicaragua, 1779–1781," pp. 164–431; Kemble to Dallings, August 26, 1780, p. 276.

17. *Kemble Papers*, vol. XVII, "Journal of Lt. Col. Stephen Kemble, Brigadier-General in Command of the Expedition to Nicaragua, 1780–1781"; entry of July 23, 1780, p. 29.

18. Ibid., entry of July 24, 1780, pp. 29–31.

19. Ibid., entry of August 5, 1780, p. 36.

20. *Kemble Papers*, vol. XVII, "Documents and Correspondence, Expedition to the Spanish Main and Nicaragua, 1779–1781"; Kemble to Dixon, September 18, 1780, p. 307.

21. Ibid., October 21, 1780, p. 319.

22. Floyd, *Anglo-Spanish Struggle*, p. 161.

23. Young, *Narrative of a Residence*, p. 54.

24. Floyd, *Anglo-Spanish Struggle*, p. 169.

25. See ibid., chap. 12, pp. 172–82.

Chapter 2

1. Peter F. Stout, *Nicaragua: Past, Present and Future* (Philadelphia: John E. Potter, 1859), pp. 169–70.

2. Orlando W. Roberts, *Narrative of Voyages and Excursions on the East Coast and in the Interior of Central America* (Edinburgh: Constable, 1827), p. 148.

3. James Douglas, "Account of the Attempt to Form a Settlement on the Mosquito Shore in 1823," *Transactions of the Literary and Historical Society of Quebec*, session of 1868–69, pp. 25–39; ref. on p. 30.

4. Ibid., pp. 38–39.

5. Ibid., pp. 32–33.

6. Ibid., p. 26.

7. *Revival of the British Settlement on the Bluefields River in Central America* (pamphlet), (London: E. Colyer, 1840), p. 21.

8. Thomas Young, *Narrative of a Residence on the Mosquito Shore During the Years 1839, 1840, and 1841* (London: Smith, Elder & Co., 1842), p. 67.

9. Ibid., p. 69.

10. Ibid., p. 70.

11. Ibid., p. 54.

12. Cited in J. A. R. Marriott, *England Since Waterloo* (London: Methuen, 1913), p. 205.

Chapter 3

1. See Gavin B. Henderson, "German Colonial Projects on the Mosquito Coast, 1844–1848," *English Historical Review*, 59 (May 1944): 257–71; p. 261.

2. Walker to Earl of Aberdeen, October 20, 1846, P.R.O., F.O. 53 (5).

3. Walker to Bunsen, November 21, 1846, P.R.O., F.O. 53 (5).

4. Walker to Earl of Aberdeen, January 9, 1845, P.R.O., F.O. 53 (2).

5. Ibid., September 19, 1846, P.R.O., F.O. 53 (5).

6. Ryder to Lambert, January 8, 1848, P.R.O., F.O. 53 (14).

7. Ryder to Munios, January 16, 1848, P.R.O., F.O. 53 (14).

8. See Samuel F. Bemis, *The Latin American Policy of the United States* (New York: Harcourt Brace Jovanovich, 1943), p. 105, and J. Fred Rippy, *The Caribbean Danger Zone* (New York: G. P. Putnam's Sons, 1940), p. 102.

9. Squier to Secretary of State Clayton, September 12, 1849, in William R. Manning (ed.), *Diplomatic Correspondence of the United States, Inter-American Affairs*, vol. III: Central America, 1831–1850 (Washington, D.C.: Carnegie Endowment for International Peace, 1933), p. 370.

10. Christie to Palmerston, August 19, 1848, P.R.O., F.O. 53 (15).

11. Ibid., September 5, 1848.

12. Ibid.

13. Ibid.

14. Ibid., September 15, 1848.

15. Ibid.

16. Ibid.

17. Palmerston to Christie, November 16, 1848, P.R.O., F.O. 53 (11).

18. Henderson, "German Colonial Projects," p. 260.

19. Christie to Palmerston, February 13, 1849, P.R.O., F.O. 53 (21).

20. Ibid.

21. Ibid.

22. Christie to Palmerston, March 22, 1849, P.R.O., F.O. 53 (17).

23. Merivale to Addington, May 5, 1849, P.R.O., F.O. 53 (22).

24. Hise to Buchanan, February 8, 1849, in Manning, *Diplomatic Correspondence*, III: 306.

25. Squier to Clayton, September 10, 1849, in Manning, *Diplomatic Correspondence*, III: 361.

26. Clayton to Squier, November 20, 1849, in Manning, *Diplomatic Correspondence*, III: 56.

27. Hubert Howe Bancroft, *The Works of Hubert Howe Bancroft*, vols. VI–VIII: History of Central America (San Francisco: History Company, 1886–1887), VIII: 262.

28. Ephraim George Squier, "San Juan de Nicaragua," *Harper's New Monthly Magazine*, 10 (December 1854): 50–61; pp. 51–53.

29. Ibid., ref. on p. 53.

30. Christie to Palmerston, October 30, 1849, P.R.O., F.O. 53 (20).

31. See Mary W. Williams, *Anglo-American Isthmian Diplomacy, 1815–1915* (Washington, D.C.: American Historical Association, 1916), pp. 81–82, and Mario Rodriguez, *A Palmerstonian Diplomat in Central America: Frederick Chatfield, Esq.* (Tucson: University of Arizona Press, 1964), pp. 323–25.

32. Clayton to Squier, May 7, 1850, in Manning, *Diplomatic Correspondence*, III: 60.

Chapter 4

1. David I. Folkman, Jr., "Westward Via Nicaragua: The United States and the Nicaragua Route, 1826–1869," Ph.D. dissertation, University of Utah, 1966 (Ann Arbor, Mich.: University Microfilms, 1971), pp. 68–69.

2. Roger S. Baldwin, "Tarrying in Nicaragua: Pleasures and Perils of the California Trip in 1849," *Century Magazine*, 42 (n.s. v. 20), no. 6 (October, 1891): 911–31; ref. on p. 912.

3. Max Harrison Williams, "The San Juan River–Lake Nicaragua Waterway, 1502–1921," Ph.D. dissertation, Louisiana State University, 1971 (Ann Arbor, Mich.: University Microfilms, 1972), pp. 192–99.

4. Folkman, "Westward Via Nicaragua," pp. 112–13.

5. Calvert to Christie, as cited in Christie to Palmerston, April 17, 1850, P.R.O., F.O. 53 (23B).

6. Vice Admiral McDonald to Secretary of the Admiralty, November 18, 1850, P.R.O., F.O. 53 (25).

7. Lord Dundonald to Secretary of the Admiralty, January 20, 1851, P.R.O., F.O. 53 (28).

8. Green to Dyke, December 18, 1850, P.R.O., F.O. 53 (28).

9. Ephraim George Squier, "San Juan de Nicaragua," *Harper's New Monthly Magazine*, 10 (December 1854): 50–61; ref. on p. 57.

10. Green to Earl of Malmesbury, August 19, 1852, P.R.O., F.O. 53 (29).

11. Wilson to Seymour, February 17, 1853, P.R.O., F.O. 53 (32).

12. Borland to Marcy, May 30, 1854, U.S. Department of State, Despatches from U.S. Ministers to Central America, 1824–1906 (Nicaragua: 1854–1873), National Archives Microfilm Publication No. 219, roll 9.

13. Hollins to the Authorities and People of Greytown, July 12, 1854, U.S. Department of State, Despatches from U.S. Consuls in San Juan del Norte, 1851–1906, National Archives Microfilm Publication No. T-348 (hereafter Despatches . . . Consuls . . . SJdelN), roll 1.

14. Fabens to Department of State, February 6, 1855, Despatches . . . Consuls . . . SJdelN, roll 6.

15. Greytown Petitioners to Queen Victoria, August 13, 1854, Despatches . . . Consuls . . . SJdelN, roll 1.

16. Folkman, "Westward Via Nicaragua," p. 198.

17. Wheeler to Marcy, February 10, 1855, U.S. Department of State Despatches from U.S. Ministers to Central America, 1824–1906 (Nicaragua: 1854–1873), National Archives Microfilm Publication No. 219, roll 10.

18. See R. E. May, *The Southern Dream of a Caribbean Empire, 1854–1861* (Baton Rouge: Louisiana State University Press, 1973), p. 134; Folkman, "Westward Via Nicaragua," p. 258.

19. See May, *The Southern Dream*, pp. 90–94.

20. Cited in letter from O'Hara to Department of State, April 26, 1897, Despatches . . . Consuls . . . SJdelN, roll 13.

21. See Walker to Heiss, September 30, 1856, in "Papers of Major John P. Heiss of Nashville," *Tennessee Historical Magazine*, 2 (September 1916): 137–49; pp. 147–49.

22. Michael Fleenen Luark Papers, Diary, 3 (December 20, 1855–January 24, 1856): 289, in University of Washington Libraries, Seattle.

23. "Reminiscences of Central America," *DeBows Review*, 29 (n.s. v. 4), no. 4 (October 1860): 410–29; ref. on p. 415.

24. Deposition, Henry Foster to Green, British consulate, Greytown, February 10, 1857, P.R.O., F.O. 53 (40).

25. See May, *The Southern Dream*, p. 135.

26. See Folkman, "Westward Via Nicaragua," p. 292.

27. Bedford C.T. Pim and Berthold Seemann, *Dottings on the Roadside in Panama, Nicaragua, and Mosquito* (London: Chapman and Hall, 1869), p. 272.

28. Ibid., p. 229.

29. Cottrell to Cass, October 31, 1857, Despatches . . . Consuls . . . SJdelN, roll 2.

30. See Mary W. Williams, *Anglo-American Isthmian Diplomacy, 1815–1915* (Washington, D.C.: American Historical Association, 1916), pp. 222–23, and J. Fred Rippy, *Latin America in World Politics* (New York: F.S. Crofts and Co., 1928), p. 105.

Chapter 5

1. In the interest of consistency, the British place name of "Greytown" will be used throughout this study, even though the port was generally referred to by its official Nicaraguan name, "San Juan del Norte," after the Treaty of Managua.

2. See David I. Folkman, "Westward Via Nicaragua: The United States and the Nicaragua Route, 1826–1869," Ph.D. dissertation, University of Utah, 1966 (Ann Arbor, Mich.: University Microfilms, 1971), pp. 363–65.

3. Cottrell to Department of State, October 6, 1862, Despatches . . . Consuls . . . SJdelN, roll 4.

4. Ibid., November 17, 1862.

5. Ibid., October 30, 1865.

6. Folkman, "Westward Via Nicaragua," appendix B, p. 431.

7. George Lawrence, "Excursion to the Lake of Nicaragua Up the River San Juan," *Nautical Magazine and Naval Chronicle* (London), 1840: 857–64; ref. on p. 861.

8. Daniel Cleveland, "Across the Nicaragua Transit," unpublished manuscript, April 15, 1868 (M65, xv, 160 leaves), in Bancroft Library, University of California, Berkeley.

9. Thomas Belt, *The Naturalist in Nicaragua* (London: John Murray, 1874), p. 32.

10. Olds to Department of State, September 20, 1872, Despatches . . . Consuls . . . SJdelN, roll 5.

11. Ibid.

12. Ibid., November 29, 1872.

13. Green, letter of certification in behalf of Cottrell, July 1, 1872, ibid.

14. Olds to Department of State, September 20, 1872, ibid.

15. Ralph Lee Woodward, Jr., *Central America: A Nation Divided* (New York: Oxford University Press, 1976), p. 178.

16. Silvio F. Pellas, "La Nicaragua Steamship and Navigation Company," *Revista Conservadora del Pensamiento Centroamericano*, 22, no. 108 (September 1969): 16.

17. Kretchmer to Department of State, December 15, 1881, Despatches . . . Consuls . . . SJdelN, roll 6.

18. Brown to Department of State, April 15, 1885, Despatches . . . Consuls . . . SJdelN, roll 7.

Chapter 6

1. See Joseph Smith, *Illusions of Conflict: Anglo-American Diplomacy Toward Latin America, 1865–1896* (Pittsburgh: University of Pittsburgh Press, 1979), pp. 92–100.

2. J. Fred Rippy, *The Caribbean Danger Zone* (New York: G. P. Putnam's Sons, 1940), p. 88.

3. Nicaragua Canal Construction Company, *The Inter-oceanic Canal of Nicaragua* (New York, 1891), p. 14.

4. R. E. Peary, "The Rio San Juan de Nicaragua," *Journal of the American Geographical Society of New York*, 21 (1889): 57–96; ref. on p. 77.

5. *New York Times*, April 8, 1888.

6. Brown to Department of State, October 29, 1888, Despatches . . . Consuls . . . SJdelN, roll 9.

7. *New York Times*, June 1, 1888.

8. Nicaragua Canal Construction Company, *The Inter-oceanic Canal*, p. 49.

9. *New York Times*, November 18, 1889.

10. Ibid., November 11, 1889.

11. Nicaragua Canal Construction Company, *The Inter-oceanic Canal*, p. 55.

12. Gilbert Gaul, "Personal Impressions of Nicaragua," *Century Magazine*, 46, no. 1 (n.s. vol. 24) (May 1893): 64–71; ref. on p. 64.

13. Ibid., p. 64.

14. *Bluefields Messenger*, March 30, 1894.

15. Nicaragua Canal Construction Company, *The Inter-oceanic Canal*, p. 8.

16. Lindley M. Keasbey, *The Nicaragua Canal and the Monroe Doctrine* (New York: G. P. Putnam's Sons, 1896), p. 214.

17. Nicaragua Canal Construction Company, *The Inter-oceanic Canal*, pp. 33–34.

18. Ibid., pp. 82–88.

19. *New York Times*, January 9, 1888.

20. Max Harrison Williams, "The San Juan River–Lake Nicaragua Waterway, 1502–1921," Ph.D. dissertation, Louisiana State University, 1971 (Ann Arbor, Mich.: University Microfilms, 1972), p. 200.

21. Brown to Department of State, January 6, 1889, Despatches . . . Consuls . . . SJdelN, roll 9.

22. Nicaragua Canal Construction Company, *The Inter-oceanic Canal*, p. 31.

23. *New York Times*, August 5, 1889.

24. Ibid., November 11, 1889.

25. Gaul, "Personal Impressions," p. 64.

26. For a listing of these pamphlets and articles, see Hugh A. Morrison (Library of Congress), *List of Books and of Articles in Periodicals Relating to Inter-oceanic Canal and*

Railway Routes (Washington, D.C.: Government Printing Office, 1900), part II: Nicaragua Route, pp. 21–51.

Chapter 7

1. James J. Parsons, "English-Speaking Settlements in the Western Caribbean," *Yearbook of the Association of Pacific Coast Geographers*, 16 (1954): 3–16; ref. on p. 11.
2. Augustus C. Thompson, *Moravian Missions: Twelve Lectures* (New York: Scribner, 1882), p. 159.
3. Cited in Mary W. Williams, *Anglo-American Isthmian Diplomacy, 1815–1915* (Washington, D.C.: American Historical Association, 1916), p. 292 (footnote).
4. Robert N. Keely, "Nicaragua and the Mosquito Coast," *Popular Science Monthly*, 45, no. 6 (June 1894): 160–74; ref. on p. 164.
5. *Bluefields Messenger*, March 30, 1894.
6. Ibid.
7. Keely, "Nicaragua and the Mosquito Coast," p. 167.
8. Ibid., p. 168.
9. Cited from Edward W. Perry, *Tropical America: Its Planters and Plantations* (1903), in William Breisky, "But Yes, We Had Bananas—Coming Out of Our Ears," *Smithsonian Magazine*, 7, no. 12 (March 1977): 101.
10. Bluefields Steamship Company, Bluefields to Bluefields Steamship Company, New Orleans, Feb. 5, 1903 (copies), in Despatches . . . Consuls . . . SJdelN, roll 20.
11. See Manuel Castrillo Gamez, *Reseña Historica de Nicaragua* (Managua: Talleres Nacionales, 1963), pp. 476–85.
12. U.S. Department of State, *Foreign Relations of the United States: Nicaragua (Mosquito Territory), 1894* (Washington, D.C.: Government Printing Office, 1895) (hereafter *Foreign Relations of the U.S.*), Gresham to Bayard, July 19, 1894, p. 126.
13. Gary M. Ross, "Mosquito Indians and Anglo-American Diplomacy," *Research Studies*, Washington State University, Pullman, 35, no. 3 (September 1967): 220–33; p. 221.
14. R. L. Morrow, "A Conflict Between the Commercial Interests of the U.S. and Its Foreign Policy," *Hispanic American Historical Review*, 10, no. 1 (February 1930): 2–13; p. 3.
15. Thomas to Baker, April 28, 1894, in *Foreign Relations of the U.S.*, p. 81.
16. Madriz to Baker, July 28, 1894, in *Foreign Relations of the U.S.*, p. 157.
17. See Castrillo Gamez, *Reseña Historica*, pp. 519–20.
18. Baker to Gresham, May 10, 1894, in *Foreign Relations of the U.S.*, p. 87.
19. Gresham to Baker, May 12, 1894, in *Foreign Relations of the U.S.*, p. 90.
20. Kimberly to Pauncefote, March 27, 1894, P.R.O., F.O. 53 (65); Bayard to Gresham, March 29, 1894, in *Foreign Relations of the U.S.*, appendix I, p. 259.
21. Gosling to Kimberly, April 24, 1894, P.R.O., F.O. 53 (66).
22. *New York Times*, May 18, 1894.
23. Ibid., August 17, 1894.
24. Bayard to Gresham, August 10, 1894, in *Foreign Relations of the U.S.*, p. 155.

25. Keely, "Nicaragua and the Mosquito Coast," p. 174; Morrow, "A Conflict Between the Commercial Interests," p. 3; Officers of Moravian Mission to Baker, April 30, 1894, in *Foreign Relations of the U.S.*, p. 83.

26. Bayard to Gresham, December 22, 1894, in *Foreign Relations of the U.S.*, p. 203.

27. Morrow, "A Conflict Between the Commercial Interests," p. 13.

28. Sorsby to Department of State, May 1, 1899, Despatches . . . Consuls . . . SJdelN, roll 16.

29. Ibid., May 3, 1898, roll 15.

30. Hill to Department of State, August 10, 1904, Despatches . . . Consuls . . . SJdelN, roll 21.

31. Ibid., May 17, 1904.

32. Copy contained in ibid., November 10, 1904.

33. Gottschalk to Department of State, October 11, 1902, Despatches . . . Consuls . . . SJdelN, roll 20.

34. Sorsby to Department of State, May 7, 1901, Despatches . . . Consuls . . . SJdelN, roll 18.

Chapter 8

1. Archibald R. Colquhoun, *The Key of the Pacific* (Westminster, England: Archibald Constable and Company, 1895), p. 216.

2. O'Hara to Department of State, June 18, 1895, Despatches . . . Consuls . . . SJdelN, roll 12.

3. Ibid., May 28, 1897, roll 13.

4. Ibid., June 30, 1897.

5. Ibid.

6. Ibid., August 31, 1897, roll 14.

7. U.S. Department of State, *Consular Reports*, 55, no. 206 (November 1897): 424–28.

8. U.S. Nicaragua Canal Commission, *Report, 1897–1899* (Baltimore: Friedenwald, 1899), p. 406.

9. Ibid., p. 411.

10. Sorsby to Department of State, July 6, 1898, Despatches . . . Consuls . . . SJdelN, roll 15.

11. U.S. Nicaragua Canal Commission, *Report*, p. 427.

12. Ibid., p. 368.

13. Ibid., p. 132.

14. Miles P. Duval, Jr., *Cadiz to Cathay* (Stanford, Calif.: Stanford University Press, 1940), p. 145.

15. Sorsby to Department of State, July 17, 1901, Despatches . . . Consuls . . . SJdelN, roll 19.

16. Ibid.

17. Duval, *Cadiz to Cathay*, cited on p. 141.

18. On the Nicaragua/Panama canal-site controversy, see also Lawrence O. Ealy,

Yanqui Politics and the Isthmian Canal (University Park: Pennsylvania State University Press, 1971), chap. 5, pp. 48–58; Gerstle Mack, *The Land Divided* (New York: Knopf, 1944), chaps. 34 and 35, pp. 417–44; Dwight C. Miner, *The Fight for the Panama Route: The Story of the Spooner Act and the Hay-Herran Treaty* (New York: Columbia University Press, 1940), chaps. 3 and 4, pp. 75–156, 189–99; Gustave Anguizola, *Philippe Bunau-Varilla: The Man Behind the Panama Canal* (Chicago: Nelson-Hall, 1980), pp. 213–28.

19. Hill to Department of State, March 24, 1904, Despatches . . . Consuls . . . SJdelN, roll 21.
20. Ryder to Department of State, July 22, 1905, ibid.
21. Hill to Department of State, July 15, 1904, ibid.
22. Ibid.
23. Ryder to Department of State, July 22, 1905, ibid.
24. Ibid.
25. Ibid., March 29, 1906.

Chapter 9

1. Clark to Department of State, July 18, 1911, *Records of the Department of State Relating to the Internal Affairs of Nicaragua, 1910–29* (hereafter *Records . . . Internal Affairs . . . Nicaragua*), National Archives Microfilm Publication No. M632, roll 69.
2. *The American*, Bluefields, Wednesday, August 6, 1913.
3. William H. Miner, *Bananas, The Story of a Trip to the Great Plantations of Nicaragua* (Sioux Falls, S.D.: Sioux Plantation Company, 1915), pp. 40–49.
4. Dana G. Munro, *Intervention and Dollar Diplomacy in the Caribbean* (Princeton, N.J.: Princeton University Press, 1964), pp. 415–16.
5. See Juan José Arévalo, *The Shark and the Sardines* (New York: Lyle Stuart, 1961), pp. 75–84.
6. Charles D. Kepner, Jr., *Social Aspects of the Banana Industry* (New York: AMS Press, 1967 [Columbia University Press, 1936]), p. 56.
7. Samuel Weil and Company et al. to Sanders, April 2, 1919, *Records . . . Internal Affairs . . . Nicaragua*, roll 94.
8. Ibid.
9. Brody to Department of State, October 29, 1920, ibid.
10. Sanders to Jefferson, April 8, 1919, ibid.
11. *La Información*, Bluefields, April 3, 1919.
12. Samuel Weil and Company et al. to Sanders, April 2, 1919, *Records . . . Internal Affairs . . . Nicaragua*, roll 94.
13. *La Información*, Bluefields, April 10, 1919.
14. Jefferson to Department of State, May 9, 1919, *Records . . . Internal Affairs . . . Nicaragua*, roll 17.
15. Sanders to Department of State, July 15, 1919, ibid.

Chapter 10

1. Thomas L. Karnes, *Tropical Enterprise: The Standard Fruit and Steamship Company in Latin America* (Baton Rouge: Louisiana State University Press, 1978), p. 120.
2. Heard to Bradley, June 7, 1921, *Records . . . Internal Affairs . . . Nicaragua*, roll 96.
3. Karnes, *Tropical Enterprise*, p. 115.
4. Heard to Department of State, August 31, 1923, *Records . . . Internal Affairs . . . Nicaragua*, roll 96.
5. Robert Hawxhurst, Jr., "The Piz Piz Gold District, Nicaragua," *Mining and Scientific Press*, 122 (March 12, 1921): 353–60; ref. on p. 354.
6. Cuthbert, Wilson, and Howell to Secretary of State, March 27, 1924, *Records . . . Internal Affairs . . . Nicaragua*, roll 94.
7. Ibid.
8. Harold N. Denny, *Dollars for Bullets: The Story of American Rule in Nicaragua* (Westport, Conn.: Greenwood Press, 1980 [reprint of Dial Press 1929 edition]), pp. 261–62.
9. Ibid., pp. 323, 353.
10. Lewis R. Freeman, "Surveying the Nicaragua Canal Route," *World Today*, 59, no. 5 (April 1932): 391–402; ref. on p. 402.
11. Ibid., pp. 396–97.
12. Carlton Beals, *Banana Gold* (Philadelphia: Lippincott, 1932), p. 325.
13. *New York Times*, April 18, 1931.
14. Charles D. Kepner, *Social Aspects of the Banana Industry* (New York: AMS Press, 1967 [Columbia University Press, 1936]), p. 67.
15. *New York Times*, April 15 and 18, 1931.
16. Ibid., April 15, 1931.
17. Ibid., April 19, 1931.
18. Ibid.
19. Ibid., April 18, 1931.
20. Ibid., April 19, 1931.
21. See Neil Macaulay, *The Sandino Affair* (Chicago: Quadrangle, 1967), p. 253.
22. Karnes, *Tropical Enterprise*, p. 139.
23. Ibid., p. 140.
24. Ibid., p. 141.

Chapter 11

1. James J. Parsons, "The Miskito Pine Savanna of Nicaragua and Honduras," *Annals of the Association of American Geographers*, 45, no. 1 (March 1955): 36–63; ref. on p. 62.
2. J. Fred Rippy, "State Department Operations: The Rama Road," *Inter-American Economic Affairs*, 9 (Summer 1955): 17–32; ref. on p. 23.
3. Parsons, "The Miskito Pine Savanna," pp. 56–58.

4. James J. Parsons, "Gold Mining in the Nicaragua Rain Forest," *Yearbook of the Association of Pacific Coast Geographers*, 17 (1955): 49–55; pp. 49, 52–54.

5. Parsons, "The Miskito Pine Savanna," p. 56.

6. Craig L. Dozier, *Indigenous Tropical Agriculture in Central America: Land Use, Systems, and Problems* (Washington, D.C.: National Research Council, National Academy of Sciences, 1958), pp. 91–92.

7. See Lazzlo Pataky, "San Juan del Norte: Una Grán Ciudad Que Hoy Está Abandonada," *Centroamericana* (Mexico), 2, no. 8 (April–June 1956): 64–67.

8. Dozier, *Indigenous Tropical Agriculture*, p. 90.

9. La Luz Mines Limited, *33rd Annual Report*, Toronto, February 11, 1972, pp. 2–3.

10. Comisión de Desarrollo de la Costa Atlántica, "Monografia y Proyectos a Organizarse en el Departamento de Zelaya," *Revista Conservadora del Pensamiento Centroamericano*, 14, no. 68 (May 1966): 7–20; ref. on p. 11.

11. Bernard Nietschmann, *Between Land and Water* (New York: Seminar Press, 1973), p. 44.

12. Ibid., p. 199.

13. See Philip A. Dennis, "The Costeños and the Revolution in Nicaragua," *Journal of Interamerican Studies and World Affairs*, 23, no. 3 (August 1981): 271–96; pp. 281–82.

14. *New York Times*, March 22, 1982.

15. *Datos Básicos Sobre Nicaragua*, SENAPEP, Colección Juan de Dios Muñoz (Managua, 1979), p. 6.

16. Dennis, "The Costeños," p. 284.

17. George Black, *Triumph of the People: The Sandinista Revolution in Nicaragua* (London: Zed Press, 1981), p. 212.

18. See Philippe Bourgois, "Class, Ethnicity, and the State Among the Miskitu Amerindians of Northeastern Nicaragua," *Latin American Perspectives*, 8 (Spring 1981): 22–39; pp. 34–36.

19. Ibid., ref. on p. 32.

20. Ibid., ref. on p. 26.

21. James D. Rudolph (ed.), *Nicaragua: A Country Study* (Washington, D.C.: Government Printing Office, 1982), chap. 2, Mary W. Helms: "The Society and Its Environment," p. 92.

Bibliography

Government Documents

Atlantic-Pacific Interoceanic Canal Study Commission. *Final Report*. Washington, D.C.: Government Printing Office, 1970.

Great Britain, Public Record Office (London). Foreign Office Series 53 (Mosquitia), 1844–1895, vols. 1–66 (microfilm).

Menocal, A. G. *Report of the U.S. Nicaragua Surveying Party, 1885*. Washington, D.C.: Government Printing Office, 1886.

United States Congress, Senate. *Report of the Isthmian Canal Commission, 1899–1901* (57th Congress, 1st session, 1901–1902, Senate Document No. 54, Part I, Serial No. 4225). Washington, D.C.: Government Printing Office, 1902.

United States, Department of State. *Consular Reports*, vol. 55, no. 206, November 1897. Washington, D.C.: Government Printing Office, 1898.

————, ————. Despatches from U.S. Consuls in San Juan del Norte, 1851–1906. Washington, D.C.: National Archives Microfilm Publication No. T-348, rolls 1–21.

————, ————. Despatches from U.S. Ministers to Central America, 1824–1906: Nicaragua, 1854–1873. Washington, D.C.: National Archives Microfilm Publication No. 219, rolls 9–17.

————, ————. *Foreign Relations of the United States, Nicaragua, (Mosquito Territory), 1894* (U.S. 53d Congress, 3d session, 1894, Senate Executive Document No. 20). Washington, D.C.: Government Printing Office, 1895.

————, ————. Records of the Department of State Relating to Internal Affairs of Nicaragua, 1910–1929. Washington, D.C.: National Archives Microfilm Publication No. M-632, rolls 17–96.

Books, Articles, Reports, Collections of Papers, and Dissertations

Ammen, Daniel. "American Isthmian Routes." *Franklin Institute Journal* 128:6 (December 1889): 409–39.

————. "Interoceanic Ship Canal across the American Isthmus: The Proposed Canal between Greytown and Brito, via Lake Nicaragua." *Journal of the American Geographical Society of New York* 10 (1878): 142–62 (paper read before the Society, November 12, 1878).

Anguizola, Gustave. *Philippe Bunau-Varilla: The Man Behind the Canal.* Chicago: Nelson-Hall, 1980.

Arévalo, Juan José. *The Shark and the Sardines.* New York: Lyle Stuart, 1961.

Bailey, Thomas A. "Interest in a Nicaraguan Canal, 1903–1931." *Hispanic American Historical Review* 16:1 (February 1936): 2–28.

Baldwin, Roger S. "Tarrying in Nicaragua: Pleasures and Perils of the California Trip in 1849." *Century Magazine* 42 (n.s. 20):6 (October 1891): 911–31.

Bancroft, Hubert Howe. *The Works of Hubert Howe Bancroft.* Vols. VI–VIII: History of Central America. San Francisco: History Company, 1886, 1887.

Baylen, J. O. "American Intervention in Nicaragua, 1909–1933." *Social Science Quarterly* 35:2 (September 1954): 128–54.

Beals, Carlton. *Banana Gold.* Philadelphia and London: Lippincott, 1932.

Bell, Charles N. "Remarks on the Mosquito Territory, Its Climate, People, Productions." *Journal of the Royal Geographical Society* 32 (1862): 242–68.

Belt, Thomas. *The Naturalist in Nicaragua.* London: J. Murray, 1874.

Bemis, Samuel F. *The Latin American Policy of the United States.* New York: Harcourt Brace Jovanovich, 1943.

Beteta Rodriguez, Virgilio. *La Política Inglesa en Centroamerica durante el Siglo XIX.* Guatemala City: Centro Editorial "Jose de Piñeda Ibarra," 1963.

Black, George. *Triumph of the People: The Sandinista Revolution in Nicaragua.* London: Zed Press, 1981.

Booth, John A. *The End and the Beginning: The Nicaraguan Revolution.* Boulder, Colo.: Westview Press, 1982.

Bourgois, Philippe. "Class, Ethnicity, and the State Among the Miskitu Amerindians of Northeastern Nicaragua." *Latin American Perspectives* 8:1 (Spring 1981): 22–39.

Britton, C. F. "Nelson and the River San Juan." *Mariner's Mirror* 28:3 (July 1942): 213–21.

Bromley, Robert. "The Nicaragua Canal Question and the Clayton-Bulwer Treaty." *Nineteenth Century and After* 49:287 (January 1901): 100–115.

Brown, Alan S. "The British Expedition to the St. Johns River and the Lake of Nicaragua, 1779–1780." *Caribbean Historical Review* 2:1 (March 1951): 26–46.

Busey, James L. *Political Aspects of the Panama Canal: The Problem of Location.* Tucson: University of Arizona Press, 1974.

Butterworth, Hezekiah. *Lost in Nicaragua.* Boston and Chicago: W.A. Wilde & Company, 1898.

Callcott, Wilfred H. *The Caribbean Policy of the United States, 1890–1920.* Baltimore: Johns Hopkins University Press, 1942.

Castrillo Gamez, Manuel. *Reseña Histórica de Nicaragua.* Managua: Talleres Nacionales, 1963.

Cleveland, Daniel. "Across the Nicaragua Transit." Unpublished manuscript, April 15, 1868 (M65, xv, 160 leaves), in Bancroft Library, University of California, Berkeley.

Colquhoun, Archibald R. *The Key of the Pacific.* Westminster, England: Constable and Company, 1895.

———. "The Panama and Nicaragua Canals." *The Graphic* (London) 61:1575 (February 3, 1900): 162.

Comisión de Desarrollo de la Costa Atlántica. "Monografía y Proyectos a Organizarse en el Departamento de Zelaya." *Revista Conservadora del Pensamiento Centroamericano* 14:68 (May 1966): 7–20.

Cox, Isaac J. *Nicaragua and the United States, 1909–1927.* Boston: World Peace Foundation, 1927.

Craig, Alan K. "Logwood as a Factor in the Settlement of British Honduras." *Caribbean Studies* (University of Puerto Rico) 9:1 (April 1969): 53–62.

Crowell, Jackson. "The United States and a Central American Canal, 1869–1877." *Hispanic American Historical Review* 49:1 (February 1969): 27–52.

Davis, Arthur P. "Nicaragua and the Isthmian Routes." *National Geographic Magazine* 10:7 (July 1899): 247–66.

———. "The Isthmian Canal." *Bulletin of the American Geographical Society of New York* 34:2 (March–April 1902): 132–38.

DeKalb, Courtenay. "Nicaragua: Studies on the Mosquito Shore in 1892." *Journal of the American Geographical Society of New York* 25 (1893): 236–88.

Dennis, Philip A. "The Costeños and the Revolution in Nicaragua." *Journal of Interamerican Studies and World Affairs* 23:3 (August 1981): 271–96.

Denny, Harold N. *Dollars for Bullets.* Westport, Conn.: Greenwood Press, 1980 (republication of Dial Press edition of 1929).

Douglas, James. "Account of the Attempt to Form a Settlement on the Mosquito Shore in 1823." *Transactions* of Literary and Historical Society of Quebec, session of 1868–69, pp. 25–39 (paper read before the Society, February 10, 1869).

Dozier, Craig L. *Indigenous Tropical Agriculture in Central America: Land Use, Systems, and Problems.* Washington, D.C.: National Academy of Sciences, National Research Council (Publication No. 594), 1958.

Duval, Miles P. *Cadiz to Cathay.* Stanford, Calif.: Stanford University Press, 1940.

Ealy, Lawrence O. *Yanqui Politics and the Isthmian Canal.* University Park: Pennsylvania University Press, 1971.

Fitz-Roy, Robert R. N. "Considerations on the Great Isthmus of Central America." *Journal of the Royal Geographical Society* 20 (1851): 161–89.

———. "Further Considerations on the Great Isthmus of Central America." *Journal of the Royal Geographical Society* 23 (1853): 171–90.

Floyd, Troy S. *The Anglo-Spanish Struggle for Mosquitia.* Albuquerque: University of New Mexico Press, 1967.

Folkman, David I., Jr. *The Nicaragua Route.* Salt Lake City: University of Utah Press, 1972.

———. "Westward Via Nicaragua: The United States and the Nicaragua Route, 1826–1869." Ph.D. dissertation, University of Utah, 1966 (Ann Arbor, Mich.: University Microfilms, 1971).

Frank, Andrew G. "The Economic Development of Nicaragua." *Inter-American Economic Affairs* 8:4 (Spring 1955): 59–68.

Freeman, L. R. "Surveying the Nicaragua Canal Route." *World Today* 59:5 (April 1932): 391–402.

Gamez, José D. "Breves Apuntamientos acerca de la Reincorporación de la Mosquitia." *Revista de la Academía de Geografía e Historia de Nicaragua* (Managua) 3:1 (January 1939): 1–51.

———. *Historia de la Costa de Mosquitos.* Managua: Talleres Nacionales, 1939.

————. *Historia de Nicaragua Desde Los Tiempos Prehistóricos Hasta 1860* (2d ed.).
Madrid: Escuela Professional de Artes Gráficas, 1955.

————. *Historia Moderna de Nicaragua.* Managua: Papelera Industrial de Nicaragua, S.A., 1975.

Gaul, Gilbert. "Personal Impressions of Nicaragua." *Century Magazine* 46(n.s. 24):1
(May 1893): 64–71.

Greely, A. W. "Rubber Forests of Nicaragua and Sierra Leone." *National Geographic
Magazine* 8:3 (March 1897): 83–88.

————. "The Present State of the Nicaragua Canal." *National Geographic Magazine*
7:2 (February 1896): 73–76.

Haupt, Lewis M. "National Influence and the Isthmian Canal." *Factory and Industrial Management* 15:4 (July 1898): 550–57.

Hawxhurst, Robert. "The Piz Piz Gold District of Nicaragua." *Mining and Scientific
Press* 122 (March 12, 1921): 353–60.

Hayes, C. W. "Physiography of the Nicaragua Canal Route." *National Geographic
Magazine* 10:7 (July 1899): 233–46.

Helms, Mary W. *Asang: Adaptations to Culture Contact in a Miskito Community.*
Gainesville: University of Florida Press, 1971.

————. *Middle America: A Culture History of Heartland and Frontiers.* Englewood
Cliffs, N.J.: Prentice-Hall, 1975.

————. "The Cultural Ecology of a Colonial Tribe." *Ethnology* 8:1 (January 1969):
76–84.

Henderson, Gavin B. "German Colonial Projects on the Mosquito Coast, 1844–
1848." *English Historical Review* 59:234 (May 1944): 257–71.

Henderson, George. *An Account of the British Settlement of Honduras, and Sketches of the
Manners and Customs of the Mosquito Indians* (2d ed.). London: C. & R. Baldwin,
1811.

Herbertson, A. J., and Howarth, O. J. R. (eds.). *Oxford Survey of the British Empire* (6
vols.). Vol. 4: American Territories. Oxford: Clarendon Press, 1914.

Hickson. G. F. "Palmerston and the Clayton-Bulwer Treaty." *Cambridge Historical
Journal* 3:3 (1931): 295–303.

Hill, Roscoe R. "The Nicaraguan Canal Idea to 1913." *Hispanic American Historical
Review* 28:2 (May 1948): 197–211.

Hoyt, Edwin P. *The Vanderbilts and Their Fortunes.* Garden City, N.Y.: Doubleday,
1962.

Huck, Eugene R., and Moseley, Edward H. (eds.). *Militarists, Merchants, and Mis-
sionaries: United States Expansion in Middle America.* Chap. 2: Conwell A. Anderson,
"Anglo-Spanish Negotiations Involving Central America in 1783." University:
University of Alabama Press, 1970.

Hussey, Roland D. "Spanish Reaction to Foreign Aggression in the Caribbean to
about 1680." *Hispanic American Historical Review* 9:3 (August 1929): 286–302.

International Bank for Reconstruction and Development. *Economic Development of
Nicaragua.* Baltimore: Johns Hopkins University Press, 1953.

Ireland, Gordon. *Boundaries, Possessions and Conflicts in Central and North America and
the Caribbean.* Cambridge, Mass.: Harvard University Press, 1941.

Kammen, William. *A Search for Stability: United States Diplomacy Toward Nicaragua,
1925–1933.* Notre Dame, Ind.: University of Notre Dame Press, 1968.

Karnes, Thomas L. *The Failure of Union: Central America, 1823–1960*. Chapel Hill: University of North Carolina Press, 1961.

——— (ed.). *The Latin American Policy of the United States*. Tucson: University of Arizona Press, 1972.

———. *Tropical Enterprise: The Standard Fruit and Steamship Company in Latin America*. Baton Rouge: Louisiana State University Press, 1978.

Keasbey, Lindley M. *The Nicaragua Canal and the Monroe Doctrine*. New York: Putnam, 1896.

———. "The Nicaragua Canal and the Monroe Doctrine." *Annals of the American Academy of Political and Social Science* 7:1 (January 1896): 1–31.

Keely, Robert N. "Nicaragua and the Mosquito Coast." *Popular Science Monthly* 45:6 (June 1894): 160–74.

Keenagh, Peter. *Mosquito Coast: An Account of a Journey through the Jungles of Honduras*. Boston: Houghton Mifflin, 1938.

Kemble, Stephen. *The Kemble Papers* (2 vols.). Vol. XVII of Collections of the New York Historical Society. New York: New York Historical Society, 1884.

Kepner, C. D. *Social Aspects of the Banana Industry*. New York: AMS Press, 1967 (reprint of Columbia University Press edition, 1936).

———, and Soothill, J. M. *The Banana Empire: A Case Study in Economic Imperialism*. New York: Russell & Russell, 1967 (reprint of Vanguard Press edition, 1935).

La Luz Mines, Limited. *33rd Annual Report*. Toronto: La Luz Mines, Ltd., February 11, 1972.

Lane, Wheaton J. *Commodore Vanderbilt: An Epic of the Steam Age*. New York: Knopf, 1942.

Lanning, John T. "Great Britain and Spanish Recognition of the Hispanic American States." *Hispanic American Historical Review* 10:4 (November 1930): 429–56.

"La Ruta de Nicaragua a través de la Historia." *Revista Conservadora del Pensamiento Centroamericano* 22:108 (September 1969): 3–13.

Lawrence, George. "Excursion to the Lake of Nicaragua up the River San Juan." *Nautical Magazine and Naval Chronicle* (London) 9:12 (December 1840): 857–64.

Lockey, Joseph B. "Diplomatic Futility." *Hispanic American Historical Review* 10:3 (August 1930): 265–94.

Long, Lewis E. "Agricultural Colonization in Eastern Nicaragua." *Agriculture in the Americas* 7:2 (February 1947): 23–26.

Lowe, Cedric J. *The Reluctant Imperialists: British Foreign Policy, 1878–1902*. New York: Macmillan, 1967.

Luark, Michael Fleenan. "Diaries, 1846–1900" (unpublished), in University of Washington Libraries, Seattle.

Lunt, W. E. *History of England*. New York: Harper, 1945.

Macauley, Neil. *The Sandino Affair*. Chicago: Quadrangle, 1967.

MacDonald, D. F. *The Age of Transition: Britain in the Nineteenth and Twentieth Centuries*. New York: St. Martin's Press, 1967.

Mack, Gerstle. *The Land Divided*. New York: Knopf, 1944.

MacLeod, Murdo J. *Spanish Central America: A Socioeconomic History, 1520–1720*. Berkeley: University of California Press, 1973.

Manning, William R. (ed.). *Diplomatic Correspondence of the United States, Inter-American Affairs*. Vol. III: Central America, 1831–1850; vol. IV: Central America, 1851–1860. Washington, D.C.: Carnegie Endowment for International Peace, 1933, 1934.

Marchant, Alexander. "Britain and the United States in Latin America before 1865." *Current History* 28:163 (March 1955): 143–47.

Maritime Canal Company of Nicaragua and the Nicaragua Canal Construction Company. *The Maritime Ship Canal of Nicaragua.* New York: Nicaragua Canal Construction Company, 1890.

Marriott, J. A. R. *England Since Waterloo.* London: Methuen, 1913.

Martin, Lawrence and Sylvia. "The World's Most Unbuilt Canal." *Antioch Review* 3:2 (June 1943): 262–70.

May, R. E. *The Southern Dream of a Caribbean Empire, 1854–1861.* Baton Rouge: Louisiana State University Press, 1973.

May, Stacy, and Plaza, Galo. *The United Fruit Company in Latin America.* Washington, D.C.: National Planning Association, 1958.

Mecham, J. Lloyd. *A Survey of United States–Latin American Relations.* Boston: Houghton Mifflin, 1965.

Merry, William L. *The Nicaragua Canal, the Gateway between the Oceans.* San Francisco: Chambers of Commerce of San Francisco, Portland, and San Diego; Board of Trade of San Francisco, 1895.

Miller, Hugh G. *The Isthmian Highway.* New York: Macmillan, 1929.

Miner, D. C. *The Fight for the Panama Route: The Story of the Spooner Act and the Hay-Herran Treaty.* New York: Columbia University Press, 1940.

Miner, William H. *Bananas, The Story of a Trip to the Great Plantations of Nicaragua.* Sioux Falls, S.D.: Sioux Plantation Company, 1915.

Morrow, R. L. "A Conflict between the Commercial Interests of the U.S. and Its Foreign Policy." *Hispanic American Historical Review* 10:1 (February 1930): 2–13.

Munro, Dana G. "Dollar Diplomacy in Nicaragua, 1909–1913." *Hispanic American Historical Review* 38:2 (May 1958): 209–35.

––––––. *Intervention and Dollar Diplomacy in the Caribbean, 1900–1921.* Princeton, N.J.: Princeton University Press, 1964.

––––––. *The Five Republics of Central America.* London: Oxford University Press, 1918.

––––––. *The Latin American Republics: A History.* New York: Appleton-Century, 1942.

Naylor, Robert A. "The British Role in Central America Prior to the Clayton-Bulwer Treaty of 1850." *Hispanic American Historical Review* 40:3 (August 1960): 361–83.

Newton, Arthur P.; Rose, J. Holland; and Benians, E. A. (eds.). *The Cambridge History of the British Empire.* Vol. II (chap. 14: A. P. Newton, "The Growth of the New Empire 1783–1870," part I, pp. 525–47). New York: Macmillan, 1940.

Nicaragua Canal Construction Company. *The Inter-oceanic Canal of Nicaragua.* New York: Nicaragua Canal Construction Company, 1891.

Nietschmann, Bernard. *Between Land and Water.* New York: Seminar Press, 1973.

Nimmo, Joseph. "The Nicaraguan Canal in Its Commercial and Military Aspects." *Factory and Industrial Management* 15:5 (August 1898): 720–26.

––––––. "The Proposed American Interoceanic Canal in Its Commercial Aspects." *National Geographic Magazine* 10:8 (August 1899): 297–310.

Nogales y Mendez, Rafael de. *The Looting of Nicaragua*. New York: R. M. McBride & Company, 1928.

"Papers of Major John P. Heiss of Nashville." *Tennessee Historical Magazine* 2:3 (September 1916): 137–49.

Parker, Franklin D. *The Central American Republics*. New York: Oxford University Press, 1964.

———, (ed.). *Travels in Central America, 1821–1840*. Gainesville: University of Florida Press, 1970.

Parsons, James J. "English Speaking Settlements of the Western Caribbean." *Yearbook of the Association of Pacific Coast Geographers* 16 (1954): 3–16.

———. "Gold Mining in the Nicaragua Rain Forest." *Yearbook of the Association of Pacific Coast Geographers* 17 (1955): 49–55.

———. "The Miskito Pine Savanna of Nicaragua and Honduras." *Annals of the Association of American Geographers* 45:1 (March 1955): 36–63.

Pataky, Lazzlo. "San Juan del Norte, Una Grán Ciudad que Hoy está Abandonada." *Centroamericana* (Mexico City) 2:8 (April–June 1956): 64–67.

Peary, Robert E. "Across Nicaragua with Transit and Machete." *National Geographic Magazine* 1:4 (October 1889): 315–35.

———. "The Rio San Juan de Nicaragua." *Journal of the American Geographical Society of New York* 21 (1889): 57–96 (paper read before the Society).

Pellas, Silvio. "La Nicaragua Steamship and Navigation Company." *Revista Conservadora del Pensamiento Centroamericano* 22:108 (September 1969): 16.

Perez Valle, Eduardo. *El Desaguadero de la Mar Dulce: Historia de su Descubrimiento*. Managua: Ministerio de Educación Pública, Departamento de Extensión Cultural, 1960.

Pijoan, M. "The Health and Customs of the Miskito Indians of Northern Nicaragua." *America Indigena* 6:1 (January 1946): 41–66; 6:2 (April 1946): 157–83.

Pim, Bedford C.T. *The Gate of the Pacific*. London: L. Reeve & Company, 1863.

——— , and Seemann, Berthold. *Dottings on the Roadside in Panama, Nicaragua, and Mosquito*. London: Chapman and Hall, 1869.

Platt, D. C. M. *Finance, Trade and Politics in British Foreign Policy, 1815–1914*. Oxford: Clarendon Press, 1968.

Powell, Anna I. "Relations between the United States and Nicaragua, 1898–1916." *Hispanic American Historical Review* 8:1 (February 1928): 43–64.

Radell, D. R. "Exploration and Commerce on Lake Nicaragua and the Rio San Juan, 1524–1800." *Journal of Inter-American Studies* 12:1 (January 1970): 107–25.

Radley, Jeffrey. *The Physical Geography of the East Coast of Nicaragua*. Berkeley: Department of Geography, University of California, 1960.

Reed, T. B. "The Nicaraguan Canal." *North American Review* 168:510 (May 1899): 552–62.

Reeves, J. S. "Clearing the Way for the Nicaragua Canal." *American Journal of International Law* 17:2 (April 1923): 309–13.

"Reminiscences of Central America." *De Bows Review* 29(n.s. 4):4 (October 1860): 410–29.

Revival of the British Settlement on the Bluefields River in Central America (pamphlet). London: E. Colyer, 1840.

Rice, Keryn A. "A River Reconnaissance in Nicaragua." *Military Engineer* 22:122 (March–April 1930): 119–21.

Rippy, J. Fred. *British Investments in Latin America, 1822–1949.* Hamden, Conn.: Archon, 1959.

————. *Latin America in World Politics: An Outline Survey.* New York: F. S Crofts & Company, 1928.

————. *Rivalry of the United States and Great Britain over Latin America.* Baltimore: Johns Hopkins University Press, 1929.

————. "State Department Operations: The Rama Road." *Inter-American Economic Affairs* 9:1 (Summer 1955): 17–32.

————. *The Caribbean Danger Zone.* New York: G. P. Putnam's Sons, 1940.

Roberts, Orlando W. *Narrative of Voyages and Excursions on the East Coast and in the Interior of Central America: Describing a Journey up the River San Juan, and Passage Across the Lake of Nicaragua to the City of León.* Edinburgh, 1827. Facsimile reprint; Gainesville: University of Florida Press, 1965.

Rodriguez, Mario. *A Palmerstonian Diplomat in Central America: Frederick Chatfield, Esq.* Tucson: University of Arizona Press, 1964.

————. *Central America.* Englewood Cliffs, N.J.: Prentice-Hall, 1965.

————. *The Cádiz Experiment in Central America, 1808 to 1826.* Berkeley: University of California Press, 1978.

————. "The Prometheus and the Clayton-Bulwer Treaty." *Journal of Modern History* 36:3 (September 1964): 260–78.

Rosengarten, Frederic. *Freebooters Must Die!* Wayne, Pa.: Haverford House, 1976.

Ross, Gary M. "Mosquito Indians and Anglo-American Diplomacy." *Research Studies of Washington State University* (Pullman) 35:3 (September 1967): 220–33.

Rudolph, James D. (ed.). *Nicaragua: A Country Study.* Washington, D.C.: Government Printing Office, 1982.

Ryan, John M., et al. *Area Handbook for Nicaragua.* Washington, D.C.: Government Printing Office, 1970.

Sanchez Pedrote, Enrique. "El Coronel Hodgson y la Expedición a la Costa de los Mosquitos." *Anuario de Estudios Americanos* (Seville) 24 (1967): 1205–35.

Sandner, Gerhard. "La Costa Atlántica de Nicaragua, Costa Rica y Panama: Su Conquista y Colonización desde Principios de la Epoca Colonial" (Translation of original, in German, in *Die Erde* [Berlin], heft 2/64. Verlag). *Informe Semestral* of the Instituto Geográfico de Costa Rica in San Jose (January-June 1964), pp. 83–137.

Scheips, P. J. "United States Commercial Pressures for a Nicaragua Canal in the 1890s." *The Americas* 20:4 (April 1964): 333–58.

Scroggs, William O. *Filibusters and Financiers: The Story of William Walker and His Associates.* New York: Macmillan, 1916.

Selser, Gregorio. *Sandino.* New York and London: Monthly Review Press, 1981. (Translation of *Sandino, Generál de Hombres Libres*, originally published by Editorial Diogenes, S.A., Mexico City, 1978).

Sheldon, Henry I. *Notes on the Nicaragua Canal.* Chicago: A. C. McClurg & Company, 1898.

Smith, Joseph. *Illusions of Conflict: Anglo-American Diplomacy Toward Latin America, 1865-1896.* Pittsburgh: University of Pittsburgh Press, 1979.

Smith, Rhea Marsh. *Spain: A Modern History.* Ann Arbor: University of Michigan Press, 1965.

Squier, Ephraim George. "British Encroachments and Aggressions in Central America: The Mosquito Question." *American Whig Review* 11:26 (n.s. 5:2) (February 1850): 188–203; 11:27 (n.s. 5:3) (March 1850): 235–68.

———. *Nicaragua: Its People, Scenery, Monuments, and the Proposed Interoceanic Canal* (2 vols.). New York: Appleton, 1852.

———. "San Juan de Nicaragua." *Harper's New Monthly Magazine* 10:55 (December 1854): 50–61.

———. (pseudonym: Samuel Bard). *Waikna; or Adventures on the Mosquito Shore.* Gainesville: University of Florida Press, 1965 (facsimile reprint of the 1855 edition).

Stansifer, Charles L. "Ephraim George Squier: Diversos Aspectos de su Carrera en Centroamerica." *Revista Conservadora del Pensamiento Centroamericano* 20:98 (November 1968): supplement, pp. 1–64.

Stephens, John L. *Incidents of Travel in Central America, Chiapas, and Yucatan.* New Brunswick, N.J.: Rutgers University Press, 1949 (reprint of Harper edition, 1871).

Stout, Peter F. *Nicaragua: Past, Present and Future.* Philadelphia: John E. Potter, 1859.

Strangeways, Thomas. *Sketch of the Mosquito Shore, Including the Territory of Poyais; Descriptive of the Country; with Some Information as to its Productions, the Best Mode of Culture, etc.* Edinburgh: William Blackwood, 1822.

Stryker, James. "Junction of the Atlantic and Pacific: Maritime and Overland Routes." *Stryker's American Register and Magazine* (Philadelphia) 2:1 (March 1849): 158–69.

Sultan, Dan I. "An Army Engineer Explores Nicaragua." *National Geographic Magazine* 61:5 (May 1932): 593–627.

Tatum, Edward H. *The United States and Europe, 1815–1823.* New York: Russell & Russell, 1936.

Taylor, James R. "Agricultural Development in the Humid Tropics of Central America." *Inter-American Economic Affairs* 24:1 (Summer 1970): 41–49.

Thompson, Augustus C. *Moravian Missions: Twelve Lectures.* New York: Scribner, 1882.

Thompson, J. Eric S. (ed.). *Thomas Gage's Travels in the New World.* Norman: University of Oklahoma Press, 1958.

Thomson, David. *England in the Nineteenth Century, 1815–1914.* Baltimore: Penguin, 1950.

"The Trade and Industry of Nicaragua and Costa Rica, and the Proposed Inter-Oceanic Canal." *Board of Trade Journal* (London) 26:150 (January 1899): 12–22.

Travis, Ira D. *British Rule in Central America: or a Sketch of Mosquito History* (publication no. 5 of Michigan Political Science Association). Ann Arbor: University of Michigan Press, 1895.

———. *The History of the Clayton-Bulwer Treaty* (publication no. 8 of Michigan Political Science Association). Ann Arbor, 1900.

U.S. Nicaragua Canal Commission. *Report, 1897–1899.* Baltimore: Friedenwald, 1899.

Van Aken, Mark J. "British Policy Considerations in Central America Before 1850." *Hispanic American Historical Review* 42:1 (February 1962): 54–60.

Van Alstyne, Richard W. "Anglo-American Relations, 1853–1857." *American Historical Review* 42:3 (April 1937): 491–500.

_____. "Britain in Latin America after 1865." *Current History* 28:163 (March 1955): 148–53.

_____. "British Diplomacy and the Clayton-Bulwer Treaty, 1850–1860." *Journal of Modern History* 11:2 (June 1939): 149–83.

_____. "The Central American Policy of Lord Palmerston, 1846–1848." *Hispanic American Historical Review* 16:3 (August 1936): 339–59.

Von Hagen, Victor W. "The Mosquito Coast of Honduras and Its Inhabitants." *Geographical Review* 30:2 (April 1940): 238–59.

Walker, James W. G. *Ocean to Ocean, An Account Personal and Historical of Nicaragua and Its People.* Chicago: A. C. McClurg & Company, 1902.

Walker, Thomas W. *Nicaragua: The Land of Sandino.* Boulder, Colo.: Westview Press, 1981.

Ward, Adolphus W. *The Cambridge History of British Foreign Policy, 1783–1919.* New York: Macmillan, 1922–23.

Webster, Charles (ed.) *Britain and the Independence of Latin America, 1812–1830* (2 vols.). London: Oxford University Press, 1938.

Whitaker, Arthur P. *The United States and the Independence of Latin America, 1800–1830.* Baltimore: Johns Hopkins University Press, 1941.

Williams, Mary W. *Anglo-American Isthmian Diplomacy, 1815–1915.* Washington, D.C.: American Historical Association, 1916.

Williams, Max H. "The San Juan–Lake Nicaragua Waterway, 1502–1921." Ph.D. dissertation, Louisiana State University, 1971 (Ann Arbor, Mich.: University Microfilms, 1971).

Wilson, Charles M. *Empire in Green and Gold: The Story of the American Banana Trade.* New York: Henry Holt, 1947.

Wilson, G. G. "Close of a Chapter in the History of Transisthmian Transit." *American Journal of International Law* 32:2 (April 1938): 329–30.

Woodward, Ralph L. *Central America, A Nation Divided.* New York: Oxford University Press, 1976.

"Work on the Nicaragua Canal." *Nation* 66:1704 (February 24, 1898): 141.

Wortman, Miles L. *Government and Society in Central America, 1680–1840.* New York: Columbia University Press, 1982.

Young, Thomas. *A Narrative of a Residence on the Mosquito Shore, during the Years 1839, 1840, and 1841: With an Account of Truxillo, and the Adjacent Islands of Bonacca and Roatan.* London: Smith, Elder & Company, 1842.

Index

ABOUT THE AUTHOR

Craig L. Dozier teaches geography and Latin American studies at the University of North Carolina at Greensboro. He received his bachelor of arts degree from the University of Wisconsin, his master of arts degree from the University of Maryland, and his doctorate from The Johns Hopkins University. He is author of *Indigenous Tropical Agriculture in Central America: Land Use, Systems and Problems* (1958) and *Land Development and Colonization in Latin America: Case Studies of Peru, Bolivia, and Mexico* (1969).